TAMING MAD DOG

JASON RILEY

Lulu Press
Morrisville, North Carolina
2023

ISBN: 978-1-7380311-0-8
Editor: Jennifer Sharman
Printed at Lulu Press
Cover & Interior Design: Katie Michiels
Cover Photos: Front Kaz Novak; back Bob Butrym

Dedicated to Mom and Dad

Ruth Marie (Peake) Riley

and

Nelson Elliott Riley

For sacrificing everything for us kids

TABLE OF CONTENTS

Foreword	p. 7
Preface	p. 9
Warm-up	p. 11
Training Camp – Growing	p. 13
First Quarter: Mad Dog Emerges	p. 49
Second Quarter: Grey Cup Bound	p. 108
Third Quarter: Street Fight in the Trenches	p. 185
Fourth Quarter: McMaster Makes History	p. 237
Overtime: Alumni Fraternity	p. 289
Post-Game Analysis	p. 293
Appendix A: Canadian Football 101: Diagram and Glossary	p. 299
Appendix B: Relaxation, Meditation and Visualization Activity	p. 309
Acknowledgements	p. 313

FOREWORD

I first met, or should I say heard of, this mountain of a man across the football field back in the early 2000s. At the time, I was the defensive coordinator at Queens University in Kingston Ontario, and Jason was coaching the offensive line unit with our arch-rival, the McMaster Marauders, in the OUA football conference. Each year, those games were fiercely competitive, emotional, and physical between two of the top offences and defences in the country. After the game, we would shake hands and give each other the "look" of respect only reserved for those who have earned it. He had that inner drive all coaches needed to win, not just on the scoreboard but in life. Passion, loyalty, technical expertise, and timely halftime adjustments all made him successful as a coach and a teacher.

Our paths have crossed many times over the years since those Saturdays in the fall. Several coaching clinics, camps, and other related football events have allowed me to gain more insight into my gridiron nemesis. Often, I have consulted with Jason to get his opinion on various historical projects archiving the legacy of the greatest games, coaches, players, and characters at the amateur, university, and professional levels. Through my role as assistant football coach and my involvement with the football alumni at UBC, I have assisted with the documentation of the 1982 national championship team and the all-time statistics and records. I had the distinct pleasure of informing him of his induction into the UBC Football Wall of Honour, being named to the 1980s all-decade teams and his selection to the Thunderbird 100th anniversary team. In the fall of 2022, he returned to Thunderbird stadium where his football heroics were celebrated at the 35th anniversary of the famed '82 season. Jason delivered an emotional and inspiring pre-game speech to the current team as they prepared for the playoffs and the Shrum Bowl. With every word and anecdote, "Mad Dog" had the 80–100 players and staff on their toes to capture it all.

This book allows the readers to get inside the head and heart of pro athletes who have reached the highest levels of success — with a thoughtful and insightful message about standing up for others and for what you believe in and living a life with purpose. Jason "Mad Dog" Riley has a raw story to tell, and holds nothing back. The themes presented provide a message of hope and direction for anyone looking for a way to overcome adversity and obstacles in their lives. He has a lifetime of joy and comfort, but like so many others he has experienced setbacks along the way. Jason wrote this book as a leader and his style of leadership stayed true when he stepped from the playing field to the classroom and eventually to the boardroom of the CFLAA.

His message of personal growth, family, and faith developed his belief with others to accomplish our goals, and to develop and maintain a successful plan for the future. Taming Mad Dog takes you on a trip across Canada, a personal journey under the umbrella of a family adventure. Each stop — starting over and fitting in, parental lessons taught through boxing and the piano — gaining momentum while asking the question, "What would I do differently?" Whether one has a hummingbird in hand or a 150-lb dumbbell, Jason proves if you live with a purpose, you can make a difference in the lives of others: from his students and his athletes, to a loyal restaurant owner and an ailing teammate.

In this book, Jason takes the reader along his journey, from Dartmouth, N.S., to Port Moody, B.C., playground to the podium, championship rings to championing a cause.

Patrick C.G. Tracey

Four-time national football champion

PREFACE

Taming Mad Dog is a memoir, the story of how childhood bullying left me with anger management issues and how football became my outlet, and ultimately, alongside my ever-supportive wife Paulette, part of my salvation. As I grew from a small, skinny, sensitive kid, who internalized my rage over the injustices of being bullied, into a wiry, strong young teenager, that rage was still there, and I essentially became a streetfighter. Football gave me the ability to channel my anger in a more positive way in the trenches of the gridiron, though I still fought off the field when bullies appeared in my life.

That anger has slowly abated over the years through the combination of my football career (and the constant struggle to gain muscle mass to play at the next level; from high school to university football to the CFL), my spiritual and personal growth, and the calming effect of Paulette and my children. I am proud to say that in my post-CFL life, in my subsequent teaching and coaching journey and beyond, I continue to convey my message of sport as both an emotional outlet and as a vehicle for personal growth, especially for our youth. How our interconnections with other people and nature help with our own personal growth and spiritual journey is another important theme – whether that happens within an organized religion, a forest, or somewhere else is your choice.

Through this writing, I was also able to reflect on my spiritual growth as it unfolded throughout my life. When some things happen in life, we tend to chalk it up to coincidence. Upon reflection, for me there seems to be just too many coincidences – this continues to add mystery for me in life.

I was weaned on jazz, and music became a big part of my life; ultimately, I became a blues and rock junkie. The songs listed throughout the book are like nostalgic landmarks in the soundtrack to my life. For me, great music improves every experience. Although copyright laws prevent me from including the lyrics, hopefully the titles, artists, and years (not always chronological) add a musical dimension to this crazy journey we're about to embark on together.

The events portrayed in this book are written from memories of my experiences and represent the best of my recollections of the events. I apologize if I have left anyone out of a particular story, or got the names wrong. Please forgive me. The stories are chosen from a lifetime of them, which I have enjoyed sharing with family, friends, and teammates over the years. At their encouragement, I began this project as a compilation of football stories for the entertainment of football fans.

However, an unexpected development occurred in the writing process; writing about my childhood experiences leading up to my football career, became therapeutic for me. I was surprised to discover that the bullying I had experienced as a small child had much more impact on me than I had first realized. Writing about this part of my life in more detail at the prompting of my editor, Jennifer Sharman, drew out all kinds of emotions that I didn't know were there. Consequently, this became an emotional form of mental health therapy for me. This is how bullying, and football as an outlet for the anger I experienced as a result of it, evolved into a major theme of the book.

Additionally, I understand that readers uninitiated to the game may find football talk intimidating – like a foreign language – because it's a complicated game. To encourage those readers to enjoy my story, a glossary of key football terms I use in the book are accompanied by a diagram in Appendix A. Hopefully, this will help take some of the mystery out of the game for you.

Finally, I feel truly blessed to have had the experiences in life that I've had; it seems now that I've had many guardian angels appear at the perfect time to help me overcome hurdles life has presented – how I got to this point seems a miracle. It's a long story, but I hope you enjoy it.

WARM-UP

We were playing against our tough league rival, the University of Alberta Golden Bears, who were favoured to win the conference that year. I was hungry to solidify my position at left defensive end, so I dredged up all my past demons, and drank a couple of coffees to send me over the top. I was so jacked-up, I was shaking as I taped up my knuckles for the game.

At left defensive end, you have the responsibility to put pressure in the face of the opposing quarterback, if he's right-handed when he's trying to throw from the pocket, and contain him in the pocket when he attempts to sprint-out to his right. Before the game, Coach Laycoe reminded me not to lose contain on this quarterback — he was dangerous on the run.

Sure enough, on the first series in the game, he rolled out my way. I knew I had to track him down before he got the ball away, or coach would chew my ass out. I shed the offensive tackle's block, then swatted the full-back past me as he tried to pin me inside. Now I had the quarterback in my sights and there was no one left to protect him. I felt a guttural growl developing in my chest as I pursued him.

He was faster than me, so my only hope was even a slight hesitation as he looked downfield to throw the ball. I used every bit of "want-to-speed" I could muster, as I worked to close that space between us, while growling to encourage him to rush his throw. Sure enough, he paused just for a moment, as he eyed his target receiver.

Desperate to stop the throw, I accelerated through him, driving my helmet and shoulder pads up through his left shoulder, just as he was releasing the ball with his right. The speed and angle of the hit instantly levelled him, knocking the snot out of him. His pass fell short of its target, incomplete.

As I got up from the collision, my teammates arrived to celebrate a great defensive hit. "Holy shit, Jason, you really de-cleated that fucker!" Cowboy chortled through his mouthguard.

Emerizer exclaimed, "You ran him down like a mad dog, Riley! When you hit him, he needed a defibrillator!"

From that day on, I was known as "Mad Dog" by my University of British Columbia teammates.

Although some may think this nickname unflattering, I was proud of it. Getting to this point in my life, and being respected by my teammates enough to earn a nickname like this was not easy. It was the culmination of much hard work and sacrifice, and hopefully a compelling and interesting story.

TRAINING CAMP

"Swingin' the Blues," Count Basie (1938)

Sports shaped my life in many ways, just as it had my father's before me. Nelson Elliott Riley, my dad, was a multi-sport athlete, competing in speed-skating as a teen, and, as an accomplished swimmer, working as a lifeguard at the Balmy Beach Club on the Toronto waterfront. In his time serving in the Royal Canadian Air Force (RCAF) during World War II, he also enjoyed taking part in the boxing and wrestling competitions that were held amongst the ranks.

At six foot four, he was an imposing figure. As a small child, knowing this gave me hope that I would inherit his size when I eventually hit my growth spurt. But Dad was also a multi-talented guy who embodied the toughness of a boxer with the artistry of a quintessential swing jazz pianist; his nickname during the war was "the Count" because he could play exactly like Count Basie, arguably among the greatest swing pianists of all time.

Later, I realized that I had inherited a dichotomy from my father. On one hand, Dad had all the sensibilities of an artist when he played the piano, on the other hand, he was capable of flattening his opponents in the boxing ring and he didn't tolerate injustice lightly. While music is in my blood, my artistic interests are in drawing and painting. So, I've always been aware of this internal tension between my creativity as an artist and the violence of a street fighter. There was constant tension between these two worlds of my life: my calm, creative side, and my angry, violent side.

Dad met and married my mom, Ruth Marie Peake, in 1951, with my oldest brother coming along the next year. My dad shared his love of sports with us four kids: my older siblings John and Janice, and my younger brother

Jeffrey. While Janice was more interested in spending time with her best friend, our mom, us boys always enjoyed sports, in all the many cities we ended up living in.

Mom and Dad married in Toronto, 1951: photographer unknown

My parents were good people, who worked hard to provide for us kids. Dad knew the value of sports for our development, so although we couldn't afford organized team sports, they both encouraged us to play locally. That's why I always looked forward to the changing seasons, which brought on the next sport: in the spring, I would look forward to diving into the local outdoor pool, at the park just down the street; in the fall I couldn't wait for the temperature to drop so Dad could flood the backyard rink. He would spend hours packing the snow as a frame and leveling the rink. Then, every night he would use the garden hose to build up the smooth ice sheet, so the next day it would be ready to go. We spent hours skating or playing shinny with our friends on that rink. The Ontario winters were consistently cold enough back then to maintain an outdoor rink for most of the winter.

The best part was Mom would never have to worry about us because she knew where we were, so we could play until it was time for bed.

Playing catch was a year-round pursuit. After a good report card in grade 4, Dad bought me a brand-new baseball glove, softball, and bat. I used to wait for him to come home from work, so he could take me to the park and pitch to me for hours, teaching me to hit and catch the ball. When I was older, John and I would play catch in the yard until Mom called us in for dinner. When Jeff was older, I would play catch with him, too. I loved the smell of that leather glove, and the ritual of playing catch with my brothers.

These early experiences that Dad shared with us gave me a deep appreciation for sports from a young age that is still with me today. I dreamed of one day playing on a team and getting my own uniform.

I was short and skinny, my freckled face displaying a permanent smile full of crooked teeth, topped off by a mop of blonde hair. I had boundless energy that I'm sure drove my family nuts at times. I couldn't sit still, unless I was doing some art work or reading a good book to calm my mind. Dad used to call me a "bundle of nerves," and Mom would say I had "ants in my pants." My sister Janice summed it up when she called me a brat!

I was also "blessed" with too many teeth for my mouth, and, in some cases, teeth growing in behind other teeth, like a shark. This gave the impression that my mouth was full of Chiclets, those once-popular squares of candy-coated gum, all pointing in different directions.

You'd think I'd learn to keep my mouth shut, but instead, I wore a permanent smile; perhaps inevitably, the kids at school used to mock me by calling me "Smiley Riley."

We couldn't afford an orthodontist. Instead, I had several visits to the dentist to pull "extra" teeth to make room for other teeth to grow in. It worked out well because my parents saved a lot of money — and my teeth ended up relatively straight.

I suppose being bullied was a fact of life for me during my formative years because my small stature and goofy appearance made me an easy target, especially after a move to a new neighbourhood where I didn't know anyone. In retrospect, it seems I was always fighting just to be accepted throughout my childhood.

In those days, I was a small kid with little self-confidence. I dreamed of getting big and strong, like my older brother John.

"In the Mood," Glenn Miller (1944)

Finding my place in the world must have been easier for me than it was for John and Janice, who were forced to grow up faster than Jeff and I because of all the moves our family made early on. After he returned from the war, Dad's career and then later financial struggles required that he move the family frequently.

To put it briefly, during the period from 1951 to 1969, Mom and Dad moved our growing family thirteen times.

John was born in Scarborough, Ontario, in 1952, before they left for California, where Janice was born in 1954. I was born back in Scarborough in 1958, while Jeff was born after our move to Port Arthur (now Thunder Bay) in 1963. After a few more moves within Ontario, we lived from Nova Scotia to British Columbia, where we settled in Port Moody in 1969. Consequently, by the time John was in grade 11, he had attended 13 schools.

All this moving about was the result of an unfortunate business deal that Dad made in California — he ended up being taken advantage of to the tune of his total life savings. And then in the move back to Canada to live with relatives while he got back on his feet, the container with all my parents' belongings was lost, never to be found again. It was only through continuous hard work, with every penny going towards whatever we kids needed, that my parents were eventually able to turn things around.

In some ways, moving this much was a blessing because, more than most people, we enjoyed the beautiful regional and cultural differences of our great country and became very resilient and reliant on each other.

But it was also a detriment because it meant that we, especially John and Janice, had no sense of attachment to the schools and friends that are so important to kids. We were constantly figuring out the new norms to fit in with a new group of friends, difficult because we weren't local. And because we were poor, we couldn't afford to buy new designer clothes to fit in, to get our hair cut in the local style. All of this also fostered the bullying behaviour bigger kids had towards me — the little goofy-looking, freckle-faced, smiley kid — resulting in emotional turmoil and anger, which was often on the verge of erupting.

Ultimately, football turned out to be the necessary outlet for my anger, as well as the beginning of my journey to self-discovery and growth. To get there, though, I had to survive the challenges of my childhood.

◇◆◇

My earliest recollection of being bullied was in Dartmouth, Nova Scotia, where we moved when I was halfway through grade 1. On that day, I got caught alone at the park by a group of teenagers, who spitefully took my hat and threw it amongst themselves, while they mocked me for being a scrawny, goofy-looking kid. When I asked for it back, they threatened me and told me there was nothing I could do about it, as they trapped me in their circle.

I felt humiliated, frustrated, and afraid of what they might do to me next; but I was determined that I wasn't going to go home without my hat. Yes, I was small, but they didn't know how fast on my feet I was. I built up my courage and waited for the kid closest to me to catch my hat, then I darted in and quickly snatched the hat out of his hand, bolting in the opposite direction between outstretched arms. They stood motionless, like a gaggle of geese, as I sprinted as fast as I could all the way home. I marched into the house out of breath, hoping my parents wouldn't notice; I was too embarrassed to tell them what happened.

◇◆◇

"All My Loving," The Beatles (1964, live on *The Ed Sullivan Show*)

After we moved back to Ontario, I had my first fight in the ditch in front of our house, in Port Credit. I'm not embarrassed to say I lost miserably — it wasn't much of a fight.

I was returning home from school in grade 3, when I found two younger boys arguing in the ditch in front of our house. One of them was bigger and bullying the other to the point of tears.

I jumped in the ditch to protect the small victim, who ran away as soon as I stepped in to help him. I continued to argue with the other boy, when a much bigger boy jumped in the ditch and pushed me back, saying, "Are you picking on my friend?"

I tried to explain what was happening, but before I even had a chance to raise my hands in defence, he started punching me in the face. He viciously punched me until my nose bled and my eyes swelled. I could taste my blood in my mouth. I ran into the house, crying like a baby.

It wasn't the physical pain that made me cry. I don't think I even felt the punches landing on my shocked face — the adrenaline must have made me immune to the pain. What caused the tears was the intense sense of humiliation I felt, while being beaten for trying to help another kid.

The unfairness of the situation, and the injustice that I was helpless to prevent, went against everything I was taught. It led to a whole range of emotions that welled up inside me, one after another: shock, humiliation, disbelief, loss of self-confidence, dwindling self-worth, anger, rage. I harboured all these things inside of me as I ran crying to my mother. When she saw my bleeding face, Mom hugged me, and quickly began to clean and dress my wounds. She lovingly catered to my physical needs, unaware of the real source of my pain, hidden deep inside.

Ultimately, although I lost my first fight, I'm proud of the fact that I stood up for what was right in protecting that young victim.

My boxing lessons began shortly after being totally annihilated in that fight. Dad had boxed in the RCAF when he was stationed in London during the war. He said, "Son, you need to learn how to protect yourself in this world."

He taught me how to hold my hands high with my elbows held in tight against my chest, turning sideways to protect my "family jewels" from kicks, while always moving left or right. He taught me how to lead with the left jab on the nose and come up with a strong right uppercut to the jaw. I was lucky to inherit his quick hands and long reach (when I grew up). My hero, my older brother John, had already graduated from Dad's boxing class — he was the toughest guy I knew.

Part of the training was to "never start a fight, but never back down from a bully, either." Dad said, "Jason, if you back down from a bully, it empowers them. The only way to stop a bully is to knock them on their ass! Hitler was a bully and the Allies knocked the Nazis on their ass to protect world freedom. Otherwise, we'd all be victims, son."

I couldn't argue with his logic. As a kid, I internalized it as "don't throw the first punch, but finish the fight."

Other non-bullying incidents also shaped me into the man I became. Ever since I was a small child, I've always felt a strong connection with nature. Mom and Dad taught us to respect all life and to enjoy nature. Although we were not raised in a formally "religious" sense, my connection with nature often seemed like a spiritual awakening. One early childhood event left me with a deep respect for the power of nature and with a sense that there is something bigger than myself that connects us.

The Black Current River in Thunder Bay was lined with a mixed forest, providing many great hiding places for our games. One day we were playing in the bush by the river and I noticed two young birch trees growing a couple of feet apart. I grabbed one with each hand and began to sway them back and forth. Soon, I heard a loud buzzing coming from high up in the trees.

When I looked up at the sound, I saw a swarm of bees leave the nest and start flying down like a tiny cyclone descending towards me. Before I could run away, they were on me. The bees began to sting me, taking turns finding the exposed flesh of my arms and legs, even crawling under my shorts and t-shirt to find more skin. I screamed in pain but could not escape the angry swarm.

A neighbour heard me screaming in pain, and rushed out to help. She bravely began swatting the bees off my body, but she couldn't get all of them. There were too many. At that moment, my mother looked out our kitchen window to see this woman beating the crap out of her son. She ran out to us, ready to confront my assailant, when she quickly understood the reality. Mom and our neighbour were able to get enough of the bees off me to drag me into the house – both receiving multiple stings, too.

I was covered in bee stings that soon began to swell into red mounds of pain. Mom applied calamine lotion to sooth the pain, then put ice packs on the worst areas of my legs and arms to help ease the swelling. She said if I was allergic to bees, I probably would have died. I still feel fortunate today that our unselfish neighbour saved me from that swarm of bees.

In fact, though a typical adult can withstand more than 1000 stings, 500 stings could kill a child (in people without bee venom allergies).[1]

In a strange parallel of events, while I was having this terrible experience with bee stings, Dad also had a near-death experience in Pittsburgh. He had driven south to pursue a new business venture in that city. While he was there, his appendix burst in the hotel. He knew from the pain that something was wrong, but he didn't know how serious it was, so he drove himself to the hospital. Because it burst, his appendix was spewing bacteria into his bloodstream while he drove; he passed out from the blood infection just as he walked into the hospital. He was told that he might have died from sepsis driving himself to the hospital. So, Mom came close to losing her husband and a son in the same week.

In retrospect, this marked an emerging sense that coincidence couldn't explain the spiritual connection I felt between me and my dad while we both survived life-threatening events at virtually the same time and survived to talk about it. Add this to my growing list of wonders in life.

When we were kids, we loved it when Mom and Dad took us swimming at the lake. Mom would pack a great picnic lunch, and after piling into Dad's gleaming family sedan (Dad always kept his cars in pristine condition, even though they were older models), he'd drive us to any lake we wanted. We could spend all day enjoying the sun and appreciating nature all around us; we had all developed a love for nature.

One time at the lake, we convinced Dad to stay for one more swim.

It was good that we stayed, because soon we saw a young boy and his sister running frantically up and down the beach trying to get help for their older brother, who had fallen off his innertube and was floundering in the lake. Dad was a strong swimmer and his lifeguard instinct kicked in. He swam directly to the boy, pulled him out of the lake, and performed CPR until first responders arrived. Dad never expected any accolades for saving the boy's life, he did it because it was the right thing to do. But if Dad hadn't been there at precisely that time, the boy would have drowned. To me, this

---

[1] Barish, R. A., and Arnold, T. 2022. Bee, wasp, hornet, and ant stings. *Merck Manual — Consumer Version*. Url: merckmanuals.com (accessed June 12, 2023).

seemed more than just coincidence, and it stirred in me a sense of awe at what my dad had done after we had convinced him to stay.

"White Room," Cream (1968)

Horses are one of nature's greatest gifts. It was around 1966 when John got a job on weekends working at Double D Ranch. It was a "dude ranch" for horseback riding, located at Jane and Steeles. He cleaned the stalls, groomed the horses, and saddled them for the public who would pay an hourly rate to ride. The owners had so much confidence in John at this young age that he would also lead the trail rides for groups of riders. The odd weekend, with our parents' permission, he took me to stay over at the ranch and help him care for the horses. I would help him with his daily routine in exchange for riding lessons and this is where I fell in love with horses: to me, they are the most beautiful, majestic animals. John taught me at an early age that I had to develop a relationship with the horse and also be confident enough to convince the horse that I was the alpha male. Once that was established, the horse would be cooperative and responsive to my physical cues from the saddle.

Eventually, I developed my riding skills; galloping on a horse, with the wind in my face, without a care in the world was a real adrenaline rush! The fact that a small kid could have complete control of such an amazing animal was very exciting and helped to build my self-confidence. I became a good rider, always looking forward to the next invitation to help my big brother at the ranch.

As a boy, I idolized John. My desire to spend more time with him also toughened me up. Whenever he made plans with his teenage friends to go into the local bush to build tree forts, play games, or to a park to sneak a smoke, I would try to follow along behind them without being noticed. The point of no return was when he had no choice but to bring me along because he couldn't send me home alone at that age. If he did, he would face the ire of our parents when I told them what happened.

The tough part was when John caught me sneaking along behind them. John would yell at me to go home, and when I didn't, he would punch me in the thigh at the perfect spot to cause temporary paralysis of the quad muscles in my leg (commonly known as a charley horse).

If I couldn't walk, I could no longer keep up with them. Once the pain went away, I would walk it off, limping all the way home. John expressed regret later on, but toughening me up this way paid dividends when I discovered football.

◇◆◇

A later event that further heightened my sense of a growing spirituality involved my older sister, Janice. I was about 8 at the time, so she would have been around 13 years old.

My friends and I often made a game out of racing through the corrugated steel culverts at the park down the street from our house. Although they were only about five feet high, they seemed like huge tunnels to us. We would run as fast as we could through them, avoiding soakers by jumping left and right over the water that streamed in the middle.

One time I slipped and fell, putting my right hand out to brace myself. My hand landed directly on the sharp upward-pointing base of a broken pop bottle. A glass shard sliced deep into the base of my hand near my wrist. I ran all the way home, with the blood dripping from my wound. When I got there, Janice was the only one home.

She calmed me down on the back porch. Trying hard not to cry, I explained to her what happened. Then, she squeezed my hand to see what the damage was. We were both startled to see the blood shoot in a stream right over the porch railing and onto the grass in the back yard — I remember thinking that it looked like Spider-Man's web in the comics, shooting out of his wrist, only mine was not a spider web, it was deep red blood!

Luckily, our neighbour was home and Janice recruited him to squeeze my wrist to stop the blood flow, while his dad drove us to the hospital. He squeezed my wrist so hard my hand was turning blue by the time we got to the hospital.

When we were in the emergency room, the nurse went into the cut with a pair of tweezers to make sure there was no glass inside before she stitched me up. She found and removed a very thin shard of glass, about the size and shape of a postage stamp, embedded in the cut. I was amazed that she found that inside my hand, and I cringed at the thought of her closing the wound with it still in there if she had missed it. She finished by putting several stitches in my hand to seal it up.

Before we left, the nurse told us that the cut was serious and, if it hadn't been for the quick actions of my sister and our neighbours, it could have been much worse. Janice had saved my life!

This whole event made me thankful for Janice being in the right place at exactly the right time. It was reminiscent of the time my neighbour saved me from the bee attack. These life-threatening events at this young age were frightening to me but they added to the mystery I felt as my life was unfolding. It sparked in me an emerging spirituality that I couldn't really understand or explain at the time, except that I felt blessed for those who were able to help me. I had a renewed wonder in the world and looked forward to finding my purpose in it.

As I said previously, John grew up fast because of our family moves due to financial struggles. When we made our final move from Ontario to B.C., John got the ultimate vote of confidence from our parents. In the summer of 1969, Dad asked John to drive the family from Toronto to Vancouver. John was only 16 years old at the time.

It was an unforgettable trip for all of us. One night, in the prairies of Saskatchewan far from a motel, and with no cellphone or GPS (this technology was not available at the time) to find one, Mom decided we would sleep in the car.

In the dark, John began searching for the best place to pull over. Eventually, he found a grassy area at the edge of a cornfield. Mom, Janice, and Jeff slept in the car, while John and I decided to sleep on the roof of the car so the others would have more room — the roof of the car seemed almost the size of a double bed, as we arranged our sleeping bags and pillows.

Soon I was thinking life doesn't get much better; me and my big brother were sleeping on the roof of our car, on a warm July night, under the Northern Lights dancing in the vast prairie sky. It was an amazing light show that added to our adventure!

The joy was short-lived, however, because in a few hours we woke up wet and shivering. As the temperature dropped throughout the night, we got soaked in the thick layer of dew that dropped out of the cooling air. When we scurried back into the car, dragging our wet sleeping bags, there was a huge commotion because we woke everyone up and got them wet, too. We were not popular brothers in the hysteria that followed, but eventually everyone got back to sleep. The next morning, we were off toward Alberta and eventually, the Calgary Stampede. I was excited when Mom said we could enjoy a whole day of events at the Stampede; the chuck-wagon races were unforgettable.

It had lasting effects on me. My mouth was watering when the cook put the heaping pile of fried onions on my hamburger. Still, whenever I smell fried onions cooking, I think of the Calgary Stampede because the entire time we were there, the delicious aroma of onions cooking on the midway grills filled the air. That beautiful smell still reminds me of all the amazing things we watched at the Stampede and the thousands of people enjoying the spectacle.

When we left Calgary, we travelled through picturesque Lake Louise, and then on through the Rockies. We saw moose and black bears in the wild along the way.

And then finally, we arrived in B.C.

The prevalence of bullying in my life had been alarming thus far, so Dad's words about knocking bullies on their asses stayed with me. Regardless of where we lived, I always tried to follow his guidelines.

When we first moved to B.C. in 1969, we lived in government-assisted income-based housing in an apartment complex with other families in various situations, each with their own stories, like us. Although the buildings were well-built, in good repair, and with well-maintained grounds, there were some kids just looking for a fight or a smaller kid to pick on. Kids from the surrounding neighborhood would often wander into the complex looking for trouble too.

Dad had chosen a large, three-bedroom apartment in a building that sat at the top of Port Moody Hill, on the border between Port Moody and Coquitlam. There were five L-shaped buildings consisting of 218 suites, which formed a maze of units and playgrounds with an indoor pool at the centre of the complex. Deeper into the complex, it wasn't always the best place to be at times, but we always had friends nearby to play with.

The view was what really sold Dad on the place. From any window in our apartment, it was gorgeous. We looked north-east towards the Coast Mountains, the virgin forests of Burke Mountain, and Buntzen Lake hidden in the trees. Years later, when I attended university, working as a park warden at Buntzen Lake would become my favourite summer job.

When we moved in, we slept on mattresses on the floor because we didn't have any furniture. John and I shared a bedroom, while Jeff shared a room with Janice. Mom and Dad had the master bedroom at the end of the hall, with an en-suite bathroom.

The only drawback was that our apartment was on the third floor and there was no elevator. Luckily everyone was in good health, so we all got a workout taking three flights of stairs coming and going. We'd help out carrying groceries up the stairs for Mom and Dad.

After our arrival, Mom took us kids for a walk to show us the route we would be walking to school every day. Jeff and I would be attending Sir Frederick Banting Elementary School, which went from grades K–7; I would be entering grade 5, and Jeff, grade 1. Janice would be in grade 10 at Sir Frederick Banting Junior Secondary, across the football field from our school.

On our way to that first visit to the school, there was an older kid loitering around the school yard path, by himself. He didn't like my haircut or my clothes and let me know it. (When we left Ontario, polyester bell-bottom pants were popular and that's what I had on. In the Vancouver area, jeans were the preferred pants. Also, my brothers and I wore brush cuts, which were popular in Ontario at the time, while the kids in B.C. wore mullets.)

This kid either didn't know I was with my mother or didn't care, because he started harassing me about how funny I looked. This led to my first fight in my new hometown. I didn't start it, but I wasn't backing down to be bullied in front of my family either, so I stood up for myself and got some good licks in before Mom broke up the fight. This set the tone for a future in the school of hard knocks for me. I'd be fighting my way through it, full of teenage angst and insecurities. Finding myself seemed like I was tracking a moving target at this point.

Later that year, there was a big bruiser in grade 7 who loved picking on kids smaller than he was. A two year gap is huge at this age, and he decided I was his next victim at recess one day and started pushing me around. He didn't like it when I stood up to him and pushed him back, so he threw me on the ground, pinned me down, and started punching me in the face. The teacher on duty grabbed us both and took us to the office, where we waited to be strapped by the vice-principal, Mr. Shantz. The school had a strapping policy for discipline and I remember being very angry as I sat waiting in that office. I thought, "I just got clobbered by a kid much bigger than I am and now I'm getting the strap for defending myself! I didn't even get to throw a punch."

Fortunately, Mr. Shantz was a fair man and, when he heard my side of the story, he didn't strap me after all. He gave me some well-meant advice about avoiding fights and, although I appreciated not being strapped, his advice didn't really apply to the real world of kids who were bullied.

It's even more frightening to think of the current victims of cyber-bullying. The kids in today's world may face bullying all day, then go home to it on social media, which could last through the night, if they choose to take their device to bed with them.

It doesn't seem to matter where one lives, there will be bullies.

Walking one summer day with my little brother Jeff to a playground in the complex, some kids told us that a local bully named Nichols and his buddies were skulking around looking for their next victim.

Nichols didn't live in the complex, but we heard about him looking for kids to beat up in the past. He was notorious among kids in the neighbourhood. He was a thick, heavy-set kid. He wore unevenly cropped scruffy brown hair, and large freckles were visible on all of the body parts that were exposed beyond his shorts and grubby t-shirt. I was small and skinny in comparison.

Suddenly, our neighbour Melanie came running up to tell us that Nichols and his buddy were beating up a friend of ours named Reinhardt in the playground. She was very upset, so we rushed to help.

When we arrived, we saw Nichols and his friends ganging up on Reinhardt. Other kids from the complex stood back and watched, too frightened to help.

When we arrived, Reinhardt was clearly relieved to see us. I told Nichols to stop. He said, "What are you gonna do about it?"

As Jeff and I stepped towards the group to help Reinhardt, one of them approached Jeff, who was the smallest kid there, and kicked him right in the balls. Jeff went down in pain.

My brother recalls me becoming enraged at that point, and running at Nichols, "slamming him over the low brick fence that enclosed the playground, where he landed on top of him and began pummelling his face with his fists. At the same time, Reinhardt got the better of the guy who kicked me. Nichols and his buddies ran away and I don't remember ever seeing them in our complex again."

After the fight, I told Jeff how grateful and proud I was of him for having the courage to stand up to the bullies when no one else would. The bullying stopped because they knew that they couldn't victimize kids in our complex anymore and get away with it. It seemed that Dad was right — "The only way to stop a bully is to knock them on their ass!"

This situation also stands out because of the memory of the absolute rage that I felt, which propelled me towards the fight. That anger in me continued to grow along with the number of bullying incidents I experienced.

One fall day, I was walking home from school after basketball practice in my brand-new winter coat. A teenager was walking down the street in the opposite direction when I felt him touch the hood of my coat as we passed each other. I turned to look at him. He didn't say anything, so I kept walking. I was still suspicious because I caught him looking back at me several times as he faded into the distance.

Before I entered my apartment building to ascend the stairs, I had the urge to take my coat off to see why he had touched my hood. It was lucky that I did because I discovered a cigarette butt burning a hole in the fuzzy lining of my hood. It was burning slowly so I didn't smell a thing until I opened my hood. I was really angry now because, if I hadn't taken a moment to check my coat, that one senseless act of bullying could have put my entire family and all the residents of our building in danger.

I imagined myself innocently hanging my coat up in the front closet with the burning cigarette igniting my coat and causing a major fire in our apartment building. It makes me angry to this day.

With each bullying incident I developed more self-confidence in fighting to match the internal anger. One day, Jeff and I were playing catch in the parking lot in front of our apartment. Some kids we had never seen before cut through the lot while we played. They picked up some loose stones from the edge of the lot as they approached and started throwing them in our direction. Jeff told them they shouldn't be throwing rocks near the cars, or us kids.

The leader of the group, who was a head taller than I was, said "Oh yeah, who do you think you are?" From across the lot, he threw a rock the size of a small hen's egg at Jeff and nailed him right in the forehead. I ran to check on him and he already had a goose egg growing out of his forehead.

He cried in pain even as he told me, "Don't worry about it, I'll be okay."

I approached the bully and challenged him to apologize for hurting my brother. He tried to ignore me. At this point, Dad appeared on our apartment balcony three stories above the fracas and yelled down, "What's going on down there, Jas (pronounced Jayce)?"

I yelled up at him, "This kid threw a rock and hit Jeff right in the head — he needs to apologize!"

Dad nodded as he understood what was happening. "That's not good," he responded. "Go to it, then!"

I pushed the kid in the chest, and again told him to apologize to Jeff. The kid said, "Fuck you, asshole!" and swung at me. I ducked and nailed him with a flurry of punches to the face, before he grabbed me in a bear hug and landed some shots to the side of my head.

Because he was bigger than me, I wasn't doing much damage, but I didn't quit and he realized I wasn't going to back down. Finally, he looked up at my dad, looked at me, then told Jeff he was sorry. He pushed past me, then motioned to his friends and they left the parking lot — we never saw them again.

Dad was still on the balcony, now with his hands clasped above his head, yelling, "Atta boy, Jas."

Unfortunately, the trend continued on my first day in grade 8. I had been dreaming about getting to Sir Frederick Banting Junior Secondary School ever since I first attended the elementary school with the same name across the field.

On this day, in my first science class, I had the ominous pleasure of sitting on the stool next to the biggest kid I'd ever seen. This monster of a kid was at least four times bigger than me, and judging by his size, he had failed grade 8 science several times before my arrival.

It's remarkable how small gestures can have a huge impact on someone, if done in just the right way. This behemoth had mastered his technique perfectly, and we had never met, so there was no other reason to do it but for intimidation and cruelty. With a smirk on his face, he simply took his huge ham-hock of a hand, grabbed a handful of dirty sand from a turtle display on the counter in front of us, and slowly poured it down the back of my shirt. I guess he thought it would be funny to see me squirm as the sand made its way down my back and into my pants. The more I squirmed, the more went into my underwear.

Abject humiliation and indignation were the result for me. This act, although small for him, seemed huge to me. It made me feel very small, and confused that someone could do this to a complete stranger for no reason, and I guess that was his objective — to make smaller kids than him feel minute in his presence.

I was so angry inside because of the helplessness I felt. The first day in my big new school had not turned out as I dreamed it would. For me, it became another day of indignation, self doubt, and rage.

I learned that people who are bullies don't just bully people. I saw kids do terrible things to animals that left scars in my mind. These types of people may grow up to have no respect for the natural world, which to me is one reason for the current state of our planet, but that is a whole other story.

My friends and I loved playing in the gulley behind our apartment complex. We used to spend hours climbing trees and building tree forts, or jumping from a tree branch into the natural sand pit we discovered in the bush. I love animals and I was taught to enjoy them in their natural habitat. We saw animals in the bush all the time.

So, it was upsetting to see sheer animal cruelty happen in the bush behind our complex. My friends and I were playing in the gulley when we came across some older teenagers with pellet guns. They were shooting at something high up in a tree. Then I noticed that their target was a large raccoon, which was stuck out on a branch, making it an easy target with no escape. There were three kids with pellet guns taking turns shooting the poor animal. Now, one shot from a pellet gun wouldn't do much damage to a large raccoon with a full coat of fur, but the number of shots they were taking was doing great harm. It was not moving and, whenever they shot it, I could hear a cry from the animal, like a deep sigh of pain. The boys acted like it was a game, as they stayed focused on injuring the animal until it fell from the tree, while the raccoon continued to hold on for dear life.

It disgusted me that someone could do this to a defenceless animal. The boys were laughing and moving for a better angle to inflict the most pain with another shot. I had to leave because I couldn't stand it any more, and I couldn't do anything to stop it. If we had said anything, the boys might have turned their guns on us, just for the hell of it. The cruelty of these boys left a lasting impression on me. At home, we were taught a great love for the natural world, and this showed me a small example of how some people don't share the same view — an early lesson on human destruction of the natural world

This experience reminds me of another summer back in Ontario. My friends and I used to catch tadpoles and frogs in the local creek by the railway tracks. We would catch them with small goldfish nets, play with them for a bit, and release them unharmed back into the creek.

One day some older teens came along and started catching frogs in the creek near where we were. What we didn't know was that, unlike us younger kids, they had malicious intent. They took firecrackers out of their pockets and took turns placing them in the mouths of these poor frogs and lighting the wicks. When the firecrackers exploded it was like a bomb to the small animals and it would blow the lower jaw right off, leaving them permanently disfigured. They even shoved firecrackers up the rectum of some frogs to watch them explode with deadly force.

Sadly, these boys had no remorse for the pain and suffering of their victims. They laughed; the more damage the louder the laughter. When they were done, they just left the injured frogs to die. It sickened me to think that kids could be so cruel; I had nightmares about it.

Anyone who intentionally causes senseless animal pain is cruel and should be charged appropriately. To my mind, it's just another form of bullying; people who act this way are trying to make up for their own lack of self-worth by harming something more vulnerable than themselves.

It's important for me to note here that these childhood experiences (witnessing these violent animal assaults, which went against my love of the natural world, and the personal bullying I continued to experience) clearly had a powerful impact on me — subconsciously.

In retrospect, I now realize the combined impact of all of it filled me with anger against injustice that I harboured deep inside. And, although a supportive family helped me heal over at the time, my repressed anxieties manifested themselves in nightmares that cracked open the scabs, allowing the pus to ooze out in my sleep. For years I had vivid nightmares, sometimes waking up my poor parents with screams.

I also suffered from a condition the dentist said was grinding my teeth at night. He explained it was a physical response to subconscious anxiety when I slept, in which I clenched my teeth so tightly, grinding them together, that it made a loud noise like a heavy axe blade grinding on a clay stone. This horrible noise woke up my entire household for years when I was a kid. It wasn't until this writing that I understood why this was happening to me.

Notwithstanding all that, I'm embarrassed to say that when I was 13 years old, I had a profound personal lesson in animal suffering, which was totally unintentional.

I convinced my parents to allow me to buy a slingshot. My circle of friends had them, but Mom insisted I could only have one for target practice – I wasn't allowed to use it on animals of any kind.

My friends and I would go to a local open-lot field and set up pop bottles or cans on a log for target practice. We would spend half our time searching the ground for perfectly-shaped stones to use as ammunition. The nice, smooth, rounded stones were the best for accuracy. We all had the yellow plastic slingshot with the ammo compartment in the handle, which we would fill up with the best stones we could find. Hollow rubber tubing formed the sling, with a leather ammo pouch to draw back and shoot.

After weeks of summer practice, we were getting pretty accurate in our target shooting. From about twenty paces, we would challenge each other to shoot the tops off the pop bottles, then blow up the midsection, and sometimes knock the base of the bottle off the log.

One day, we were walking back home from target practice through the complex. There were always pigeons around somewhere looking for scraps of discarded food. I was feeling cocky at the time because I was getting pretty good at hitting bottles with my slingshot. Showing off to my friends, I told them I could hit a pigeon we saw pecking at food on the ground about fifty paces away. To make it even more unlikely, I said I would turn my back on the target, spin, and hit the pigeon without stopping to aim. In my mind, I thought there was no way I could hit the pigeon from there, even without spinning to shoot. Unfortunately, I was wrong.

With my friends egging me on, I spun and shot. To my surprise, I drilled the poor bird directly in the side of the head. It immediately began trying to fly, but it just kept spinning in circles as it flapped its wings on the asphalt. My heart sunk like a rock and I felt pangs of guilt building in my stomach. When we approached the floundering bird, there was a trail of blood from its injured head as it hopelessly flapped its wings.

I felt no joy in hitting the bird, only guilt for going against my parents' wishes and injuring a helpless animal. I knew I needed to take responsibility and rectify the situation, so I ran home and grabbed the empty hamster cage we stored in the closest after Jeff's hamster died. I put the injured bird in the cage and walked it to the nearby veterinarian clinic to hopefully save the bird and ease my conscience. I remember the long wait in the waiting room being like waiting for the strap in the principal's office.

When I got to see the vet and explained the situation, he told me there was nothing he could do for the bird. My shot had rendered the bird permanently brain injured and it would never be the same. When I asked him what I should do, he told me the only option was to take it to the bush, hit it over the head with a stick to put it out of its misery, and bury it.

Alone with the suffering bird in the cage, I walked back toward the gulley to do my penance. This gave me time to reflect, and I realized the veterinarian probably had two reasons for giving me this single option. One, it prevented him from administering drugs to euthanize the bird and creating an expensive bill for my parents, and two, he was forcing me to take responsibility for injuring the bird.

When I got to the edge of the bush, I took the bird out of the cage and laid it on the grass. I found a suitable stick and, and as the bird looked sadly into my eyes, I whacked it over the head, ending its pain and suffering. Then, I buried the bird in a shallow grave and vowed I would try to never hurt another animal. Even to this day, I find myself using the catch-and-release method with spiders I find in the house.

"Limehouse Blues," Teddy Wilson (1957)

Throughout this early period of my life, it was my home life that kept me sane. Mom always made a beautiful Sunday dinner, so whoever was available would be there. Her roast beef, mashed potatoes, and gravy, with homemade Yorkshire pudding was always excellent. After dinner, Dad would play a swing session on his upright Yamaha piano.

We'd enjoy Mom's homemade apple pie with ice cream, sitting around the piano as Dad played. He had such big mitts and long reach that he literally rocked the piano when he played. I'm not a pianist, but Dad described his stride piano style as syncopated rhythm.

His large hands helped him hit notes that would be difficult for smaller hands. The thing he loved most about swing was the improvisation, which allowed him to play any of our favourite songs differently than the last time whenever we requested them. Us siblings would catch each other's eye occasionally and share a look of pure pride in Dad's musical genius. At that moment no one had it better than we did. I often got goose bumps listening to Dad when he was in full swing, creating musical euphoria. It was unreal.

These were the things that made our family so close. We had been through a lot together with all the moves, new schools, adjusting to new norms, and simply trying to find our path in life. But Mom and Dad's love was what kept us together and our family unity was instrumental for our success. It kept us pointed in the right direction in life.

Inevitably, I would experience more bullying, and even as an adult in the work place, there were events that could be considered the same. This story is about how I was able to use sports and, specifically, football to overcome my personal insecurities, which I attribute to being a victim of bullying as a youth.

Mom and Dad always taught us to be fair, to stand up against injustice and help those in need, and I had experienced bullying behaviour regularly throughout my life to this point. But I had always internalized it; I never told my parents or anyone else about most of it. This led to inner turmoil for me, as my subconscious mind tried to reconcile the humiliation and anger of being bullied with my obligation to do the right thing.

Though people who know me now might say that I am an eternal optimist, in my transition from adolescence to teen hood, that inner turmoil resulted in an anger management problem. Even though I tried to never start a fight as Dad had taught me, I was quick to fight if someone took a swing at me. With a quick temper, my disposition changed instantly; I turned into an angry street fighter.

Consequently, by the time I left high school, I had already been in many fights, usually against bigger guys, defending myself from bullies.

I suspect that I might have landed in jail for assault later on, if it wasn't for football. Fortuitously, football saved me from my demons most of the time by giving me an outlet for my inner hostilities and aggression. Years later, it would be my wife Paulette who kept my rudder steady in the water of my turbulent career.

When I reflected on it, there were more examples of bullying in my childhood than I thought; evidently, I was stowing the negative experiences away in the back of my mind, while I struggled to find my own personal identity, self-esteem, and self-confidence. It was only while writing this book that I realized how much bullying I actually experienced as a child. This shows a pattern that is frightening for young kids who have suffered from bullying in the past; how much harm does the repression of bullying incidents do to adolescent minds?

The effects of bullying have been studied, and there is evidence that when those kids who are bullied are adults, they have an increased risk of experiencing mental health issues such as anxiety, depression, suicidal ideation, as well as higher rates of attempted and completed suicides.[2,3] Not only that, adults who were bullied as children were found to self-report their general health as lower than those not bullied, and have more bodily pain and headaches.[2,4] There were also socioeconomic impacts: adults who were often bullied as kids had lower levels of education, fewer social supports, and earned less money than non- or less-bullied peers.[2,4]

But, given that these studies took place over many years, with the kids under study being bullied decades ago before the internet existed, if this is an indication of past norms, can you imagine how much more harm is done through today's ubiquitous social media platforms? Now, kids can't escape cyber-bullying, they are not able to turn it off by going home to a supportive family, like I could. If these bullying victims don't turn off their devices, they continue to be targets at home. I believe that society, including the major social media corporations, need to be proactive to mitigate the harm to mental health that bullying does, and its impact on our youth.

Finally, in no way do I want to imply that I am the "greatest victim of bullying who ever existed," because I know there are many people who have suffered much worse situations than me. However, I can only tell you the story from my perspective and how I am just learning about much of this myself, as I type these words.

Writing this book has actually become cathartic for me, in that it has allowed me to reflect. I'm now learning more about myself, and realize the

---

[2] Wolke, D., and Lereya, S. T. 2015. Long-term effects of bullying. *Archives of Disease in Childhood* 100: 879–885.

[3] Takizawa, R., Maughan, B., Arseneault, L. 2014. Adult health outcomes of childhood bullying victimization: evidence from a five-decade longitudinal British birth cohort. *The American Journal of Psychiatry* 171: 777–784.

[4] Wolke, D., Copeland, W. E., Angold, A., and Costello, E. J. 2013. Impact of bullying in childhood on adult health, wealth, crime and social outcomes. *Psychological Science* 24: 1958–1970.

bullying had more impact on me than I suspected. I think it's human nature to lock negative experiences into a vault in one's mind and try to move on. In my case, I think this resulted in resentment, anger, and anxiety in the back of my mind that has stayed with me.

I've never received any psychotherapy, but now I think that it may have helped me process those angry dark thoughts that lingered in my mind.

A side effect of being bullied and that lesson from my dad to always finish a fight was that it toughened me up physically. As a result, although I was still small upon leaving elementary school, I was strong and wiry for my size. That turned out to serve me well in the next phase of my life.

When I finally got to Banting Junior Secondary, I was very excited to be going to the "big school" on the other side of the football field from our elementary school. Now I could play on the teams I used to watch on the field after school! In reality, it was a small school because it only went from grade 8 to grade 10, but in my mind, it was huge. Also, Banting had a great teaching staff, who volunteered to coach every sport you could think of.

This meant that in my first year of high school, a cornucopia of sports was suddenly available to me. Playing school sports was free and we got awesome uniforms!

I saw this as my chance and I took full advantage of my opportunities. In grade 8, I played rugby, football, track and field, soccer, volleyball, basketball, gymnastics, and wrestling. We also played intramural floor hockey every lunch period. I had so much energy that I needed to be constantly active, and I loved the structure and teamwork of sports.

Wrestling with my brothers all my life had made me a good wrestler, in spite of my size — my small size and weight is etched into my brain because in grade 8, I wrestled in the lightweight 115-lb weight class.

Dad had encouraged us to wrestle when we were young. When Mom tried to stop us, he would say, "It's okay, Ruthy, it's like bear cubs in the wild, it makes them stronger and more able to defend themselves." His words were so true; we wrestled with each other constantly and if we were lucky, Dad would show us his moves too.

I loved all the sports I played, but the one that really hooked me that year was football. When I tried out for the junior football team, and I got to put on my own helmet and shoulder pads for the first time — I was in another world.

That year I was one of the smallest guys out there, but I could run like a mouse on hot sand. Coach Odynsky decided to give me a shot at returning punts. I wasn't very good at it, but I was happy he found a spot for me to play on the team.

Soon, I learned that one of the best things about the game is there is a position for every body type, so anyone can play. The more I learned about football, the more I enjoyed the sport: the teamwork, the discipline, the camaraderie, and the platooning of offence, defence, and special teams (all the units that deal with the kicking game — see Appendix A). I looked forward to growing bigger, so I could play other positions in the future.

I was very proud at the end of my grade 8 year, when I received the "Big Block Award" at the school assembly; it wasn't for being the best at any of the sports, it was for playing in all the sports. The large embroidered capital "B," for Banting, was meant to be sewn onto the school jacket, and was usually reserved for senior students. I didn't even have a school jacket, but Mr. Roberts and Mr. Odynsky wanted to recognize me for my participation in almost every sport in the school.

I was so proud of that "B" I was bursting at the seams when I rushed home to share it with my parents. This is a true testament to the positive power of sport on young kids.

All sports are good for the healthy development of kids, but I learned that football is tops. One of the key things that makes football the best sport in the world for adolescent young men, as shown in my case, is that there is a position for every body type. Generally speaking: the biggest and strongest players play the offensive and defensive line positions; the intermediate sized athletes play running back and linebacker positions; while the smaller, faster, athletes play the receiver and defensive back positions. No other sport is like this. Most sports have a specific "cookie-cutter" body type that is required to meet the demands of the sport (for example, basketball, gymnastics, soccer, and hockey), whereas football is totally inclusive to everyone, regardless of size.

Another factor that makes football so attractive to young men is the size of the rosters. There is no other sport that incorporates so many players in so many different ways at the same time to make a play successful. In Canada, there are 12 players on offence, 12 players on defence, and 12 players on special teams, along with another group of players backing up all these positions.

Football is also the most complicated of team sports, like a chess match with human pieces. Everyone must work together on either side of the ball attempting to make the coaches' strategy work. If one player on either side doesn't do their job, the play doesn't work.

Thus, players have to develop self-discipline and a sense of responsibility to their teammates in practice to execute their job on any given play — each position having a unique skill set and job.

Therefore, scoring points on offence, or stopping your opponent on defence, is a by-product of team work, discipline, and trust in your teammates for success. The team that does this most consistently on game day wins the game.

All this requires great dedication to the team for the coordination demanded between all the moving parts to make a play successful.

Because of all this, football is the closest thing to a military experience for civilians; it is excellent for adolescent young men to grow out of their natural impetuousness and into responsible young men.

Once a player gets hooked by the sport, like I did, they learn all the necessities for success in life after football.

Finally, football is also an excellent outlet for the pent-up anxiety and aggression in adolescent boys. The hard, physical work required to play the game is therapeutic in itself, but add the fact that the play only ends when the ball carrier is on the ground, and you have a very physical sport.

While the players on offence are trying to keep the ball off the ground until they cross the goal line, the players on defence are trying to accomplish the opposite, by putting the ball carrier on the ground. Heavy physical contact is the result.

The beautiful thing about it is that the equipment and the training are so good that players can knock the crap out of each other, then go back to the huddle for the next play. Generally, if this behaviour took place off the football field (the gridiron), kids would end up in jail; while inside the white lines of the gridiron, players just dust themselves off and go back to the huddle with impunity.

I finally hit the growth spurt I was praying for between my grade 9 and 10 years. I grew straight up several inches, although I was still thin and wiry. Mom was a great cook, but my metabolism was so fast that I ate constantly and still didn't put on much weight. Nonetheless, as I grew bigger and stronger, the bullying lessened accordingly.

In fact, I was now able to defend kids in the school who were victimized. I was very aware of how much harm it can do to a person's self-esteem, so I would stick up for the kids that were bullied. Now I was getting into fistfights defending kids who bullies tried to put into garbage cans or squeeze into lockers, trying to humiliate a victim to build up their own ego.

My pent-up aggression, the anger stored away in my psyche would be released during these confrontations. I hated bullies.

Thankfully, my therapy was putting on my football equipment and flying around the gridiron with wild abandon — or as my future nickname suggested, like a mad dog.

"Smoke on the Water," Deep Purple (1972)

On a lighter note, in 1975 we were in grade 10 and my friend, Cliff Chappell, told me his dad was picking up his new sports car at lunch one day; a brand new 1975, Datsun 280Z, all white, with black interior. We planned to be out in the teachers' parking lot when Mr. Chappell arrived with his car. I remember the crowd of grade 10 boys swarming around the car like ants around a crumb when he drove that car into the lot. From the moment I saw the car; I fell in love with it. Mr. Chappell allowed Cliff to take it out for joy rides later on when he got his licence and I went on several with him — the car's handling and performance was ahead of its time. I dreamed of someday having the money to purchase it from Mr. Chappell.

Besides owning the car of my dreams, Mr. Chappell had another major impact on me. He was widely recognized as one of the best teachers at Banting Jr. Secondary and then Port Moody Senior Secondary schools, and I enjoyed his art classes for five consecutive years. He had a way of evoking the best from his students, in a humorous and engaging way. Because of his influence, I have enjoyed creating art ever since.

My enjoyment of art somehow seems in opposition to my physicality, which was borne of anger, but perhaps the connection is in the sensitivity that made me feel anger at the injustice of bullying; that same sensitivity connects to my creative and artistic side. Suffice it to say that during the football season when I was in constant "combat mode," I found it difficult to be creative, but in the off-season, it seemed my creativity flourished — maybe it was just the change in focus.

My love of music is another extension of that: I was weaned on jazz at home and my love of music continued to grow as I grew up. In high school, I fell in love with rock and roll at a Heart concert in the Banting gymnasium, and I've attended countless concerts ever since. We also enjoyed some kickass high school dance parties, with rock and roll blasting from the stereo.

Sadly, bullying extends into all realms of life. At one high school party, most of my friends and I were dancing. I noticed a tough-looking guy, who must have been somebody's uncle because he seemed twice as old as everyone else, sitting on the couch. He kept staring at me as I was dancing. Finally, when I got close enough to hear him over the music, he called me a "fucking faggot."

Although I'm not gay, this was my first experience with homophobia and I was shocked — totally broadsided emotionally. It was such a great party until this asshole completely destroyed my mood. I felt humiliated and told my friends I was leaving because I didn't want to ruin the party with a fight. I left the party indignantly and cooled off as I walked home in the cool night air. During my walk, I considered how difficult it must be for someone who was gay to navigate life facing this type of hostility daily.

"Bennie and the Jets," Elton John (1973)

In my senior year at Port Moody Senior Secondary, football was the only sport I played and I was becoming pretty good at it. I had an unquenchable hunger for the game and I brought a toughness to the football field that came from deep inside my psyche. The game allowed me to play with an edge that came from letting all my inhibitions loose as an outlet for my anxieties and pent-up aggression. When I think back on it, it's clear that this latent aggression stemmed from all the bullying I had experienced; football was my chance to let it out in a legal way by knocking my opponent on his ass, without really hurting him. It was glorious. Conversely, I learned how to roll with it when someone got the better of me with a good hit.

I also adopted the mentality that playing defensive line against mostly bigger offensive lineman was like a street fight. I tried to defeat my opponent on every play, for all four quarters. Before every game, I mentally prepared myself by convincing myself that I was the toughest guy on the field. Whether it was true or not, no one was going to out work or out hit me. I didn't play the game like a gentleman; I used the game as an emotional release. I played angry and the more I could do to build up that anger before a game, the better. I began to visualize the events and people in my life that caused me to be angry in the past, summoning that anger brought adrenaline, I could unleash on the field.

By now I was almost 6'4" but I was still only 185 lb. I had started weight training on the Universal Gym weight machine we had in the basement of the school and I was eating my parents out of house and home, but it was difficult for me to gain any weight.

All the other guys on the senior defensive line were at least 20 pounds heavier than I was, around 205 lb, so I had much work to do. I was fortunate enough to be voted captain of the defence, mostly because of my physical attitude toward the game.

Our head coach of the Port Moody Blues, Al Jones, taught us to "be tough and aggressive on the field, but be gentlemen off the field, outside the white lines of the gridiron." He'd say, "Men, you have to learn to turn it off when you're outside the white lines, or it will get you into trouble."

Coach Jones encouraged me to continue playing football and reinforced the fact that I needed to get bigger and stronger in the weight room to play at the next level. People telling me this repeatedly had already given me a complex about being undersized; after all, that was the root of much of the bullying I had experienced. Now my coach was encouraging me to do something about it.

At that point, I was determined to play in university and I decided that I would work as hard as necessary to gain the size to make it happen. A fringe benefit would be the end of bullying once and for all, or so I thought.

Back in the 1970's there was no internet to Google information at the touch of a button, and unless you were a Hollywood movie star, there were no personal trainers or private dieticians to help a young kid like myself learn how to gain healthy muscle mass. Everyone had to do their own research.

Subsequently, I made several trips to different libraries to research the material I needed. On top of that, I searched out and spoke to coaches of various sports on successful training techniques, and I approached successful people I met at the gym to discuss their approach. I became passionate about educating myself on the physiology of sport, diet, and training techniques to not only add muscle mass, but to develop the quickness, agility, and flexibility I would need to play.

"Lonely Time," Led Zeppelin (1971)

Now that I had my mind set on playing university football, I had to decide where to play. We lived about a twenty-minute drive from Simon Fraser University (SFU), which is perched on top of Burnaby Mountain. At that time SFU was in the National Association of Intercollegiate Athletics (NAIA), so they bussed to all their away games in the U.S. I figured I could save a lot of money if I played at SFU because I could live at home, so I made an appointment to meet the head coach, Bob DeJulius. I had received a couple of letters of interest from American schools, but I wanted to stay home and play for a Canadian school. I knew that if I played at SFU I wouldn't be playing against Canadian schools, but I would enjoy playing close to home with a strong program. However, SFU had never recruited me, so I planned to make my case as a walk-on.

I had barely walked into DeJulius' office when he started chuckling at me. He said, "You don't look big enough to play at this school, Jason." It was embarrassing. He was like everyone else who had told me I was too small to play the game. Adding salt to the wound, after a cursory look at my transcript, he added, "You probably don't have the grades to get in here anyway." Funny, if he'd taken the time to look at my transcript more closely, he would have seen that I was an honour student and I could easily have been accepted to SFU — their entrance requirements were much lower than those of the University of British Columbia (UBC). So, in the short time I had been in his office, this coach who had never seen me play decided that I couldn't play for his program. Then he made a similar assumption about my grades, with only a brief glance at my transcript.

We really had no other meaningful interaction before I left DeJulius' office. When I left, I felt completely humiliated, disappointed, and angry — like I had been emotionally ambushed. As I left campus, I looked at the grey concrete architecture with new eyes. Instead of the opportunity I saw in them when I arrived, now these buildings resembled a prison. At that moment, I made a personal vow that somehow, I would find a way to prove DeJulius wrong.

As luck would have it, the next week I met someone who would become one of my most influential mentors. Coach Frank Smith, head coach of the UBC Thunderbirds, called me. Essentially, I had contacted DeJulius, only to receive a hasty dismissal from his office, while Coach Smith personally called me, and asked if I would be interested in going for lunch with him to discuss playing for him at UBC.

The following week, Coach Smith drove the 45 minutes out of his way to take me for lunch in Port Moody. Over lunch, he told me that right now he thought I was undersized to play the defensive end position I wanted, but he could tell from my frame that I had great potential to grow into the position, and he had confidence that eventually I could contribute to his program. It seemed to me that he had an eye for the potential of a recruit when he saw them, and to me, that connection we had was positive from the start.

What an emotional turn-around for me: from abject rejection at SFU, to the exhilaration of actively being recruited by its cross-town rival, UBC. I immediately felt committed to play for Coach Smith, who took the time to scout me and showed genuine interest in my future. And at the same time, I knew that playing at UBC would give me the opportunity to prove DeJulius had made a mistake. At that time, UBC and SFU played an annual grudge match called the Shrum Bowl — I was already motivated for those games!

No doubt, it was partly this innate recruiting skill that led to Coach Smith being inducted into the Canadian Football Hall of Fame (CFHOF), in 2019. He is considered one of the greatest Canadian university coaches of all time.

I registered for the education program because my long-term plan was a career in teaching. I had really enjoyed my school experience because of good teachers and coaches, despite the bullying that I experienced.

"Bad Moon Rising," Creedence Clearwater Revival (1969)

My path to UBC didn't go quite to plan due to a needless knee injury that happened during my end-of-the-year school camping trip; I did not end up playing for Coach Smith in the fall after my 1977 high school graduation.

In my final semester at Port Moody High, our PE class took a camping trip to Alouette Lake, in beautiful Fraser Valley. There was an all-girl class and our class of boys, both celebrating our senior year on this trip.

After we arrived and set up the tents and the fire pit, the first activity the teachers had us do was a game of tackle football, boys against girls. Unfortunately, the grass that we were playing on was sloped down towards the lake and there were trees dispersed throughout — not an ideal football field. But as spirited high school kids, we didn't think twice about it, we just got right into the game.

I had a crush on a girl named Denise at the time, and when she got the ball, I didn't want to hurt her, so I gave her a big bear hug. As we laughed, her girlfriend came up behind us and playfully pushed me in the back to free Denise. When our combined weight transferred onto my downhill left leg, I heard a sudden pop and felt pain in my left knee. I tried to walk it off, but now my knee was completely locked.

I limped to the teachers to tell them what happened. Without even looking at my knee, they chuckled and said, "Don't be such a wimp, Riley." They badly misread the situation, adding, "We're going on a five-kilometre hike after this. So, suck it up!"

All I could think of was that I was on the way to play at UBC in a couple of months, and they didn't believe I was hurt playing their silly game: I was in shock.

I actually tried to go on that hike by cutting a Y-shaped branch off a tree to use as a crutch. I got about fifty metres down the path and gave up, limping back to the campsite. When I got back, a beautiful girl had decided that she didn't feel like hiking either. We had never spoken and it was fun for the two of us to have the entire campsite to ourselves for a few hours to get to know each other. Unlike the teachers, she was very sympathetic towards me because of my injury.

When I went to my family doctor after the injury, he gave me crutches and said I should be fine in a couple of weeks. The swelling eventually went down and I could bend it again after I was off the crutches. It was business as usual. I worked all summer and partied with my friends and trained to get bigger and stronger for my first university football season.

But by the end of that summer, my knee was swollen like a balloon and the family doctor finally sent me to an orthopedic surgeon. Dr. Hunt quickly diagnosed it as a torn meniscus and scheduled me for surgery. Another trap door had opened around the corner, to use my dad's phrase, but this turned out to be a blessing in disguise.

I had surgery at the end of August, with UBC camp starting shortly afterwards. Dr. Hunt found that the medial meniscus was torn completely in half, so he removed it entirely. This is what they did back then, before the orthoscopic techniques were developed to repair cartilage instead of just removing it. The meniscus is the spongy pad between the bones, which cushions the joint and prevents the bones from rubbing directly onto each other when the joint is rotating. When they remove the meniscus completely, they are making the joint more susceptible to bone-on-bone friction, which leads to the development of arthritis. (As I write this, I've had a complete left knee replacement because of the arthritis build up in my knee after 43 years without the cartilage. Luckily, I was blessed with tight ligaments, which helped support my knee without it.)

The fact that I had the surgery so late in the summer benefitted me too, because I decided I didn't want to waste a year of eligibility if I couldn't play football. I decided to take a year off and work to save money for school.

This also allowed me to focus on my training, get bigger and stronger, and make myself more competitive for camp. When I informed Coach Smith of my situation, he simply told me to get well and come back when I was at one hundred percent so I could help the team.

For the most part, up until now, I had been undersized for my age. Now that I had experienced my growth spurt straight up, I was working hard in the weight room to put on muscle mass. This also made me less likely to be bullied, and I found myself defending those who were victims, because I had empathy for them. These experiences made me tougher mentally and physically, and stoked that adolescent rage I had inside of me. Now, I was even bigger and tougher than my hero, my big brother John, and I developed a physical confidence in myself that would serve me well in the future.

As Dad said, "Jason, you graduated from the school of hard knocks, where we learn more about life than from books at school. Shit, if I didn't have "boarding house reach" (long arms), I wouldn't have eaten at the Air Force boarding house in London. The food would be put in the middle of the table, on big trays. It was everyone for themselves, and the short guys got skinny, real quick!"

"Carefree Highway," Gordon Lightfoot (1974)

In the meantime, my sister Janice's husband Larry, who I had always admired and respected, got me a job driving a delivery truck for a large plumbing supply warehouse, in Surrey, B.C. I would load the truck with bathtubs, water closets, bundles of copper pipe, and anything else the work order required, then deliver and unload the material at the job site. It was very physical work, but I embraced it because I knew it was making me stronger; I thought of it as an extension of my training.

In a typical day back then, I would drive from my home in Port Moody to Surrey (about a half-hour drive), then work all day loading and driving the truck all over the Fraser Valley, drive home for dinner, then drive to the YMCA in New Westminster (about a half hour in the opposite direction) to work out for two hours in the gym. I did this religiously four times a week because "the Y" was the closest gym to my house in those days.

It wasn't easy because I was usually really tired from working and driving so much, but I stayed committed to my training. Ultimately, I was able to put about 15–20 pounds of muscle mass on my growing frame every year, thanks to Mom's good cooking. My research and hard work were paying off.

For a short time, I moved in with my friend Mike Wood in Surrey to be closer to work. This gave me some time to take a few courses at Douglas College to get a head start on my university degree.

There, in my first psychology course, the professor did something that would always stick with me. He engaged us with a hands-on study that he called biofeedback. In a quiet room, he hooked us up individually to a machine that monitored our heart rate on a wrist band (similar to an early electrocardiogram), and provided our audible pulse on a speaker, accompanied by a numerical heart rate on a digital screen. Then he took us through a relaxation activity, demonstrating how we could actually lower or increase our heart rate with only our minds.

I learned to use this technique to help calm myself as part of my personal mental health improvement plan. I would use it whenever I needed to bring my levels down a notch: at night if I couldn't sleep, for example, or between shifts at work or practices if I needed a power nap, and before games if I felt myself overdosing on caffeine. It also became a good tool decades later when I shared it with my students and players, to help them with their mental health.

Similarly, as part of my knee surgery rehabilitation plan, I signed up to play defensive line in the Canadian Junior Football League (CJFL), with the Vancouver Meralomas that summer. If I was going to be competitive at UBC, I needed to improve my football skills, not just get bigger.

One of my teammates on the Meralomas was Gerald Roper, who was also preparing to play ball at university in the fall. We had mutual friends in football circles, and Roper would also become an All-Star offensive guard in the CFL, so this was the beginning of a long relationship in the football fraternity.

Roper and I had a good season together that summer, he on offensive line (a.k.a. OL) and me on defensive line (a.k.a. DL), winning the BC provincial championship. However, we were beaten badly in the Western Conference Final, when we flew to Saskatchewan to play the Saskatoon Hilltops. A positive memory for me in that game came when we were backed up on our own one-yard line on the last play of the game.

From my defensive end position, I shot through the "B" gap (see Appendix A), tackling the running back in the backfield, preventing him from getting to the end zone and running up the score even more. Who we are as individuals is a result of our past experiences, and I was developing mental and physical toughness through football. The game had already taught me many things, especially to never quit.

After that summer CJFL stint, I looked forward to the opportunity of playing at the next level, for UBC. But I needed to keep training to make it happen.

Before training could continue, though, I would have to overcome another injury. Loading and unloading that Cronkhite Supply truck with heavy plumbing supplies had wrecked my back. I couldn't afford to miss training for camp my rookie year, but it was so painful that I couldn't even sit down. Luckily, there were soft bark-mulch trails in the local park to reduce the pounding on my lower back when I ran. I was off work and going to both a chiropractor and physiotherapist to try to recover before UBC camp started in August.

FIRST QUARTER
MAD DOG EMERGES

"Foreplay/Long Time," Boston (1976)

I finally got to UBC training camp in 1979. My training had added 20 lb of muscle to my frame, so I weighed in at around 205 lb. This was the moment I had been anticipating since Coach Smith had recruited me. I had worked so hard in the gym to get bigger, and saved my hard-earned money to pay for my tuition. It should have been an event to celebrate.

However, instead of finally stepping on the field of my dreams to show that I belonged, I was faced with the frustration of a pretty serious lower back injury. The combined physiotherapy and chiropractic treatment wasn't helping anymore. I couldn't practice because of the pain.

When I went to tell Coach Smith the news that I may have to sit out another training camp, I knew he must have been having doubts about me by then. But he never wavered; he reiterated that he still had faith in me. He said, "Jason, just get healthy and come back when you can help the team."

Years later, he reminded me of that conversation when he said, "Looking back at that point, Jason, you looked like a drowned rat with a bad back."

"Beast of Burden," The Rolling Stones (1978)

Fortunately, when I saw the team doctor, he recognized my frustration and prescribed some horse pills (not literally, of course) that had muscle relaxant and painkiller in them to settle down my lower back spasms. The drugs helped relieve the pain so that I could actually practice; that was the solution. The more I practiced, the stronger my back got and the less pain I had. By the end of training camp, my back felt as good as new: this was the opportunity I was praying for.

I was still the lightest defensive lineman on the roster, so I didn't play much defence at first, but I was quick, agile, and loved to hit. This allowed me to thrive on special teams, which is how most young players earn a spot on the roster.

Unfortunately, I had one really negative side effect from all my training to gain body mass: chronic shin splints. I didn't even know what they were until I got them. Suddenly, whenever I tried to run, I felt sharp stabbing pains, like red-hot tent spikes were being driven up from my ankles into my shin bones and the pain travelled up each of my tibias into my knees every time a foot made impact with the ground. I couldn't even run across the street, let alone play a football game. It was clear that if I wanted to continue playing, I either had to find a cure or a way to manage the pain. If I didn't, my career would be over before it started. This quest for a cure began in my second year; unfortunately, I played with severe shin splints for the rest of my career.

Luckily, UBC had a sports medicine clinic on campus. The doctor told me he wanted to do a bone scan because he suspected I had stress fractures in my shin bones (the medical term for this is "medial tibial stress syndrome"). The scans were negative, but the radiologist said that my tibias were expanding to compensate for my increasing weight — since high school, I had now added about 40 pounds of good weight. He recommended anti-inflammatories before going on the field, and ice treatments after practice to reduce the inflammation and pain. He also prescribed custom-fitted orthotics for my shoes to help prevent my lower legs from torquing when I ran, but the orthotics had no effect at all.

I soon realized that there was no cure, unless my tibias eventually enlarged themselves enough to compensate for my added weight. But I was trapped into constantly gaining more weight. By now, I was gaining about twenty pounds of "good weight" each year, and each year, I had to start running before training camp started, which made my shins flare up again. My shin splints had become the biggest hurdle for me to continue playing.

It was a catch-22. The only real solution was to stop running completely, and I couldn't do that, so I continued to search for ways to adapt.

One thing I knew was that I had to reduce my intake of heavy anti-inflammatories because, if I didn't, I'd wreck my gut. I experimented with other forms of painkillers and prescription drugs, but nothing worked — except aspirin. Amazingly, I found that four regular-strength over-the-counter aspirin removed the pain completely. If I took the aspirin with food, usually a banana, one hour before a game or practice, my shins would be pain-free for about three hours. Then, right after I got off the field, I would wrap ice bags on my shins, or stand in the ice tub for about 20 minutes to reduce the inflammation.

These methods never eliminated the cause of the pain, but through trial and error, I learned how to manage the pain enough so that I could keep playing the game I loved. Nonetheless, it was very frustrating for the rest of my career, every year hoping that they wouldn't flare up again, only to have them return after my second training run. Essentially, before training camp even started, my shin splints would return in full force every single year until I stopped playing.

They were especially painful in training camp because we had two practices every day, so my legs got no rest from the pounding. Because of this pain, I dreaded the start of training camp every year. Luckily, for the majority of my off-season training, I could ride the bike at the gym for my conditioning, which eliminated the pounding completely.

In hindsight, I should have done an aspirin commercial because Bayer Aspirin saved my career.

Having a smart coach helped too. Coach Smith was a hard-nosed, old-school coach, who didn't mince words and expected results on the field, but he also took advantage of every opportunity to make the team better. He knew I'd run through a wall for him and my shin splints weren't just a ploy to get out of conditioning. Accordingly, whenever my shin splints were severe during the season, he allowed me to do alternative conditioning — when the team was running wind sprints on the field, I would be in the training room doing an interval workout on the stationary bike. This eliminated the pounding on my shins and reduced the pain, before I jumped back into the ice tub, once again.

Whenever I rode the stationary bike in the training room, I drew motivation from the 8x10 photos framed and mounted on the wall of all the past UBC football grads who went on to play in the CFL. Great players like Kevin Konar, Dave Kirzinger, Doug Mitchell, Cal Murphy, and Neil Quilter were among that stellar group, and they all achieved excellence after they left campus. I wasn't aware at the time, but all these members of our alma mater would in some way have some impact on my career down the road.

My good friend Pat Brady's dad, Bob Brady, could have been up there too, because he played at UBC as well. I met Pat Brady on UBC campus one summer when he was staying at his parents' place in Vancouver for the summer. Pat had chosen to go to Western University, in spite of his dad being a UBC alumnus and encouraging him to attend his alma mater. Brady's choice would have ramifications later in our intertwining lives.

Coach Laycoe had mounted these pictures on the wall to inspire us. It worked, because I was motivated to ride hard in their presence.

I rented a room in a fraternity house on campus that year. I didn't join the fraternity — I simply paid room and board to stay in the house. I shared a room with a teammate, who was a member of the fraternity. This ended badly because on nights before weekend games, the whole fraternity would literally go out on panty raids at campus sorority houses. When they returned from these frat escapades in the middle of the night, they would do a victory march through the house, banging pots and pans, so I got no sleep at all. I'm sure that the members of the fraternity will remember those as some of the most fun years of their lives, but for me, it wasn't good. I needed a good night's sleep for games, so I had to get out of there.

I moved into a basement suite in Kitsilano at the start of my second year, just a ten-minute drive from Thunderbird Stadium. It was fully furnished and I paid $300 per month. The best part was it was only two blocks away from what would become my favourite restaurant, Olympia Pizza, on Broadway. The second-best thing about it was that it was only a five-minute walk from Kits Beach, on Vancouver harbour. I stayed in that basement suite for the rest of my time at UBC. I moved home during the summers, to save the rent. My landlord saved the room for me every year because he said his wife and daughter felt safe when they knew I was in the basement.

Now, I was about 225 lb and I was starting to get strong. I was training hard and eating five meals a day because I was determined to prove that Coach Smith was right about me. One of those meals was a high protein milkshake in the evening, but breakfast had to be fast so I could get to my early classes. This often consisted of a quick meal of five raw eggs guzzled from a glass and chased with a glass of milk to wash them down. We went to the movie *Rocky* in the late 70s, and when Rocky drank raw eggs out of a glass, the audience gasped because they were grossed out. I wondered what all the fuss was about because I had been doing it long before the movie came out. I was determined that I was going to play varsity football for the UBC Thunderbirds and help the team win; if I had to gain protein by guzzling raw eggs, so be it.

I decided early on that I'd rather guzzle raw eggs than take anabolic steroids to get bigger. In that era, there was no drug policy regarding steroid use whatsoever and it was a totally unregulated industry. This led to athletes in many sports using them to gain an advantage.

Due to the physical demands of the game, many football players at all levels (high school, university, and professional) began using steroids and growth hormones. The black-market performance-enhancing drug trade exploded with dealers seeing huge profits.

I considered doing steroids at the time, because I saw the benefits that powerlifters, bodybuilders, and others were gaining from using them. After researching the topic and doing my own cost-benefit analysis, I found some information on both sides of the steroid issue.

On the plus side, anabolic steroids are considered performing-enhancing drugs because when used in concert with a proper heavy-weight training program, they can result in increased muscle mass and strength in most people. They can also reduce the time it takes to recover from muscle injuries, reducing the time an athlete is sidelined due to injury.

On the negative side, however, I found that long-term use of steroids can damage the user's internal organs, especially the heart, kidneys, reproductive and immune systems, and lead to connective tissue injuries. An example of the latter would be when muscle strength exceeds ligament strength and pulls the ligament right off the bone. These types of injuries usually require surgical repair to reattach the ligaments, thereby increasing missed playing time.

The worst thing was that because it was so unregulated, young guys would "stack" steroids (take several different anabolic steroids at the same time, sometimes along with growth hormones) to get a competitive advantage, often doing serious harm to themselves. Steroid abuse has also been linked to mood swings and violent behaviour off the field.

Lyle Alzado, the former NFL defensive-line great, became the "poster child" for the damage steroid abuse can do to the body and mind. He did steroids and growth hormones throughout his college and NFL career. He declared, "If you're on steroids or human growth hormone, stop. I should have."[5] Sadly, at the young age of 43, Alzado died of brain cancer, which he believed was caused by his steroid abuse. His second wife also accused him of dramatic mood swings and physical abuse, attributed to steroid use.[6]

Hence, after thoroughly researching it, I made a personal decision to abstain from steroid use. I figured it would take longer, but if I worked hard enough, I could still build my size and strength up enough to play the game without them.

Nonetheless, throughout my career I had some teammates and opponents at all levels who used steroids. Some guys at gyms I worked out at dispensed them from their lockers and offered them to me whenever I had even a slight injury. "Jason, come into the change room, I've got some stuff that'll help you heal faster and make you stronger," they'd say. I just thanked them for the offer and declined.

This was a personal choice that I made based on my own needs and experience. I certainly didn't need steroids to increase my aggressiveness on the field, for example. I had learned that with a couple cups of coffee, I could conjure up all the aggression I needed, using that inner anger I harboured from my bullying experiences. It was like a candle of fury always waiting in the background of my mind, which I could light up when I needed it.

---

[5] Alzado, L. 1991. I'm sick and I'm scared. *Sports Illustrated Vault*. Url: vault.si.com/vault/1991/07/08 (accessed April 13, 2023).

[6] Puma, M. Not the size of the dog in the fight. *ESPN Classic*. Url: espn.com/classic/biography/ (accessed April 13, 2023).

To conclude this discussion of performance enhancing drugs, it's good to see the league and player's association taking action to control their use to help protect athletes and level the playing field. Part of the current CFL/CFLPA collective bargaining agreement states, "Players who test positive or fail to provide a sample face a two-game suspension for a first violation, a nine-game suspension for a second violation, a one-year suspension for a third violation, and a lifetime ban for a fourth violation.[7]

Eventually, with my increasing size and strength, I was getting more competitive and earning more playing time at defensive line. My hard work in the gym (and in the kitchen) was finally starting to pay off.

And I was still able to get my adrenaline fix on the punt team, flying down the field with reckless abandon, and blowing up opposing punt returners. I loved special teams.

Bob Laycoe was an outstanding coach and even better person. He was a positive role model for everyone on our team. I was proud to have him as my defensive coordinator for my four years at UBC. I learned much from him about my defensive line position, defensive systems, and dedication to the sport. He was a true gentleman of the game, who led with a quiet demeanour and brilliant intellect.

Like all great coaches, he spent long hours breaking down film of our next opponent and instructing us, in the meeting room and on the field, on how our unit would be successful in defending every play they ran against us. He made sure we were in the right position to be successful.

But something Coach Laycoe was really good at, and that many other coaches at the time didn't do, was grading our performance in the previous game. He watched every position and gave every player a percent-grade after the game. He posted these grades on the bulletin board for complete transparency. One time in third year, I questioned my grade after a game. He didn't take offence. He said, "Jason, come in tomorrow morning and we'll grade it out again together, and by analyzing and reflecting on your play, it will help you reach your potential as a player."

---

[7] Canadian Football League (CFL) News Release. February 3, 2023. *Hamilton's Colin Kelly suspended for violating CFL/CFLPA drug policy*. Url: press.cfl.ca (accessed July 17, 2023).

We went through the film together the next day. I couldn't believe that I graded myself lower than he had; I learned that when you think you've had a great game, it usually wasn't as good as you thought, and vice versa if you've had a bad game.

Coach Laycoe and Coach Smith complemented each other extremely well. Sometimes we suspected they conspired to work the good cop, bad cop routine; if not, they fell into it very naturally. At half-time, if we happened to be losing and needed some added motivation, Coach Smith would hustle into the dressing room and cuss and yell and rant to the point that his carotid arteries would appear to want to burst from his neck. Depending on how pissed he was at the time, these episodes became known as either a "single or double blue-veiner," which indicated how pronounced the arteries were on his neck. In fear for one's life, no one wanted to go near him after a double blue-veiner!

Then, after a moment to let our tongue-lashing sink in, Coach Laycoe would step in and say his piece. In a complete contrast to Coach Smith, he would say something like, "Okay, gentlemen, this is what we need to do." And he would calmly explain the error of our ways and how to correct them. I don't remember him ever swearing. The net result of these two coaches working in unison was generally very effective in correcting and motivating us to be successful in the second half.

"A Horse With No Name," America (1971)

In my quest to put myself through school, I worked as often as I could; the only time I didn't work was during the football season. I gained a lot of diverse work experience during these years, some of which could be quite physical at times, making for a bit of extra "training."

During summers, I worked weekends as a bouncer and occasional disc jockey at a pub in Coquitlam, called the Caribou Trail Hotel. We called it "The Boo" for short. At the same time, my full-time summer job was assistant park warden at Buntzen Lake Recreation Area (Park).

Compared with the combination of the hectic pace of university studies, the grind of training constantly, the pounding music and cigarette smoke of my pub job, this job became something I looked forward to every day.

Buntzen Lake, owned by BC Hydro, was close by my parent's place, where I stayed to save money in the summer months. The hydro company built a dam at the northern end of the lake, to generate hydroelectric power for the Vancouver region. At the opposite end of the lake, they built a beautiful park, with imported white sand for an amazing beach and public swimming area. The crystal-clear water averages about 30 metres in depth and is stocked for fishing every spring.

Being a park warden's assistant was one of my all-time favourite jobs. Among other things, I joined a crew to start building hiking trails around the lake. Warden Johnston would load up the tools in his powerboat (his was the only powerboat permitted on the lake), and drop us off on the far side of the lake for the day. He'd pick us up at a designated time afterwards. We had a walkie-talkie for emergencies.

I would arrive at the park early each day tasked with opening the park and cleaning up the beaches before the public arrived. Although I never saw a bear that summer, there was usually evidence in the morning of bears tearing apart garbage cans that had been locked the night before.

It eased my soul to be the first arrival to this picture-perfect postcard every morning: the emerging sun fighting through the morning dew; the mist-covered forest of the Coast Mountain foothills reflected in the still, glass-like water; the steam eerily rising up from the lake's surface into the crisp morning air; a welcoming cocoon of silence enveloping everything; the mystery of the new day confirmed by the enigma of the loon's call, suddenly breaking the silence. It was beautiful.

The peace and tranquility it offered, amongst a world of chaos, provided a connection with my spirituality, which surprised me at first. I began to embrace the lake's ability to help calm my mind and body, opening myself up to the mystical journey it presented.

In that vein, one day, we were working loudly with shovels and pick-axes on the hiking trail, when we looked up to find an entire family of deer standing silently, watching us work. The family was literally only about 10 metres from us. It was so amazing that they were not frightened by the noises we made. We all stopped working and stared at them for what seemed like a long time, but was probably just a few seconds. Then they bounded into the bush and disappeared from our view, like they were never there.

We concluded that they were unafraid because they had not seen humans before, but it definitely left us with a strong feeling of being closely connected with our natural surroundings. The job was filled with these special moments, which were beautiful distractions from our labour, especially for me after a crazy shift at the pub the night before.

Another experience that added to my ever-growing sense of connection with wildlife occurred when we were eating lunch in the lunch room inside Warden Johnson's headquarters. It was attached to the fenced compound where all the park service equipment was stored. I was sitting with my back against the wall beside an open window. The large garage bay door was left open, creating a sort of wind tunnel, so there was a nice cool breeze flowing though the building on a hot day.

Suddenly, as I took a bite of my sandwich, I saw what I thought was a large bumble bee streak into the room, following the flow of air, and without hesitation, it zipped toward the open window. We were startled by a bang and small explosion of body parts as the bumble bee hit the closed side of the window beside my head. It fell to the ground, motionless beside my chair.

I leaned over in my chair to take a closer look at the biggest bee I had ever seen. It was not a bumble bee at all. It was a beautiful hummingbird that had hit the window in full flight, losing many feathers and apparently dead from the impact. We didn't think anything could live after such a high-velocity impact with the window.

I picked up the tiny bird and placed it in the palm of my hand. On a hunch, I wrapped my right hand around it gently but firmly to warm its body, while I stroked its head with the tip of my left index finger, and breathed gently into its face. Then, I got goose bumps as, amazingly, it opened its eyes and stared straight into mine. "It's alive, can you believe that?" I exclaimed, incredulously.

A moment later it began to rotate its head back and forth to survey the room. When I opened my hand, it stood up on my palm and blinked at me. It flapped its wings a couple of times while resting there, as if to test them out. Then, it raised itself up and hovered above my hand, with its tiny wings flapping at an invisible pace. I was convinced that it would take off, terrified by the monster that held it captive, and never look back after its near-death experience.

Amazingly, it did the opposite. Several times, it hovered above my hand and landed again, like it was the trusted pad for a tiny helicopter. Then, it hovered in front of my face and looked directly into my eyes, as if to say thank you in its silent elegance. Finally, it flew out of the warden's centre the same way it came in, returning to the safety of the park.

The hummingbird was the topic of our crew's chatter for the rest of the lunch break. None of us could believe that such a tiny bird could live after hitting the window with that much velocity. Later, I found one of its feathers on the floor. I kept it as a tiny memento of that moment when the smallest of creatures blessed me with its presence. The brief but strong connection I made with this creature remains a mystery. Perhaps it was absolution for my guilt resulting from my shameful treatment of that pigeon as a boy, so long ago. Without doubt, it was a spiritually uplifting experience for me.

I am no saint, but Mom and Dad always taught us to be fair. Still to this day, when I see injustice in the world, I get angry. "Never start a fight, but never back down from a bully, either:" Dad's motto was great on the football field because I could legally unleash my inner rage. Inside those white lines of the football field, I could play like a mad dog, frothing, growling, and knocking people down for an entire game with impunity! Luckily, football allowed me to vent my emotions this way most of the time — enough to keep me out of jail, anyway. Unfortunately, there were times that I just could not contain myself when I saw shit happen off the field.

One such occasion occurred after a hard day of trail-building at Buntzen Lake. I was driving home in my little Chevy Vega through rush hour traffic in downtown Port Moody. I had the windows down because it was a hot day and the car had no air-conditioning. The cassette player was cranked up loud with rock and roll. All the traffic stopped at a red light.

As I waited for the light to change, I heard a deep rumble over my stereo. At first, I thought it was thunder, but the sky was clear. I checked my rearview mirror to see two idiots on motorcycles driving between the stopped rows of cars. They looked like typical biker-gang members, in ragged jeans, black helmets, full black leather jackets, chains dangling from their wallets, full beards, and dark shades so you couldn't see their eyes. They rode Harley Davidson choppers with extended chrome front forks.

I first thought, "What assholes, driving between cars to get ahead because they think they are the kings of the road, better than everyone else. They think they are above the law, so they can fuck everyone else. These guys are totally disrespecting everyone else on the road." They passed me to the right, between my car in the left lane and the car in the adjacent lane. Their exhaust pipes snarled, completely drowning out the stereo in my car.

Right after they passed my car, I saw a large gelatinous green-yellow blob of snot and mucous running slowly down the inside of my windshield. I was confused at first, thinking "How did that get there?" Initially, I couldn't comprehend anyone doing something like this unprovoked to a complete stranger. After processing what had happened, I realized that one of those bikers had the audacity, the sheer disrespect, to spit into the open passenger window of my car. I felt completely violated.

I thought, "Fuck! I'm not going to let them get away with it." I immediately went into an unmitigated rage. I knew from their driving that these assholes showed no common courtesy or respect to the general public, but now they had made it personal. Using human bodily fluid to demean another person is disgusting. To do it to someone like this, with the noise of their bikes masking their degenerate actions, was over the top — something only the lowest bullies would do. I couldn't let it go.

I was a couple of cars back from the light when it turned green. I accelerated and negotiated through the traffic to catch up to the bikers, the whole time working up the biggest gob I could muster in my mouth. I didn't know which one of them had spat into my car, but it didn't matter. To my thinking, they were both complicit in their assault on common decency.

As soon as I reached the first biker, I pulled as close as I could without hitting his bike and honked my horn to get his attention. When he looked from his Harley saddle into my open driver-side window, I looked directly through his shades and I spat the entire mouthful of gob I had built up in my mouth, straight into his face!

He was so shocked that he almost lost control of his bike. He weaved back and forth across the road until he regained control; unfortunately, he didn't put his bike down. I turned right down the next street, and pulled over to the side of the road, hoping they would follow. I stayed in my car, with my right hand on the handle of the baseball bat I kept behind the passenger seat, just for occasions like this.

Both thugs pulled up to the end of the street that I was now waiting on. I could see in my rearview mirror that they were debating what to do next, so I hailed them to come to my car with a wave of my arm. I imagined that they had trouble rationalizing what just happened to them. I figure the conversation might have gone something like this:

"What the fuck just happened, you almost put your bike down?"

"That fucking asshole just spit in my face!"

"What the fuck? Let's go take him out!"

"Well, I spit in his car at the stop light, and he seems like a fuckin' lunatic — look he's inviting us to come to his fucking car!"

At that exact moment, a Port Moody police cruiser drove down the next street at the end of the block I had stopped on. I don't even remember the cops looking in our direction, but I know the bikers saw them cruise by and might have concluded their brief discussion something like:

"Holy shit, look, the pigs just drove by!"

"Let's get the fuck outta here!"

As I watched the bikers drive away in the rearview mirror, my adrenaline-fuelled rage began to dissipate and I felt torn. At first, I was so angry from my disappointment that they didn't turn down that road so we could finish the fight, but then I was relieved that the situation didn't escalate into a violent street brawl.

Fortunately, I never did have to use that baseball bat, but it was always good to know I had some back-up in case I was outnumbered like this. There had been news reports of gang activity in the area — which, in my mind, can be translated into "bullies victimizing innocent people" — and I wanted to be vigilant, to protect myself from bastards like this. It just wasn't in me to look the other way.

After I calmed down, I had some time to reflect. I thought about how crazy I was to do what I did, but at the same time, didn't they deserve to be held accountable for their actions? Those bikers could have been armed with more than a baseball bat, what if they were packing guns? What are the odds of that cop car driving by right at that specific moment? What would have happened if that cop hadn't driven by? Once again, could it be just coincidence, or was there something greater at play here?

Regardless of these thoughts racing in my mind, I had a smile on my face all the way home because I felt that I had stood up for common decency and, just maybe, those bikers might show more respect to people they encountered in the future. The music on my tape deck sounded sweet all the way home.

"Move It On Over," George Thorogood and the Destroyers (1978)

Bouncing at the Boo was distinctly different from the park warden job — the contrast was striking. With the large crowds, pounding music, and smoke-filled air, the pub atmosphere was diametrically opposed to the wide-open space and fresh air of Buntzen Lake Park, nestled in its natural oasis.

The Boo pub was a local landmark, with great shows on summer weekends, featuring the likes of Long John Baldry, Powder Blues Band, Doug and the Slugs, Corey Hart, and Jan and Dean, who all played to sold out shows over the years.

The Boo was also known for its greasy-spoon "Boo burgers" with fries, which John the chef would make for the staff for a buck. John's burgers were great and us bouncers would often go to the hotel cafe on our breaks to briefly remedy our inexorable appetites.

The manager of the pub, Batiste, was a smart guy who recruited some of the biggest and toughest guys from the SFU and UBC football teams. Many of the players worked summer jobs as bouncers. Some of the SFU boys I remember working with were linebacker Richard White, offensive linemen Tony Antunovic and Dennis "Mount" Guevin, defensive linemen Derek "Fadge" Faggiani and Rick Klassen, and linebacker Dan Rashovich. Kelly Stinson was a former player who was the assistant manager of the pub. The UBC contingent included offensive lineman Don Adamic, George Piva, and Jerry Dobrovolny, linebacker Steve Harrison, and defensive linemen Dean Claridge, Carey Lapa, Rob Waite, and myself. There were many other staff that were not from one of these schools, but for a few years, we formed a formidable group. The irony of it was that although we (the SFU and UBC team members) were sworn enemies on the field when we played against each other, we worked as a team backing each other up at the pub. We had a lot of memorable nights at the Boo.

An infamous example was when a pissed-off patron who had been kicked out earlier in the night for intoxication came back with a gun and shot up the Backstage Club, our late-night dance club adjacent to the Boo, which was open after the pub closed.

Richard White tells the story of how Rick Klassen probably saved his life because he pulled Richard back from the door just before this asshole shot up the place. I was not there to experience the chaos that night, but luckily, no one was hurt.

After that happened, if a guy ever made a threat to the staff about bringing back a weapon, we would subdue him before he got to his vehicle and confine him in the office until the police came. Depending on the situation, this could be a matter of life and death and we weren't leaving it to chance. Management recognized this too and made sure we were treated well for working pub security.

"Songbird," Fleetwood Mac (1977)

I met my beautiful wife, Paulette, during my first year at UBC, in 1979. She worked as a teller at the CIBC Bank on campus, where I held my student loan. I saw her the first time I walked in and lined up waiting for a teller.

She caught my eye because she was the prettiest girl in the building; with beautiful, smooth skin, a pert little nose, hazel eyes, auburn hair cut in a blunt hairstyle just above the shoulder, and bright red lipstick framing her mischievous smile. A stylish white cashmere sweater and black dress pants accentuated her small but strong frame. Her sparkling personality as she interacted with her clients only enhanced her appearance.

I didn't ask Paulette out on a date right away because I needed to get to know her better. I usually waited in line until she was free, just so I could talk to her. She was always very patient with me when I came into the bank with some lame question or other about my student loan.

She liked my long, flowing mullet haircut, which she described as "business in the front and party in the back."

Eventually, I decided to ask Paulette out on a date. To which she promptly said, "No." I must have asked her out a half a dozen times, before she finally said yes and agreed to come to a game on campus. I remember it distinctly because I was walking towards the bank exit with a big smile on my face, when she exclaimed across the room, "But, Jason, don't think this is a date or anything!" All her colleagues and the customers laughed at my expense, but I was undeterred. "This girl has a great sense of humour!" I thought as I left the bank.

As it turns out, it was a date. We won the game, and afterwards we joined the rest of the team at the student pub on campus. I was impressed with Paulette's knowledge of the game as we talked over drinks, cocktails for her and lagers for me. She credited her father and brother with this knowledge, because if she wanted to watch TV on Monday nights, it was *Monday Night Football* or bust, so she learned to enjoy the game with them.

Knowing how much I loved beer, Paulette began the ritual of bringing a six-pack of Heineken beer to every home game, easily concealed in her large black leather purse. As I quenched my thirst in the parking lot, I couldn't believe how generous this woman was, but also how well she understood me. Already.

I had no idea at that time that this woman would become the answer to my prayers, bringing an understanding and patience for my shortcomings, taming the rage that was built up inside me, like a soothing emotional balm.

The team had an excellent defence that year, coordinated by the great Bob Laycoe, and we competed at every position with games within the game. When the boys found out that Paulette was bringing me a six-pack to every game, we made a deal that whoever got a sack or made a big defensive play in the game got beer in the parking lot. We would remind each other during the games whenever someone made a big play: "Hey, that's a Heineken for me!" Hence, opposing quarterbacks can blame Paulette indirectly for motivating our defensive line to be even more thirsty for blood than we already were.

Another thing that endeared me to Paulette was her kindness in helping feed me. Having made sure that I waited for her to help me at the bank all those months, she knew how limited my resources were, so I was the benefactor of her pity. She would go to the Granville Island Market on Saturday mornings and pick up all the fresh ingredients for a meal she wanted to cook for me. She also knew I had limited cookware and kitchen utensils in my basement suite, so she would often bring her mom's pots and pans to cook with. She would make me meals that were the envy of all my teammates. After all, she learned from the best. Paulette's mom, Roxine, was an outstanding cook and she taught her daughter everything she knows in the kitchen. I just happened to be the lucky recipient of that culinary knowledge, as Paulette continued casting her spell on me.

"Takin' Care of Business," Bachman-Turner Overdrive (1973)

Speaking of food, one night in 1980, my second year in the program, the UBC physical education department held a dance at the gym on campus, to which I invited Paulette and some other friends to enjoy a night of music and dancing. I didn't know at the time that the night would end up with yet another example of bullying and violence.

After the dance, we went to Olympia Pizza. I loved their food, so I ate there as often as I could. Olympia was also open till 3 a.m. — later than most other restaurants at the time — so it got the late-night crowd, after the bars closed.

George Kerasiotis was the original owner, and it's still in the family. I met George the first time I discovered the restaurant after moving into my basement suite. I introduced myself after enjoying the best lasagna I had ever tasted. George told me he personally came into the restaurant early every morning to make the pasta sauce for the day using an old family recipe. As I got to know George, I learned that he is one of the kindest and most generous people I know. He is a short, Greek-Canadian immigrant, who wears an eternal smile on his face.

The night of that dance cemented the now forty-year-long friendship between George and me after George was a victim of bullying and I was able to help him.

While Paulette and I, along with my old room mate Mike Wood, waited for our large "Royal" pizza, Mike and I reminisced about our time living together in a basement suite in Surrey before I left for UBC.

Shortly after ordering our food, we heard voices being raised at a booth on the other side of the restaurant. I saw George go to speak to the four noisy guys sitting in the booth, but the din in the busy restaurant made it hard to hear what was going on.

I watched closely to see if George needed my help, but Paulette told me to ignore it and let George handle it. She rightfully didn't want me to escalate the situation, so I listened to her and waited. But I was now fixated on the situation. Suddenly, I heard even louder taunts coming from the four jerks. That's when I told Paulette and Mike that I could wait no longer — I couldn't sit and watch while a friend was being bullied.

I walked up behind George and put my hand on his shoulder to reassure him that I had his back. That's when I noticed an entire serving of lasagna sliding down the wall of their booth, after being thrown by one of these assholes. "Who invited the big, blond gorilla?" one of them asked, as the others laughed.

I looked each of them in the eye, and said, "Is everything okay here, George?"

George said, in his Greek accent, "Thank you, Jason, but don't worry about it. I can handle it. You go enjoy your food."

The bullies now understood that George was not alone, so I took his advice and returned to my table. In my experience, bullies are really brave when they outnumber their victims, so now they knew the odds were more even. However, their intoxication offered false bravado.

By now everyone in the restaurant was aware of what was going on; we were all relieved when they got up and walked to the cashier station at the entrance to the restaurant. Then, voices were raised again; now they were refusing to pay their bill and George was attempting to calm them down and have them pay for the food that they had ordered but were too drunk to enjoy. Finally, George told them all to leave the restaurant because they were making more of a disturbance than it was worth.

I saw George actually go out the door with the four of them and close it behind him. I thought, "What a brave individual he is at his size to face four drunken assholes by himself so that the rest of us can eat in peace."

Then the ringleader of these clowns opened the door and yelled inside, "Come on out here, you big, blond gorilla! I have something for you."

Paulette encouraged me to sit down and not get involved, but I just couldn't ignore the injustice happening right before our eyes.

When I got outside the front door, George grabbed my arm and said, "It's okay, Jason, let it go." But I couldn't let it go. These four guys had bullied my friend, thrown his food against the wall, tried their best to ruin the meals of everyone else in his restaurant, refused to pay their bill, and then physically threatened George in front of his establishment.

I said, "George, I'm glad you're okay. Please go back inside and let me handle this."

I stepped toward the group and noticed that one of them had a small dog on a leash. Thankfully, he quickly ran away with his dog — I don't like to see animals put in harm's way. When I took another step towards them, two more decided they didn't want to be involved and ran away.

That's when the one with the big mouth took a swing at me. That was a mistake because I was ready for a fight. After watching these clowns treat a man as nice as George so rudely, I was angry.

I quickly delivered a flurry of punches that put him down on the sidewalk. I told him to fuck off and never bother George again. Thinking he'd got the message, I stupidly broke the bouncer's code and turned away from him to rejoin Paulette and Mike in the restaurant; I hadn't realized that they were already behind me. With my back turned on this asshole, he staggered back up on his feet with a knife in his hand. Luckily, before he got to me, Mike saw the knife and showed tremendous courage. He shouted, "Look out!" as he stepped around me, and nailed him with a hard right uppercut.

After George called an ambulance for the guy, he told us how much he appreciated what we did to support him. He told us to walk home before the police arrived, took my address, and said he would have the pizza delivered. When the pizza arrived and I tried to pay the driver, he told me George said it was on the house to thank us for the help.

For the first couple of visits to Olympia after that, I thought it was a kind thank-you when George covered my bill. But then it started to get embarrassing. Though I didn't want to take advantage of his generosity, George knew I was a growing student-athlete and continued insisting that I eat for free.

To this day, whenever I'm in Vancouver, I visit George and his family at Olympia Pizza to catch up with the news, and to help pay him back for his generosity when I was a student. His food is as good as ever, so our family and friends enjoy dining there as often as we can. And you know what? George still goes in early every morning to make his pasta sauce.

◇◆◇

Another friend I met that summer was Rick Moor, who was later the catalyst for another drunken incident where the angry streetfighter in me emerged and nearly derailed my university football career (it certainly thwarted later training plans). We met at a construction site where we were both hired as labourers for the summer, working on the construction of a large complex of condominiums.

Rick was a fitness-conscious insurance executive who wore glasses, so I nicknamed him “Clark Kent.” We got on well because we were both athletes who took the physical labour as a challenge to get stronger.

So it was that Clark and Mad Dog paired up to embrace the tough physical work that some others avoided whenever the foremen needed something done quickly. Once, we needed to move a pile of gravel into a foundation before the cement truck arrived. Shovelling gravel is one of the toughest jobs on construction sites, so we knew it would be a lot of work, but also a great workout; to up the ante, we pushed ourselves to move the gravel as fast as we could.

We both shovelled gravel into the wheelbarrow, then took turns moving it into the building and dumping it onto the dirt floor. Some of the other labourers were on break when they circled around us, leaning on their shovels, and cheered us on as we created a flurry of dust and stones. When we had moved the pile, we took rakes and leveled the gravel, so the cement could be poured. We finished this just in time for the cement truck to arrive.

“Badlands,” Bruce Springsteen (1978)

And now the drunken incident: one night, when I wasn’t scheduled to work at the Boo, Rick and I decided to meet at the pub to enjoy some cold beers. We stayed too late, got drunk, and went to the Denny’s restaurant located across the parking lot for something to eat. It was open twenty-four hours a day, so it was packed with the post-pub crowd. The hostess asked us to wait for a table in the small lobby area, just inside the front entrance.

The front entrance had two sets of double glass doors, with a few feet of space between them for insulation. The doors opened towards the outside.

So, there we sat, two drunken jocks dressed in jeans, sneakers, and t-shirts. We were just getting to know each other, so I didn't really know how Rick would behave when he was drunk, though from our work together, it was clear that he liked a physical challenge. But up to this point, he had been a complete gentleman and we were just having a good time, looking forward to some food.

Then, two really attractive girls walked in the side entrance. We elbowed each other where we sat, thinking, "Look at those babes...wink, wink, nod, nod."

The girls were soon followed by two guys in full biker regalia, wearing long beards and heavy leather jackets — the only thing missing was their official gang colours. They were both formidable-looking characters. That's when Rick's attitude changed and he decided to verbalize what we were both thinking; loudly enough for the bikers to hear, he grumbled, "Too bad those two babes are with those fuckin' bikers!" The bikers immediately walked towards us with malice in their eyes.

Standing up to face these new enemies, we were now the drunken assholes who initiated their hostility. I turned toward Rick, wondering, "What the fuck were you thinking?" Unfortunately, the copious amount of alcohol we had consumed made me slow on the draw.

When I turned back toward the biker, he was now squarely in front of me, "Fuck you, asshole!" he said, as his fist came at my face. He hammered me squarely in the mouth, the force of impact snapping my head back. In his hubris, he seemed to think he could put me down with one shot. Rick apparently agreed with him because he instantly lunged at the guy and latched on to him.

However, I stayed on my feet and shook my head. Instead of putting me down, the punch woke me up and things quickly changed pace for me. I knew Rick was overmatched with this asshole, and I needed to take out the second biker quickly, so he wouldn't jump me from behind when I got back to the object of my rage. I knew I had to do it fast, because I believed Rick's life was now in danger.

The situation created a sudden urgency in my mind, which the second biker now had to endure. I delivered a relentless combination of punches, knocking him through the first set of double glass doors. He was belligerent and attempted to swing back at me, so the brawl continued as I knocked him through the second set of glass doors onto the sidewalk outside the entrance. I had delivered blow after blow smashing his head and face repeatedly, with blood splattering everywhere. But he was a tough son-of-a-bitch, and refused to go down. In desperation, knowing I needed to get back to Rick, I kicked him in the head and knocked him out. I rushed back into the restaurant, hoping Rick was still alive.

As I burst back through the doors, I was immediately grabbed by two bouncers I worked with at the Boo. Rick was fine, and the first biker was surrounded and restrained by more Boo bouncers. Still raging, I momentarily considered lunging over the top of the group separating myself from the object of my anger. As if they read my mind, my colleagues just increased their grip on my arms and ushered me aggressively into the men's room. They said, "Jason, settle down man, we need to check you out." They mistakenly thought that I was covered in my own blood.

These guys stayed with me in the bathroom to calm me down. I noticed that my right hand was beginning to swell. I thought, "No big deal after all the punches I threw."

Later, Rick told me he thought the biker had knocked me out, so he just bear-hugged him and hung on for dear life until my bouncer compatriots broke them up. Personally, I was really pissed off that I never got to finish what the first biker had started.

When I went to the Royal Columbian Hospital emergency room in New Westminster, they took x-rays of my swollen right hand. When the doctor had the results, he told me I had shattered the fourth metacarpal and fractured the third metacarpal in my hand. I would need surgery to put a plate on my fourth metacarpal to maintain proper function of my hand.

After I had the surgery on my hand a few days later, the surgeon said it went well, and the new plate would make it stronger than it was before. The other fractured bone would need a few weeks to heal. The important thing for me was that I could still do bench presses by placing the bar on the heel of my hands, so I wouldn't have to miss any training. I also went back to bouncing soon because I needed the money.

In the meantime, I went to see Coach Smith to tell him what happened and not to worry because the hand would be fine by the time my third-year training camp started. He was disappointed that this may affect my training, but he was happy that it would be healed in time for camp. "Just stay out of trouble for the rest of the summer, so you can help the team, Jason," he said.

Coach was right. After all the work I had put into my training, I was finally getting close to the size and strength I needed to be successful. However, if I didn't control myself and manage my anger outside the white lines of the football field, I could jeopardize everything being injured in a fight. We both knew I needed to get 100% healthy to have the type of breakout season I was hoping for.

A few weeks later at my follow-up appointment the doctor re-x-rayed my hand. He told me it was good to go. He literally said, "You can go back to boxing." I thought, great, now my hand is one hundred percent so I don't have to worry about it at work anymore.

As luck would have it, one night near the end of summer, about a week before training camp at UBC, I was back at the front door of the Boo for one of my last shifts. Jan and Dean, an influential 1960s group known for their beach party music, and almost as famous as the Beach Boys, were playing, so it was a very busy night. Rick Moor would be there with his brother that night. I didn't know Rick's brother, but Rick assured me he would behave himself.

As the night went on, the place was hopping. Although we managed the crowd with a line at the front door, we were often over the seating capacity for the pub when a big-name band was playing — this increased the gate receipts, which management loved. The crowd was generally well-behaved and loved to party. Girls would often dance on the tables, until we asked them to climb down. Strategically, as long as we had a lineup out front, the police knew we had the crowd under control.

One of the reasons the crowd was usually so well-behaved for these shows was because the manager, Kelly Stinson, would employ as many of the biggest and toughest of the SFU and UBC football player-bouncers as possible. So, there would be about five monsters of humanity at each door when we allowed the patrons to come into the pub for the show. People commented about the size of our bouncers all the time, and it was well-known that if you got caught fighting, you had your ass thrown out for the night, if not longer.

Later in the evening, with everyone having a fantastic night enjoying the band, I scanned the crowd for trouble from my station at the front door. Unexpectedly, I saw a chair being raised by someone up above the crowd's heads. That could only mean one thing, so I started working my way through the crowd as quickly as I could toward the chair in the air, after letting my colleagues at the door know, just in case. When I got closer to the suspect, I saw him swing the chair down on someone's head. The victim was Rick's younger brother, who was my guest for the night. Apparently, brawling ran in the family!

I grabbed the chair bandit in a bear hug and began to escort him out of the pub. We were almost out the front door when he twisted away and took a swing at me. I dropped him with a right cross, then two bouncers came to remove him; he was banned for the night. Later on, I noticed that my hand began to swell again.

When the x-ray results were in, my third metacarpal was fractured again. The doctor said I could still play and compete in training camp, but only if I wore a cast on my hand until further notice. I thought, "Maybe if you hadn't told me I could go back to boxing so soon, I wouldn't have reinjured my hand so close to training camp." I didn't say it though, because I knew I could only blame myself.

Of course, when I went back to Coach Smith to explain my new predicament, his stern face said it all. "Unfortunately, I broke my hand again," I told him, then followed that with what I meant as a "silver lining" comment: "I'm so glad that I won't have to have surgery again and miss training camp, Coach."

Coach Smith only had one thing to say: "Dammit, Jason, when are you gonna learn how to kick?"

"Long Train Runnin'," Doobie Brothers (1973)

The story doesn't end there, however. I went to our trainer, Ron "Shooter" Mattison, to speak to him about designing a removable cast, so I could wear it for practices and games, and take it off when I wasn't on the field. He said he recently learned that you could make a rubberized cast out of silicone caulk. I thought that was a great idea, it would protect my hand from impact, but would be light and more flexible than a traditional plaster cast. We arranged for him to do it before our upcoming camp.

When the time came, I went to see Shooter to have the new-style rubber cast put on my hand. First, he applied a gauze wrap to protect my skin from the caulk, wrapping several layers on my hand and wrist. Then he snipped the point off the tip of the silicone caulk tube and began to cover the gauze with it. He used large tongue depressors to spread it and smooth it over the gauze. He used two containers of caulk to get the thickness he wanted, then he shaped it at the ends and curled the gauze up around my wrist and fingers. It was a work of art.

Shooter told me to go to a movie or something to pass the time, because it would take 2–3 hours for the silicone caulk to cure. Following doctor's orders, I invited Steve Harrison, our All-Star inside linebacker, to join me for a movie at the local theatre. It would keep my mind off the hand and let the silicone set. After the movie, we planned to go for a beer and talk about our important training camp coming up in a couple of days.

About half an hour into the movie, my hand started to itch. Steve said, "Don't worry about it, Shooter said it had to cure." I thought, "Okay no problem, let's keep enjoying the movie."

An hour into the movie, my hand started burning. Stubbornly, I decided to bear with it and hope the caulk cured soon. Shortly after that, I noticed an acrid smell coming up out of my cast. That's when I lost it. "Steve, come on, we have to get back to my place and cut this fucking cast off my hand. It smells like it's burning my skin."

We left the movie in progress, and the funny thing is, I don't even remember what movie we went to. We rushed back to my place and I grabbed the scissors for Steve to cut the cast off. He carefully cut down one side of the cast, and as he did, we could smell the burned flesh even more.

As Steve removed the cast, we could see that the gauze that Shooter had applied to protect the hand was now absorbed into the calking and the silicone was in direct contact with my skin. The skin was now bright red and swollen where the caulk had burned the entire area the cast had covered. We could feel and smell the heat coming off my skin. I ran it under cold water to try to relieve the pain, but it didn't do anything to stop the chemical burning of my flesh. I was really disheartened now. I had a steel plate in my fourth metacarpal, a newly fractured third metacarpal, and now I was going to lose most of the skin off the entire hand and wrist.

When Steve looked at it, he couldn't believe it. He asked what I was going to do now. I told him I didn't know, but I was going in to see Shooter first thing in the morning to show him the results of his experiment and figure out next steps. I could not afford to miss practice. This was a pivotal year for me and the team.

I showed up at the training room at the scheduled taping time before practice and there was a lineup to get taped. My situation was urgent, so I broke my own rule (I don't like people who cut into the front of lineups) and butted into the front of the line. I stepped into Shooter's taping room and closed the door. Shooter took one look at my face and his eyes got big. I told him I wasn't happy with what happened to my hand last night. When I pulled back my sleeve to show him my hand, he was speechless. By now the hand had swelled and blistered; the bright redness of my skin camouflaged the fresh scar from my surgery weeks prior.

Of course, I knew that Shooter had been trying to help me by trying something innovative, so he had totally good intentions, but, as Dad used to say, "The path to hell was paved with good intentions." The end result was that the injuries to my hand had been made worse. I was pissed off at the situation, and the trouble this would cause me for the rest of the season, not to mention the pain I was suffering.

Though I had intended to calmly show Shooter the damage and find out what we could do to correct it, my angry demeanour alongside my size must have been too much for him, because the next day, Coach Smith called me out for intimidating Shooter. I was walking across campus with my blue Adidas book bag with the red handles. I carried my books to class in it every day — I preferred it to the backpacks everyone else used. Suddenly, I heard Coach Smith's voice; he said seriously, "Come over here? I need to talk to you." He asked me to tell him the whole situation with my hand and how it was going to affect my play.

After I told him the story, he said, "This is an important season for you and the team, Jason. We can't have you intimidating the trainer."

I said, "What do you mean? I didn't intimidate Shooter — I didn't threaten him in any way."

He said, "Shooter told me you were angry when you went to see him yesterday, and he felt very intimidated."

Shit, of course I was angry. But really, I was angrier at the situation than at Shooter. He just happened to be the lightning rod for my emotions at that moment. I knew I had only myself to blame for the entire situation by getting into a brawl at Denny's in the first place.

The next day, after apologizing to Shooter for scaring him, he built a fibreglass cast for me, then cut it off with a cast cutter by slicing incisions down each side of the cast. This way, he could tape it back onto my hand before every practice and game, but I didn't have to wear it when I wasn't on the field. Shooter gave me some ointment to help my skin heal, and applied gauze with Vaseline to my hand whenever he put on my cast to protect the raw skin underneath the fibreglass.

I wore the cast like that for the rest of the season, whenever I was on the field. It was awkward at first because Shooter would tape the cast on, then cover it with foam padding to protect opposing players. And because I used a right-handed stance, I had to adjust how I put it on the ground in my three-point stance (see Appendix A). Shooter made sure when he formed the cast that I could bend the last two knuckles in all my fingers, but I could not squeeze my hand fully into a fist or use it to grab any cloth when I was making a tackle. It was a disadvantage I had to learn to work around if my third season was going to be a good one.

"Dance the Night Away," Van Halen (1979)

During this 1981 season, my third year, the team had high expectations. The core of the team had been together for three seasons and we continued to gel and get better each year. Now we were playing with confidence, developing trust in each other, and expecting to win. That's why it was so disappointing when we lost our opening game in Saskatchewan.

Fortunately, next game we beat our Western Conference nemesis, Coach Jim Donlevy's University of Alberta Golden Bears. Jerry Dobrovolny and the boys in Gage Residence threw a victory party for the team in their quad — every floor of the residence had four residence apartments in each corner, known as a quad, with a common area in the centre.

Most of the team was in Jerry's quad for the party. They had set up speakers in each corner of the quad for excellent stereo sound and cranked the music up loud. We ordered pizza, and beer flowed from all four corners.

The party really sprang to life. Everyone was in a great mood after the win — the team became totally engulfed in the victory party atmosphere. We beat Alberta! So, we sang our beer-chugging song and cheered into the wee hours of the night. As the evening went on, it morphed into a pulsating organism of celebration. I always loved parties like this, and never wanted them to end.

In this vein, when we began to run out of beer, I recruited a couple of teammates to help stock the fridge. We jumped on the elevator to the bottom floor and invited every resident from the ground up to join the party — quickly returning to the party with reinforcements, of beer and more party-goers.

Now, the place was really jammed and the bathrooms full. Four of us decided we needed to empty our beer-engorged bladders, so naturally, we made the executive decision to simultaneously piss off the balcony! Soon, we were standing shoulder-to-shoulder on the balcony with our peckers over the railing and relief on our faces as we relieved ourselves in the cool night breeze.

At that moment, we heard a quartet of engaging high-pitched giggles above us. We all looked up together to see four pretty young ladies from the quad above enjoying the scene they witnessed below.

We knew they must have a great sense of humour, if they were amused by our shenanigans. We yelled up to them in unison, "Come on down to the party!" And so, the numbers at our party continued to grow. I'm sure there were close relationships created of all kinds that night, both short-term and long-term.

"Locomotive Breath," Jethro Tull (1971)

At about three in the morning, the party began to break up. We all tried to ignore the reality of the next morning rundown at 10:00 a.m., our morning post-game practice, where the conditioning coach led the team through a running and stretching program to release the lactic acid and soreness that accumulates in major muscle groups during games. (Many of us would jump into the ice tub for a few minutes after the rundown to flush our muscles even more — this was essential for me to manage my shin-splint pain.) So it happened that all the guys on our defensive line were leaving the quad together. It was a foggy night — the misty fog moved across the dead-calm parking lot, in stark contrast to the raucous party we had just left. But the quiet whispers of the night air did not completely quell our lingering desire to celebrate as we approached the parking lot.

At that moment, somebody said, "Hey let's flip over a car!"

I said, "What are you talking about? Why would we do that?"

"Come on, man, didn't we beat Alberta today?"

Naturally, the four of us clasped arms, looked each other in the eye and said, "Let's flip over a car!" A drunken pact was made.

The four of us powerful defensive lineman walked up to the first parked car that we saw, a little grey Honda Civic. Shoulder to shoulder, we squatted down, reached under the body of the car, said together, "One, two, three!" and in unison, dead-lifted the car effortlessly onto its side, where it settled and stayed.

Someone said, "You wanna push it all the way over on its roof?"

Even in our inebriated reasoning, we agreed that we didn't want to do damage to the car, we just wanted to make a statement and it looked pretty good on its side the way it was. We didn't want to cause damage — it was the exclamation point on the fact that we had beaten Alberta. As we walked away from the car in the fog, we could see a row of cars in single file, with two tires eerily perched above their roofs. Then, we all went our separate ways to get some sleep before rundown.

The next morning, my head was still full of party. I was in recovery mode, clumsily sorting out the gear from my laundry bag to get ready for practice. I had my head down, oblivious to the memento we had left in the parking lot the night before.

At that moment, Ken Munro, our record-setting kicker, came up to me and asked in a louder-than-usual voice, "Hey, Mad Dog, why did you guys flip over my car?"

"Kenny, we would never flip over your car. You're our teammate!" I said incredulously. "We flipped over some random little Honda."

"That was my car, man!" he protested, as he pulled out a bunch of Polaroid pictures taken from one of the quad balconies above the car that morning. He flipped through them slowly under my nose to make his point. Sure enough, there was his little grey Honda on its side, with about 10 or 12 people around it, setting it down gently so the shocks wouldn't crash through the fenders when they put it down.

Once again, my heart sunk. "Here we go again into emergency recovery mode," I thought. "Kenny, I'm so sorry. We didn't know it was your car! We'll make it up to you and pay for any damages we caused to your car."

Unbelievably, Ken started laughing. He laughed loudly as more of the players crowded around, listening to our conversation. He said, "Don't worry about it, Mad Dog! There was no damage to the car. The only thing that happened was my ashtray emptied all over the interior, but other than that, nothing. There's nothing to worry about, I already cleaned it up!"

Ken Munro's car flipped on its side, from the 8th floor, Gage Residence, UBC, 1981: Ken Munro photo

A group of Ken's friends putting his car down gently, UBC, 1981: Ken Munro photo

I couldn't believe that we randomly picked a teammate's car to flip, and there was no damage done — no harm, no foul! The team had an up-tempo practice, continuing to embrace the joy of victory over Alberta and, importantly, without the coaches finding out about our shenanigans. Although I remember some puking during rundown that day, it was time to bear down for a great week of practice to prepare for our next game.

The coaches were intelligent men and, although we made sure they didn't know the details of our escapades, they knew we needed to be reined in sometimes. Coach Smith used many techniques to maintain his command of the team, so before a Sunday morning rundown at the stadium, he decided to set an example. This is how Laurent DesLauriers, our All-Star defensive back and receiver (he could do it all), Carey Lapa, the other starting defensive end, and I became his victims. We were having a conversation in the dressing room as we waited for practice. We knew we weren't late for practice because George Piva's clock, which sat in the top shelf of his locker, was always accurate.

Going by George's clock, we had a few minutes to continue our conversation before the 10:00 a.m. practice started. The rest of the guys had already filtered out of the room to head down to the field. It was only a light post-game rundown, so all we needed was shorts and t-shirts — no big deal.

At about two minutes to the hour, Carey said, "Guys, we better head down. We don't want to be late and piss Frank off." The three of us headed out to the stadium stairs leading down to the field. As we approached the top of the stairs, we noticed the team had already started warm-up, which wasn't a good sign. Coach Smith looked up from the field and yelled to us, "You guys are late, go home!"

We looked at each other and shrugged, thinking that coach must be joking, and took a step down. Again, Coach exclaimed, "You're late, go home!" We looked down at the team stretching silently as Coach looked up at us, "I'm serious," he declared. "You guys are late, go home!" The three of us turned like children and shrank back into the dressing room.

All three of us were really shocked. Laurent was a starting wide receiver and the best athlete on the team. Carey and I were starting defensive ends on one of the best defences in the country. Yet, we were being sent home for being questionably late for practice! We knew George's clock was always right. Why would Coach start practice early?

As we changed into our civvies, we talked about our possible collective fates. We all knew Frank Smith was a hard-ass coach, but would he really bench three starters for this? We all wanted to play on Saturday and began to think the worst. We were all committed athletes and we were embarrassed that we had let the team down. Who knows what Coach Smith would decide to do to consequence us, sending a message to the team? That night the three of us talked on the phone, we all agreed to meet the next morning at the stadium to apologize to Coach Smith — we couldn't stand the uncertainty.

In the morning, we nervously knocked on the door of Coach Smith's stadium office. "Come in," he said from his windowless, concrete bunker. When we opened the door, there he was, sitting in a pitch-black office, breaking down game film on his 8 mm projector. As we entered, he just kept rolling the film back and forth, staring at the screen, until he was satisfied with his analysis. When he finished his notes on the play, he looked up at us from his desk. "What's up, guys?" he said, with a broad smile on his face.

"Well, Coach, we wanted to apologize for being late for practice yesterday. We thought we were on time, we thought..."

"Shit, fellas, I forgot all about that. Gentlemen, what's the lesson in this for you? Always set your watch by the head coach's watch!" he said, grinning as he pointed to his watch. "I always set my watch five minutes fast, so I'm never late. And I always start practice by my watch. Have a great day and I'll see you boys at practice tonight."

So, that was it. The three of us had lost sleep over this and the whole team was worried about what Coach Smith was going to do with us. He didn't "forget all about it," he sent a clear message to the team about being early for every team function, while giving three of his starters a day to rest our legs. This is just one example of the psychology that Coach Smith used to keep everyone on their toes; it was part of his winning formula. These tactics didn't sit well with everyone, and he pissed off a lot of players over the years, but it sure got results.

Another time, I thought I was the victim of similar coaching tactics when the team arrived at Vancouver airport, returning from a road trip. I urgently needed to use the restroom after the flight and I couldn't wait the twenty minutes it would take to get to campus from the airport. I asked two different players to tell Coach Smith I was in the bathroom, so he'd hold the bus for me. After all, when you got to go, you got to go, right?

By the time I got out to the loading area, the bus had left the terminal. I was pissed off, thinking that Coach knew I was in the bathroom and still decided to leave me behind to set another example for the team. I jumped into the first cab available and said, "Follow that bus!"

The cabby caught up and drove behind the team bus back to Thunderbird Stadium. When we arrived, I was planning to give Coach Smith a piece of my mind for leaving me behind. I was convinced that he had gone too far this time, and now it was costing me money I couldn't afford to pay for the cab. I jumped out of the cab and headed straight for him, as he got off the bus. "Coach, why did you leave me at the airport? You knew I was in the bathroom! I asked two different guys to tell you where I was."

"Shit, Jason, I didn't know you were in the bathroom. No one said anything to me," he shrugged innocently. "I thought you were on the bus with the rest of the team. Here's some cash to pay the cab driver." He handed me a $50 bill from his pocket. "Keep the change," he said. Since the short drive only cost me about $15, I pocketed the rest to buy groceries for the week. I really needed that money, but I hadn't mentioned anything to him about my finances.

Given the circumstances, this was the last thing that I had expected from Coach Smith. He completely took the wind out of my sails, and showed me the understanding a good parent would have for their son. It made me regret my self-righteous behaviour and it endeared Coach Smith to me all the more. I wanted to play a game tomorrow and kick some ass for him, just to show my gratitude for his kindness.

He found other ways to help me out, too. Being fully aware of how hard I was working in the gym and how much I ate to continue to pack on weight, during team meals, he would often place a whole plate of food in front of me, before I had even finished the plate I was eating at the time. "Keep eating, Jason," he'd say. "You need to fill out that frame."

"School," Super Tramp (1974)

Fortunately, after losing that first game to Saskatchewan, we managed to turn the season around, finishing the rest of the season undefeated, resulting in a 7–1 record. Finishing first overall in the Western Intercollegiate Football League (WIFL) gave us the opportunity to play the Hardy Cup at home against our old nemesis, the University of Alberta, whom we had finally beaten in the regular season game.

This Hardy Cup became a bellwether for things to come. We outplayed Alberta in the game, but some mistakes and a late fumble turned the momentum in their favour, allowing them to take the game away from us.

Naturally we were angry with ourselves for ending the season this way; we came up short on the scoreboard after we allowed Alberta only eight first downs in the entire game. The loss was such a gut-wrenching end to a promising season that I was really angry after the game. I went into the locker room with my game face on and let my emotions get the better of me.

My teammate, All-Star safety Dave (Singer) Sidoo, put it this way:

> When we lost to Alberta in that game, you came into a dead silent locker room and went from the offensive side to the defensive side and yelled out loud, 'Never again will we ever let anyone get close to us in a game. NEVER! We dedicate ourselves to doing everything we can, from this day on, to NEVER let anyone get close to beating us again!'
>
> And the rest was history. We never did! That is why we won the Vanier Cup, in 1982. In the weight room. At practice. We all dedicated ourselves because we either respected you so much and what you said made sense, or we were terrified of you. Probably a little of both.
>
> Another thing I remember from that season, is how you would say, when I returned a punt after we would stop an opponent on

> offence, 'Everyone, block your asses off for Singer,' and everyone did because they thought you would kill them the next day in practice if they didn't do their job. In some cases, when I returned a punt there was no one within 10 yards of me.

Though my teammates knew that I would do anything to help any of them, it is interesting to hear the perspective of a smaller player — Dave was a defensive back — who was not a fighter, in seeing me in a rage after that loss. Notwithstanding any feelings of intimidation in the face of my anger (which the team knew was not directed at them), he knew I'd back him up no matter what.

That is how our third year ended, in a stinging and emotional loss to a promising season, and with a pact amongst ourselves to never let it happen again. After all the issues with my right hand and wearing a cast all year, I was not expecting to have any personal accolades for my play, either. So, for me, it helped soften the blow of our playoff loss when I was named WIFL All-Star, All-Canadian defensive end, and the WIFL nominee for the J. P. Metras Trophy as best lineman in the country.

These were all first-time honours for me and it was gratifying to realize that my training was starting to pay dividends. Now I looked forward with confidence to next season, my senior year, when I could finally play without any physical constraints, and with another twenty pounds on my frame. My new goal was to play the next season at 260 pounds, which would mean I had packed on 75 pounds of muscle since leaving high school, 15–20 pounds each year.

My size and strength had benefits off the football field, too. In the spring of 1982, a friend I played high school football with, Paul Jaheny, invited me to join his hand-pump rail car team to compete in the annual Golden Spike Days Rail Car Race.

The Golden Spike Days celebrates the 1885 completion of the Canadian Pacific Railway, which runs from Montreal to Port Moody, and was the dream of Sir John A. Macdonald, Canada's first prime minister. Port

Moody was chosen as the western terminus for the line, resulting in city leaders celebrating this rich history in the annual Golden Spike Days Festival. This history is part of the tough, blue-collar culture of the area that became my stomping grounds growing up.

One of the main events they held at the Golden Spike Days Festival each year was the World Hand-Pump Rail Car Championship, which was open to teams from all over the world, but mainly comprised teams from B.C. and the western U.S. Teams were made up of five people, four pumpers and a pusher.

Teams competed by pumping their hand-car 300 metres down the track in the fastest time possible. Similar to Olympic bobsleigh, a key to success in the event is a fast start. The pusher is critical to get the car moving as quickly as possible from a standing start. Once the car is moving, the four pumpers use this momentum to cover the distance in the least amount of time possible. Paul recruited me to be his pusher because he knew how hard I had trained to gain size and power for university football.

I got ready for our race the same way I got ready for a football game; I channelled my inner rage to explode. When the starter's gun sounded, I pushed our car off the start with all my might. As I got up and brushed myself off, I saw the four pumpers pumping the car like hell down the track. The car was moving fast and I sprinted to meet the team at the finish line. By the time I got there, the crowd was cheering wildly for the local team, all graduates of Port Moody High School.

We won the event. Our car travelled the 300-metre distance in 33.54 seconds, faster than any other team. We were named the 1982 World Champion Hand-Pump Rail Car Team! Sponsors presented each member of our team with a brass rail spike to commemorate our championship, which I still cherish. For me, it was not only a symbolic tribute to the unique history of our small city, but also a personal affirmation of the commitment I had made to my training.

This gave me hope that I could attain even higher goals, if I kept working hard.

World Hand Car Championship spike, Port Moody, 1982: Jason Riley photo

That was the same summer that Jerry Dobrovolny and I went to a B.C. Lion's game at old Empire Stadium, in Vancouver. It was an exciting game, and Jerry turned to me with a decisive look on his face. "Jason, I want to play in this league. It would be so much fun. Look at this crowd. It's going wild. It would be awesome to be on that field right now," he said.

At that moment, I think we both decided that it was our new goal to play in the CFL. Personally, I had never really considered it to be a realistic goal for me, because of my lack of size at every level I played. Now I began to think that if I continued to work and train hard enough, I might be able to play at the next level. I set a new personal goal just to prove all the naysayers wrong: to play at least one game in the CFL.

"Eye of the Tiger," Survivor (1982)

Coach Frank Smith was the quintessential university coach for his era. He was an outstanding recruiter, who saw the potential of players when others could not. I was a case in point. He provided the leadership and the role model for us young men to reach our potential and work towards something great. He was also a perfectionist with a great mind for football, and demanded the best from all members of the program: players, coaches, and support staff. His success spanning decades is why he was inducted into the Canadian Football Hall of Fame as a builder.

At the end of that summer, when the 1982 training camp finally arrived, the entire UBC football program was full of anticipation for the season to begin. Coach Smith's mission was well underway. Right from the first team meeting in training camp, he asked us to recall the previous season: "Remember the disappointment we all felt at the end of last season, we don't want to experience that again." He never once mentioned the Vanier Cup. "We need to take each game of the schedule as its own challenge and not look beyond any of them. Men, if you take an opponent for granted, that's when they bite you in the ass! We need to focus on the team in front of us each week, and not beyond, to get where we want to go."

That's the approach the team took. After the heartbreak at the end of our '81 campaign, we all redoubled our dedication in the weight room to prepare for our senior year. Now the core of the team had been together for four years and we were full of confidence. Yet the previous loss to Alberta in the Western Conference final served us well; we were not cocky or smug in our approach to the new season. We all knew that we had to play our best football consistently throughout the season to reach our ultimate goal. What we thought we could achieve the previous year turned to bitter disappointment when we lost the WIFL final to a team that we should have beaten. Now, we all knew our team had worked hard all off-season, growing in talent and confidence, sensing that the team was on the verge of something great.

Every morning throughout training camp, someone put a boom box at the end of the hall in the players dorm, blasting the then-new hit, "Eye of the Tiger," as a wake-up call. It was our "Reveille," rallying the troops and setting the tone for each day of camp, right from the start.

Accordingly, practices were very intense from the start of two-a-days in training camp. The depth of talent and leadership that we had at all positions was really impressive. The veterans on defence included Mark Beecroft, Bernie Glier, and Dave Sidoo at defensive back; Mike Emery and Steve Harrison at linebacker; Carey Lapa and myself at defensive line.

On offence, there was a trio of outstanding running backs pushing each other to get better and help the team: Pete Leclaire, Kent Bowling, and Glenn Steele. All of them were great competitors and athletic backs who could score. Steele set several records in our championship year, but all the running backs were talented and any defence we played against had to prepare accordingly. Unfortunately, Pete Leclaire broke his leg in our first game, which put him out for the season. He was a tough kid; he played most of the game before succumbing to the pain that day. The team honoured him by wearing his number 23 on our helmets for the rest of the year.

Laurent "Lou" DesLauriers and Rob Ros led a talented group of receivers. Finally, Jerry Dobrovolny, George Piva, and Pieter Vanden Bos were all seniors leading the offensive line.

Dobrovolny's nickname was "Dobro," because no one could pronounce or spell his name. He was an outstanding offensive tackle (OT) and teammate. His commitment in the weight room to increase his size and strength helped to drive the players around him to get better. Vanden Bos' nickname "Bronco" was given to him by Kevin Konar (our former teammate, who later became an All-Star linebacker for the BC Lions), when Pieter was still a running back because he was like having a horse in the offensive backfield, such was his speed and stamina. Bronco became an excellent offensive guard and many of our running plays were designed for him to pull around the corner and lead the running back to the perimeter of the opposing defence — he would often personally escort our backs all the way into the end zone.

Pat Cantner was our prototypical fullback (FB), built like an undersized offensive guard. His nickname was "Apeman" because there was no limit to his energy and he was always up to something to either motivate or entertain us. He was more than just a blocker because he could carry the ball and run routes as well, but blocking was his forte. He was like another offensive guard coming around the corner on a toss to block a linebacker or hammer the defensive end on an off-tackle power (see Appendix A). He was quirky, fearless, and tough, endearing himself to his teammates.

Harrison's nickname was "Cowboy" because, aside from being one of the best linebackers in the country, he rode wild horses in competitive rodeos. He was relentless in pursuit of the ball.

Mike Emery's first nickname was "Bull" because he was like a wrecking ball on the field and in film one time Coach Laycoe said he played like a bull in a China shop. His second nickname, coined by yours truly, was "Emerizer" because he hit guys so hard, I'd tell him that he "Emerized" them. These nicknames were used at his teammates' discretion; but Mike was such a classy, unselfish, and committed leader on the team that he could have handled any number of nicknames without developing an ego. Emery was twice named President's Trophy winner, as the best stand-up defensive player (see Appendix A) in the nation – he always humbly shared the praise he received for an award with his entire defence.

Knowing that Emerizer and Cowboy were patrolling the middle of our defence, always ready to pursue to the ball and tackle whatever we funneled to them, gave the entire defensive line confidence in doing our jobs. We developed a strong mutual trust between all the members of our defensive front seven, which also included outside linebackers Greg Kitchen and K.C. Steele, to round out our tough 3–4 front (three defensive linemen and four linebackers).

We also had great depth at defensive back. Mark "Beaker" Beecroft led the WIFL in interceptions that year. David "Singer" Sidoo set the example on the field with his fearless punt returns and excellent defensive coverage. He was drafted into the CFL in 1982 and had a six-year pro career. Bernie "Ort" Glier was an All-Star defensive back, who was drafted in the first round of the 1982 CFL draft and played seven years with the BC Lions. They all led by providing athleticism and leadership in the defensive secondary, blanketing the opposition's best receivers.

My nickname was "Mad Dog," as given to me by my teammates (I have no idea why!). My defensive line-mates were Dwayne "Derbs" Derban, an outstanding rookie at nose guard, and Carey Lapa, the opposite bookend from me, at the right defensive end position. He was an excellent player, drafted by the Hamilton Tiger-Cats, and an even better person.

The senior players set the tone on and off the field for the younger guys in their positions. I would go to war with any one of them. It made the coaches' jobs easier knowing that they had such strong leadership at every position.

Derban recalled his rookie year with us like this: "Trent Edwards, Paul Zanni, and I, the Kamloops rookies, were gobsmacked at the number of senior guys who all were amazing leaders — not just the four captains. It began with Carey Lapa and George Piva seeking us out the summer before the season in Kamloops and training with us. And for me to play nose guard between you and Lapa, with the incredible linebackers behind us — I felt like I had won the lottery!"

Derban went on to tell me one of his first on-field memories: "On the field, it began with Lou DesLauriers, with his massive thighs and incredible stride, returning the opening kickoff on the first play of the game about 100 yards for a touchdown. And then it just continued."

Derban added, "Off the field, one of my first memories was sitting having a quiet pre-game movement in a T-Bird stadium bathroom stall. You sat down in the stall next to me and said 'Derban?' and then proceeded to give me your strategy for the D-line for the upcoming game. That's dedication!"

Personally, I don't remember that particular story, but it fits with Male Toiletry 101, which we all subscribed too. I have no reason to doubt Derbs on this one — we used every minute we could to get an edge.

Similarly, I know that practicing against All-Stars like George Piva, Jerry Dobrovolny, and Pieter Vanden Bos on the offensive line every day made us better. Each of us, on both sides of the ball, took it personally if we lost a one-on-one rep (see Appendix A) in practice, privately keeping track of who beat who, and studying their technique. Then, when we went to team drills, the competition escalated even more — competition made everyone better.

The coaches were focused, with a plan to take advantage of the talent that we had, and the players were self-motivated and driven; we pushed each other in every drill. These guys all had good character and were outstanding student-athletes, whom Coaches Smith and Laycoe recruited for those reasons.

From my perspective, our whole defence loved and respected each other like brothers so much that we simply never wanted to come off the field! This became the main ingredient in the chemistry for the best defence in the country. We truly swarmed to the ball as a unit. However, the better we played, the less time we spent on the field. Our defence became so dominating, we often had "two and out" series (when the defence stops on offence after two plays, so they have to punt on the third down), which helped keep our offence on the field more to break all those offensive records. It became a mutual admiration society between the offence and defence.

"He Ain't Heavy, He's My Brother," The Hollies (1969)

To illustrate this steadily-growing brotherhood, I played left defensive end and George Piva played right tackle on offence, so we were often lined up against each other during team periods in practice. George was a very good offensive lineman and a student of the game. He knew the defensive linemen were taught to "read the hat" of our opponent to anticipate which direction they were going to step when the ball was snapped. We were expected to watch the helmet of the lineman we were lined up against and step in that direction to defeat their block. Although I was never considered to be fast in a 40-yard sprint, I had good reaction speed, so I was quick off the ball, with good lateral movement. I was good at "reading the hat" and defeating the block.

Because George knew our technique, one day he decided to use it against me. We were near the end of a competitive inside-run period and the coaches were getting heated because of some mistakes being made. The tempo (the level of intensity of practice) kept rising with each rep, as the coaches' voices got louder. Now it was down to the last play, and whoever lost the rep, either offence or defence, would have to do twenty push-ups. On the snap of the ball, I read George's hat as it moved inside to my right. I immediately stepped hard to the inside gap to nullify his block, he then turned and easily drove me down to the inside. The ball carrier ran for a first down right where I had vacated, as George giggled the whole time. George had intentionally given me a head fake, knowing that I would take the bait, then he used my own momentum to take me out of the play.

"Goddammit, Riley," one of the defensive coaches bellowed. "You can't get caved in like that! Defence, do your push-ups!"

I learned from George that day and it's an example of good players making their teammates better. Our whole team followed this philosophy, as it was embedded into us by the coaches; constant competition and repetition of correct technique makes everyone better. I still maintain that I would have been fine, if George hadn't cheated!

On another note, George had a black pickup truck and he used to pack as many guys as he could into the back (it was legal in 1982) and take us to the Dairy Queen on Broadway for milk shakes. This was a great way to replenish the calories we had lost in practice, and grew into another tradition that brought the boys together off the field. The best part was that being a rich farm kid from Kamloops, George never asked us for gas money!

We did a lot of things off the field together to build camaraderie during training camp. This off-the-field bonding was a lot of fun, and it also helped galvanize our team into a tightly-knit unit, working toward our ultimate goal — winning the national championship.

◇◆◇

We played hard on the field and we partied hard off the field.

Indeed, we could eat and drink as much as we wanted to because our young metabolisms were burning off so many calories every day. Mine as much as anyone's — that's why I had so much trouble gaining weight. It stands to reason, then, that most of our off-field events included food. In camp, the training table (see Appendix A) ensured we always had three square meals a day, but usually, we needed to top up our intake later in the evening.

In my case, the day of the "boat races" turned out to be a bad time to have that extra evening meal. Boat races were a training camp tradition that had nothing to do with boats. It was a drinking competition between the vets and the rookies, which took place at a campus pub called the Pit. Every vet would be matched up with a rookie to see who could chug a 16-ounce glass of draft beer the fastest then slam the empty glass upside down on the table. I could normally chug beer with the best of them and I was looking forward to the boat races that night. It was a matter of pride that the vets would win their boat race. If they didn't, they were subjected to major jeering by the onlooking team members, as the newcomers were cheered; this ensured much loud machismo and peer pressure was displayed for the duration of the event.

My mistake was that I had decided to go to my favourite burger restaurant, P.J. Burgers, on Broadway, for my evening calorie top-up before I went to the boat races. I ordered my usual: the Hulk Burger, which included a half-pound patty of beef, with a fried egg on top, and all the fixings. It came with a side of carrots and celery, with blue cheese dip. I inhaled that puppy and made sure I finished all my veggies. Then, I went straight to the Pit to make sure I didn't miss my boat race, although I was hoping my name would be called later, so my meal would have time to settle.

That didn't happen. Almost as soon as I arrived, my name was called to take on a rookie challenger in a boat race. I stepped up to the table and, as the team called out the countdown, I mentally prepared to chug that beer as fast as possible — after all, my reputation was on the line. It is a skill to chug beer — one has to pour the beer down their throat as quickly as possible, and hold their breath at the same time, or one could drown oneself (though drowning in beer is a fate that most of us could only dream about during a hot afternoon practice).

On cue, I lifted the glass and chugged that beer like an All-Star. When the glass was empty, I slammed the glass down on the table, just before the rookie's glass came down. The team cheered me on; as expected, Mad Dog won his heat.

Unfortunately, the Hulk Burger I had consumed earlier, with little time to digest, now occupied most of the space in my stomach, and the 16 ounces of beer I chugged so quickly had now exceeded the space available. Suddenly, my stomach began to churn and I felt gas bubbling in the bottom of my throat. I knew there was only one possible outcome, so I quickly excused myself to the bathroom, casually concealing the urgency as if nothing was out of the ordinary. After all, I couldn't let the guys, especially the rookies, know that I had trouble chugging one beer — that would have been very embarrassing for the Mad Dog!

When I was clear of the team, I rushed towards the bathroom. It became clear that I wasn't going to make it. Instead, I saw the exit sign above the back door and made a bee-line for it. As I pushed the door open, the beer frothing in my stomach made its exit. I did a power-puke that seemed like a bathtub faucet on full blast, ejecting the entire contents of my stomach on the bush beside the stairs. It was so forceful that I had carrot pieces in my nostrils that I had to blow out of my nose afterwards. It was disgusting, but I didn't get anything on me. My main regret was losing that beautiful meal.

When I turned to go back into the pub, I was locked out. Ignominiously, I walked around to the main entrance and rejoined the team to watch the rest of the boat races. I ordered another beer to drink at a normal pace and enjoyed the rest of the evening with the boys, who never really knew the sacrifices I had made for the team that night. Later on, I got something to eat at the pub — after all, I wasn't used to an empty stomach.

"One Bourbon, One Scotch, One Beer," George Thorogood and the Destroyers (1977)

After losing the previous year in the Hardy Cup, ending our 1981 season on such a sour note, the coaches saw how our disappointment fueled the team's hunger to win, they saw our renewed commitment in the gym that off-season, led by our determined veterans, and they sensed that we were ready to take the final step.

So, right from 1982 training camp, the coaches knew that if they game planned to put us in successful positions, no one could beat us. Consequently, the offence set records all season with a balanced attack, and the defence was relentless, taking every point-against our team as an insult. It was an amazing feeling being part of a team that was so self-motivated, with adrenaline our jet fuel, ignited by the excitement of just playing together every week.

On Saturday, October 9, 1982, in Winnipeg, we beat the University of Manitoba to go 6–0 in our regular schedule. The team stayed over night at the Polo Park Inn in Winnipeg, waiting for our return flight the next morning. This gave us time to really enjoy the victory. Too much time, apparently.

The Polo Park Inn had a pub attached, just off the lobby of the hotel. Many of my teammates agreed to meet for a beer after the post-game team dinner. We occupied several tables throughout the pub and everyone was in good spirits after the win. We were having a good time replaying the details of the game over beers and looking forward to our next game and a successful stretch drive to the playoffs. As the evening went on, the team got livelier, while the beer disappeared.

It must have been close to midnight when one of the boys came running up to me from the direction of the men's room. He yelled, "Jason, K.C. Steele just flooded the bathroom and he's in big trouble!"

I said, "What happened?" as we ran toward the men's room.

When we got there, we saw about an inch of water covering the entire bathroom floor, with water still gushing out of one of the toilet stalls. When I tiptoed in, so my pants didn't get soaked, I saw that one of the large toilets had been completely ripped off the floor. The supply line, previously attached to the toilet, was now shooting water like a fire hose.

K.C. was gone, but I was relieved to know that he was not hurt, which was my original concern. K.C. was an integral part of our record-setting defence, and his health was important to the future success of the team. I was also pissed that he had done such a crazy thing to ruin the night that the rest of the team had been enjoying.

I found out later that K.C. and some teammates were in the bathroom bragging, and in their inebriated state, one of them challenged K.C. to deadlift a toilet off the floor. In his state of mind, unfortunately, he accepted the challenge. He had on his big Dayton boots, so first he kicked the bolts until they loosened, then he used his incredible lower body power to deadlift the toilet clear off the floor bolts. Now, when you think about it on the one hand, that's an impressive feat of strength — but unfortunately it is also an act of vandalism.

Did I mention that the hotel manager just happened to be using the urinal in the men's room, precisely when K.C. decided to take up the challenge to remove the toilet? All I could think was "What would happen if Coach Smith found out about this?" What would be K.C.'s fate, and, more importantly, what would be the repercussions for the team? Would K.C. be charged by the local police? It would be hell, no getting around that.

I automatically went into full team-recovery mode. In that moment, I learned that a crisis like this can sober you up very quickly. I knew we had to get to the manager before he got to Coach Smith. First, I went around to everyone on the team who was in the pub and explained the situation. I collected all the cash they had left on them, which wasn't much after a night of drinking beer — after all, we were students. At most, this equated to some small change or a few bills from each of us. When I counted the money, I was surprised that I now had almost $90 in my hand.

Next, I went directly to the front desk in the lobby, in search of the manager. I spoke to the clerk and he said he would call the manager down to see me right away.

Within less than five minutes, the double doors to the lobby crashed open and the Winnipeg Police Emergency Response Unit (a.k.a. SWAT team) poured into the room and surrounded me, their rifles pointed directly at me. The unit leader barked to me, "Freeze! Put your hands up!" My heart jumped into my throat, and my pulse skyrocketed as I looked down the barrels of those rifles and thought I was about to die.

When I explained the situation to them in a stammering voice, they turned their attention to the clerk. Instead of calling the manager as I had asked him to do, he explained to the police that he had prematurely pressed the emergency "riot button" behind the front desk. He had been told about the damage in the washroom and got trigger-happy with security, thinking I was the main suspect in a pub brawl. The unit leader was very stern when he told the clerk, "If it ever happens again, we will no longer respond to your emergency riot button!" They exited smartly out the same door they had come in.

After I cleaned the shit out of my pants, I explained my plan to the manager. I gave him all the cash I had collected from the team for the down payment on the damage, and told him that we would cover the rest of the repair bill when he forwarded us the final invoice. I gave him my contact information in Vancouver. I also appealed to his sense of compassion: "We need to prevent our head coach from hearing about this issue, because it could destroy a very promising season for the entire team."

To his credit, he agreed with my terms. In doing so, he showed his empathy for young athletes who sometimes make stupid mistakes in the strangest circumstances. We've all been guilty of it at some time or other, but in this case, no one was physically hurt or harmed in any way. The manager recognized this and didn't press charges with the police, or contact Coach Smith about the incident.

The next day at the airport, I explained to K.C. about the deal I made with the manager in his absence. He agreed to pay the full amount of the balance for the repair bill, and he was grateful to his teammates for bailing him out with the down payment.

Weeks later, I got the bill for the remaining costs from the manager in the mail. It was almost $300, including parts, labour, and taxes — a hefty amount for a student in 1982! K.C. promptly sent a cheque to the manager for the balance and no one spoke about the matter again for the entire season for fear that Coach Smith would find out. To this day, I don't know if Coach ever heard that story — I don't want to know what he might have done if the hotel manager had not honoured our deal.

This event can also be seen as a testament to the power of teamwork and the friendships we shared. There were no questions asked when one of our teammates was in trouble — we did what needed to be done. I can now see that this was also a healing experience for me; after all the bullying from my youth packed away in my subconscious, it was like an emotional balm every time I was able to provide support for my brothers.

Mission accomplished.

After finishing the 1982 regular season undefeated and winning the WIFL championship, we earned the right to go to the national semi-final Atlantic Bowl (now Uteck Bowl), in Halifax, N.S., where we would play the Atlantic Conference champion, the St. Francis Xavier X-Men. If successful this week, we would go straight to Toronto to play the winner of the other national semi-final, the Mitchell Bowl — either Western or Concordia University. At that time, we were embarking on the longest road trip in duration and distance in the history of CIAU (now U Sports) football. Before we left Vancouver for the East Coast, Coach Smith instructed all the players to get written permission from our professors to miss two weeks of classes. We did this in great anticipation of the incredible adventure the team was embarking on.

We arrived a few days before the game to adjust to the time zone and practice on the game field. One night after meetings, a few of us decided to go to the local pub in Sackville for a pint of beer and some relaxation to get our minds off the big game for a while. As we walked to the pub from the hotel, we passed a street named Sackville and one of the guys said, "Hey, Mad Dog, since you're leading the nation in sacks, you should take this street sign as a memento of the season for your rec room. I'm sure the city won't mind."

In the passion of the moment, I jumped up and grabbed the street sign with both hands. It came down easily from its moorings on the pole. I slid the sign inside my jacket and we continued to the pub. When we got to the pub, we all took our coats off at the coat check, where I carefully slid the street sign down my sleeve, thinking that the lady wouldn't notice and I had impunity — after all, the street sign was good karma, right?

Suddenly, I felt a heavy hand on my shoulder. A deep voice said, "Son, I think you have something that belongs to us in your coat!" I don't know how he knew, but I turned around to see an N.S. police officer with a glint in his eye. He obviously knew who we were when he said, "Why did you take that street sign?" When I explained the personal significance of the sign to me, he said, "Well, I understand your point of view, but if you give me the sign now, you can continue the evening with your teammates." I gave him the sign without another word and, as he walked back to his car, he turned back and said, "Good luck in the game!"

My impetuous act could have had negative consequences for me and the whole team. Thankfully, the officer understood that I had no ill intent, it was my passion for the game that made me act like an idiot. I can't even begin to imagine the alternative; if the police officer had been less forgiving, the very least he could have done was report me to Coach Smith, and I'd have had to face Coach's wrath in the most important week of the season.

"I'm Your Captain," Grand Funk Railway (1970)

We were coached to never take a team lightly, and to always focus on the game at hand: "Never overlook your opponent because if you do, they'll bite you in the ass!" So, initially, we were quietly confident going into the Atlantic Bowl game, but very aware of the urgency to win the game to reach our ultimate team goal. Although everyone looked toward the game with high anticipation, we did our best to keep our emotions in check before the biggest game of our lives.

Then, St. Francis' coach, John Musselman, made a strategic error at a press conference a few days before our game. In attempting to build his team's confidence for our game, he stated publicly that, "The only reason UBC was undefeated in season play is because they play in the weakest conference in the country." If he had said this in the dressing room and not to the media, it may have had good results.

However, when Coach Smith read it in the local newspaper, being the motivator that he was, he posted the article with Musselman's quote on the bulletin board in our dressing room. Every time we walked into the dressing room to prepare for practice that week, we saw that article on the wall. It really pissed us off. After all we had done during the past four years to get here, the hard work in the weight room, the sweat and blood spilled on the field, the film work in meetings every night, and injuries overcome in the damn ice tub, our team collectively would not stand for it. The weakest conference in the country? We knew it wasn't true and we planned to prove it.

Consequently, by the time kick-off arrived, we were so fired up that we didn't want to just beat the X-Men, we wanted to beat the crap out of them. Our defence was so well-prepared by the coaches and so motivated psychologically, that we smothered everything they did on offence. Similarly, our offence rolled over them with our big OL knocking them off the ball consistently to open holes for our running backs.

I remember on one run-pass-option play (see Appendix A) early in the game, no one blocked me, so I screamed into the backfield from the backside (see Appendix A), just as the QB and the RB still had their hands on the ball. It helped set our team's tempo for the game when I drilled the QB and laid him out. When I got up off the QB, I wasn't disappointed that I hadn't made a sack, because the running back with the ball was nailed for a loss on the play by the rest of the boys on defence.

We won the game 54–1, and Western won their game 17–7, to set up the Vanier Cup next weekend in Toronto.

"Let's Dance," David Bowie (1982)

Finally, we were where we wanted to be: in Toronto, preparing to battle for the Canadian National Championship. Most of the senior players that Coach Smith and Coach Laycoe had assembled while building our team had been together for four years now, continually developing and improving under their tutelage. The coaches also added some excellent talent into the mix by recruiting character guys, who were coachable and team-oriented, providing depth. All the players bought into the culture of working hard to get better on and off the field. At this point, we had spent so much time together supporting each other through the tough physical, intellectual, and emotional battles required to win consistently over time that we had grown even stronger bonds. The byproduct of this process was that, collectively, we were brothers in arms and we were prepared to fight for each other.

This camaraderie that we experienced created a cycle of positive peer pressure for our teammates, always working towards the common goal of winning a championship, which in turn led to greater team unity. After all the work we put in for the past four years, we were finally at the doorstep of greatness, and we could taste it.

In this vein, the team's emotions continued to build up through the week of preparation in Toronto. This includes everyone in the program, from the training and support staff to the players and the coaching staff. Obviously, the coaches couldn't exchange film of the game until after the games were played the previous weekend – the Mitchell Bowl, which Western won, and our Atlantic Bowl – and the opponents for the Vanier Cup were determined. As soon as they received the film, the coaches spent many hours breaking it down during late-night meetings. So, it was with this heightened sense of urgency, anticipation, and emotion that we prepared for the opportunity to take our school's first Vanier Cup. We players were totally focused on the coaches' game plan; once again, we were facing a team we had never played before, so the coaches prepared us well in meetings and practice for everything they saw in the game film.

One of the premier events of the Vanier Cup festival is the annual awards banquet, usually held on the Thursday night before the game. Both teams are invited to attend, along with the VIPs associated with CIAU (now U

Sport) football. Pat Marsden was an iconic sports broadcaster, having called CFL game play-by-play for decades, who also embraced Canadian college football and was working the broadcast of our game that weekend, along with Leif Pettersen as colour commentator.

Marsden's table at the banquet was adjacent to Pat "Apeman" Cantner's table. Pat, being the friendly, gregarious, raw-boned fullback that he was, struck up a conversation with this sports icon beside him. By the end of the night, Marsden knew all the nicknames on our roster.

Apparently, Apeman made an impression on Marsden. Armed with this new information, Marsden used the nicknames of our players throughout the broadcast of the game, which made it even more entertaining for us when we watched the recording. Marsden commented at one point in the game after I sacked Western's quarterback, Andy Rossit, "They really let the 'Mad Dog' out of his cage that time, didn't they!"

Cantner even credits Marsden's commentary for boosting his career:

> Marsden mentioned All-Star running back Glenn Steele when he broke a run for about forty yards through the teeth of the Mustang defence, then added, 'And look at that fine young man Pat Cantner, his teammates call him Apeman, who sprung Steele with a great block at the point of attack!' Marsden's calls in our game elevated my spotlight and was one of the reasons that I was drafted by the Winnipeg Blue Bombers and enjoyed a five-year career in professional football!

"Don't Stop Believing," Journey (1981)

Meanwhile, the major national award-winners and the All-Canadian team were announced at the banquet. The national award-winners included Mike Emery, my esteemed teammate, as the Presidents' Trophy winner for the best stand-up defender (see Appendix A); and Peter Langford, of the University of Guelph, who was chosen over me as the J. P. Metras Award winner, as best down lineman in the country; and also, the great Bernie Custis of McMaster University, who years later would become a mentor of mine, who won the Frank Tindall Trophy for coach of the year. Those who received All-Canadian honours from our team included Mike Emery, Dave Sidoo, and myself on defence and Jerry Dobrovolny, Glenn Steele, and Pieter Vanden Bos on offence. I used the fact that I was overlooked for the Metras award as personal motivation for the upcoming game.

As we prepared for the game throughout that week, we were aware that the venerable old Varsity Stadium, in the heart of the biggest city in the country, held its own special character: like the personality of an old castle, with its hidden secrets of the past, the cold damp concrete was alive with the spirit of so many players before us, who fought for the national championship; the echo of the fans from the past could be heard cheering in the stands for their beloved teams. It spoke to us in a tangible way, and we recognized the stadium possessed the unique opportunity to fulfill our team's destiny; we knew we had to honour the old girl by playing our best game on Saturday.

Game day arrived — November 20, 1982. The weather was chilly with some light snow, comfortable for the players. Most of the crowd of around 15,000 might have been cold, but they stayed warm by cheering for the Ontario team. It was a loud and high-spirited atmosphere for the game.

Accordingly, our defence was well-prepared by our coordinator, Coach Laycoe, and his assistants. We were ready, both physically and emotionally, with a great game plan. The senior team leaders had now been the core of the team for 4 years and were extremely focused; this permeated the entire roster.

Our entire defence played on another emotional level that game — we would not be denied. Emery recalled, "Western's first offensive play of the game was a 25-yard completion on a go-route, straight down the right sideline. This sent the message that we were playing a good team and we needed to play hard to limit their offence." He continued:

> The coaches had prepared us well for the game. Western loved to pull their guards on the running game, so Cowboy and I were coached to shoot the gap whenever the guards pulled.

> On one play, [Pat] Brady pulled to our right on a sweep, and I shot the gap and made the tackle for a 5-yard loss. Normally it would be difficult for me to do that, because I'd feel like I was leaving my area open to attack, but I had so much confidence in my teammates on the defensive front that I knew if I made a mistake, my teammates would make up for it — it took any doubts about it away because I knew someone would make the play. We all relied on each other and when you have trust in your teammates like that, everyone plays with more confidence.
>
> That's why when I accepted the President's Trophy at the awards banquet, I accepted it on behalf of the whole defence; we had such a talented group that I genuinely believed the entire defence shared it.

Western gave it their best shot and never quit, so we knew that Western's head coach, Darwin Semotiuk, and his staff had them well-prepared, too. One play late in the game exemplifies this. They ran an "inside-trap" play to my side. (The trap was one of their bread-and-butter plays, so we had prepared all week to defend it). On a trap, the backside guard pulls down the LOS to block the first defender past the centre. The play is a "quick hitter" designed to spring the running back just behind the pulling guard's kick-out block.

Brady played left guard in Western's offence, on the opposite side of the centre from me, which meant that on this play, Brady pulled to block me. I was running a cross-stunt with our outside linebacker, Greg Kitchen, on the play, but I saw the running back with the ball in the backfield so I slanted inside hard. As I zeroed in on the running back, Brady caught me with an excellent trap block, knocking me back, but as I sprawled backwards, I managed to get a hand on the running back's foot, just enough to slow him down so that "Emerizer" and "Cowboy" could finish him off after a short gain up the middle. I remember that trap play clearly because it was the hardest hit I received in the game!

Our team broke several records that day. Just to name a couple, our defence allowed the "least passing yards against" in a Vanier Cup game, and our offence set a record for most first downs in a championship game. The entire team was relentless in every aspect throughout the game in pursuit of UBC's first championship. The passion that we had for each other and the game was something that Western could not match that day.

When the final whistle blew, the scoreboard read "UBC 39 – Western 14." I had a huge rush of adrenaline in my excitement after completing our four-year quest. We dominated the championship game against an excellent opponent, after an undefeated season!

In the mosh-pit of celebration that followed, Harrison and I picked up Coach Smith like a priceless trophy and put him on our shoulders, carrying him around centre field to acknowledge his team's ultimate victory. The uncontainable emotion was palpable. Some guys were screaming, others crying with joy, while everyone got bear hugs from their coaches and teammates, ignoring the dirt, sweat, blood, and spit that dripped off every one of us.

1982 Vanier Cup Champions, Thunderbird Stadium UBC, 1982: UBC archives

◇◆◇

"Break On Through (to the Other Side)," The Doors (1967)

After the team was herded and corralled, still delirious, into the dressing room, Coach Smith gave the team a well-deserved victory speech, congratulating everyone soundly for the team's unprecedented accomplishment. We had every right to bask in the glory of our win, which was the result of standing on the shoulders of the generations of Thunderbirds who preceded us, our victory that day forever cementing the legacy of the UBC program (the oldest football program in the WIFL).

Then, he brought us back to reality:

> "Now you have a decision to make. Remember, the season isn't over yet." While he spoke these words, he knew the character of his team and how we'd respond. "You can sit back and wallow in your victory, drink beer and party all night, then take your time getting back home, and let SFU kick your ass in the Shrum Bowl and claim the national championship, or you can pack your bags for an early flight home and start preparing to play a school that will be well-prepared to take your championship away from you next weekend. It's up to you!"

Although SFU played in the American NAIA Conference, we all looked forward to playing them every year in this annual exhibition game called the Shrum Bowl. The Shrum Bowl transcended its official designation as an exhibition game, taking on a life of its own as a very emotional cross-town rivalry for both programs. The winning team's spoils included bragging rights (especially at the Boo Pub!), higher local ranking of programs by the media, with obvious implications for recruiting on the line. For me personally, ever since my humiliating visit with their head coach DeJulius back in high school, it was always a very important game on my calendar.

This year, the game was scheduled when both teams' seasons were over. As our coaches stated, SFU would have a clear advantage in practice and preparation time this year because their season ended sooner than ours. But we were battle-hardened, so that was in our favour. We voted unanimously to pack our bags, get home as quickly as possible, and prepare for our last game. Coach Smith knew that we weren't about to relinquish our hard-fought championship to our cross-town rivals!

Fred Hume, the UBC athletics historian, recorded Coach Smith's statement that we had to "complete unfinished business in Vancouver." That Shrum Bowl took on immense importance despite and because of our historic Vanier Cup win: we were putting our "unblemished Canadian record of 11–0 and [our] national championship on the line."[8] Our travel-weary team now fully embraced the challenge to prepare for yet another battle, with all the passion we could muster after such an emotional championship run. And although SFU was a skilled and highly motivated team, fortunately for us, we had been forged into a formidable band of brothers who overcame in a 19–8 win in this Shrum Bowl to formally end the greatest season in UBC history.

Apparently, the CIAU governors were so pissed-off at us for leaving Toronto so quickly after our Vanier Cup win and missing the post-game agenda they had planned for us, that they changed the league rules, so that no team could schedule a post-season exhibition game after that. One would think they might have understood that we were actually fighting to validate the legitimacy of their league.

"Thunderstruck," AC/DC (1990)

Years later, while watching the Vanier Cup game with my family at the Skydome in Toronto, Peter Langford, the 1982 winner of the J. P. Metras Trophy who had attended the University of Guelph, approached me out of the blue. He said, "Jason, I just wanted to tell you that I think you deserved the 1982 J. P. Metras Trophy. Your stats were better than mine, and you led the nation in sacks and tackles on an undefeated championship team. The only reason you didn't win it was because your teammate, Mike Emery, won the President's Trophy and they don't like to give two major awards to one team."

It meant much to me for Langford to say that. Although I had felt honoured that I had been nominated for the J. P. Metras Award as the WIFL representative the previous year (wearing the cast), I knew I didn't deserve it then. However, after my senior year, and our championship season, I had

[8] Hume, F. 2003. *1982 UBC Thunderbirds Team*. UBC Sports Hall of Fame. UBC Thunderbirds website. Url: gothunderbirds.ca (accessed April 26, 2023).

earned it. Langford was a class act to say what he did, and I don't mind losing it to a character guy like that. This remains my only regret in this incredible season.

Nonetheless, the most important thing to me was that I could "help the team win," as Coach Smith put it 5 years earlier. I was and still am grateful to Coach Smith for seeing my potential when no one else did and for his unwavering faith that I would eventually help his team win. Ultimately, the award that I was most proud of from the 1982 season was winning the *Thunderbird Lineman of the Year Award*, as voted by my teammates. With all the talent we had on the team and the trust and love I had developed for my teammates over the years, it really legitimized my personal transformation from a "drowned rat with a bad back," to a respected member of a championship team.

Our championship season was also transformative for the UBC program. The first national football championship for a proud university is something that no one can deny. It elevated the institution of UBC to a new level because the three-hour national broadcast of the Vanier Cup was like a free three-hour commercial for the school — priceless national exposure at the time, considering television was the primary advertising platform before social media was even a concept. Further, it transformed the football program by making it that much easier for the coaches to recruit top student-athletes, committed to winning.

During the 1997 Vanier Cup game telecast on TSN, commentators Rod Smith and Jamie Bone agreed that in their opinion this '82 UBC team was the best football team in CIAU (now U Sport) history.

Stu Laird, the long-time anchor of the Calgary Stampeder's defensive line, offered this about our team:

> "Even today, I am still in awe of your 1982 T-Bird team, that I had the distinct displeasure to play against when I was at the University of Calgary. I don't have the same knowledge of college football history that I do of the CFL (I am a bit of nerd) but in my humble opinion, there was never before or since a better college team in Canada."

Individually, the four-year journey to a championship taught us players everything we needed to know to be successful at whatever career path we chose to pursue, and it bolstered our confidence to do so. If you look through the team roster, our players became successful doctors, engineers, teachers, firefighters, entrepreneurs, and many other community leaders who continue to make a positive impact on society. I don't think it's coincidence. Once again, it illustrates the binding power of the human spirit in hard work, self-discipline, teamwork, commitment and personal sacrifice, and those connections between us that are bigger and grander than our individual selves.

SECOND QUARTER

GREY CUP BOUND

"Jason, you were on [the roster] the day of your first practice...I remember hearing the "pop" of your helmet in drills. I had never heard that from any of those other linemen...none...I'm getting giddy thinking of that now. Wow!"

Ben Zambiasi,
Canadian Football Hall of Fame linebacker

"Burning Down the House," Talking Heads (1983)

After this unprecedented season for the UBC football program, we had the best draft in CFL history. Five of us went in the first round of the 1983 CFL draft: Jerry Dobrovolny was drafted first overall, by Calgary; Steve Harrison went second overall, to Ottawa; Mike Emery went third, to Saskatchewan; Pieter Vanden Bos, fourth, to Edmonton; and I went seventh, to Winnipeg. Others drafted that year included Pete Leclaire in the second round; Carey Lapa, in the third; Pat Cantner, in the fourth round joining me in Winnipeg; George Piva, in the fifth; and kicker Ken Munro, in the eighth round. Several other players from that team were also drafted in other years – Bernie Glier and David Singh (1982); Laurent Deslaurier and Greg Kitchen (1984); Don Adamic, Bruce Barnett, Terry Cochrane, Roger Deslaurier, Rob Ross, Glenn

Steele (1985) - for a record 20 players taken from our championship team over 4 different CFL drafts.[9]

Everyone in the draft had worked so hard to get to this place where we might finally experience our dream of playing in the CFL. Personally, I had already worked my butt off to overcome my shortcomings just to play the game. Now that Winnipeg had made me a first-round draft pick, I knew I would need to redouble this effort moving forward to overcome the challenges professional football would bring. In reality, I had no idea that I'd be facing the craziest roller-coaster of emotions imaginable in the upcoming calendar year.

One early event perhaps should have served as warning for the highs and lows to come; it certainly added to my ever-growing sense of the mysteries of life — the unexplained blessings we receive that often go unappreciated.

There was an annual tradition at UBC to celebrate the CFL draft. Naturally, we held our celebration at the Boo Pub. Unfortunately for us, we decided to meet early for dinner at the pub, which meant we had all evening to drink to our heart's content. We chugged beer together, pounded countless celebratory shots, and sang drinking songs into the night. We went way overboard.

After several hours of this we were all smashed. Of course, in the early eighties, although drinking and driving was illegal, people stupidly tended to think it was okay to do it despite its illegality. At the time, it was considered by many, especially testosterone-fueled young men, to be a "sport," by which one's manhood could be measured. People used to brag about how many beers they could drink and still drive home.

Accordingly, when it was time to go home, I eagerly got into the car with a friend who was driving despite having consumed as much alcohol as I had. We headed home along the Lougheed Highway. On Lougheed, there is an industrial park in Burnaby, partway to UBC. At the time, there were exit lanes on the right with corresponding entrance lanes, which were separated by triangle-shaped medians like islands between them. On each of these islands, there was a concrete lamp post positioned right in the middle of the grassy median, which was rimmed with a concrete curb.

---

[9] CFL Draft Archives. *Draft Tracker: 1983*. Url: cfl.ca/draft-tracker/1983 (accessed July 17, 2023).

The music on the radio was loud as we sped down the highway, discussing the events of the night in loud voices. At one point, we both realized that the car was in the exit lane, heading off the highway into the industrial park to the right. We were now hurtling towards the island, with the concrete lamp post in the middle of it, and no time for the driver to even hit the brakes. All we could do is accept our fate and pray for the best.

The car hit the curb on the near side of the island at full speed, causing an explosion of sound. The car became airborne, and time slowed down. We seemed to float towards the lamp post in slow motion.

Then we watched the lamp post sail inches to the left of the car, along the entire length of the vehicle, with no contact. The car crashed down onto the far curb, bouncing onto the highway entrance ramp, on the far side of the island. Both of us were speechless as we limped along the highway toward home — the crash landing had badly damaged the undercarriage of the car.

We looked at each other in a state of suspended reality, with disbelief on our faces — what had just happened? How did we avoid hitting that post and becoming a statistic? The thing we were most concerned with after coming to terms with our own mortality, was the stain that our violent deaths would have had on our families and the UBC football program, forever placing an asterisk beside our championship team. The headline would have been something like, "UBC Vanier Cup Champions Die in Crash After Drunken CFL Draft Party!" Unfortunately, at the time, the machismo of men outweighed any concern for safety on the roads. It is miraculous that we survived, in spite of our now-diminished hubris. In retrospect, even worse than our own deaths, we might have injured or killed other innocent people with our recklessness on that dark highway, and this would have been unforgiveable.

Later, when we drove by the site in the light of day, we both agreed that there was no explanation for missing that post; the exit lane leads directly to the island and the post is dead centre on the island. Based on rudimentary physics, the car should have been cut in two, at the angle, direction, and speed that we travelled. But somehow, we missed it. Some would say it was just "dumb luck," but I got the feeling that there was something more at work. For me, this added to the mystery of life, for which my appreciation continued to grow. Our friendship has been forever bound by this terrifying experience, and the unspoken shame we both try to conceal.

"Radar Love," Golden Earring (1973)

My CFL dreams seemingly about to be realized also allowed me to fulfill one of my teenage dreams. After being drafted by the Winnipeg Blue Bombers and signing my contract, the first thing I did was call my former teacher, Mr. Chappell, to see if he was interested in selling his car. Ever since I saw him drive into our school parking lot back in grade 10, I had wanted to buy that white Datsun 280Z. Now, finally I could afford to make him an offer.

Luckily, when I called him, he was preparing to retire from teaching and wanted to buy a van to hold supplies for mural painting, which he planned to do in his retirement. I was so excited that the timing was perfect and he wanted the car to go to someone who would take care of it the way he did. I told him there was only one caveat: if I didn't make the team, I'd have to use my signing bonus to pay the rent!

Cal Murphy was a first-year head coach for the Blue Bombers in 1983. His first training camp was a war of attrition. At the time, there were two weeks of two-a-days and four exhibition games before the start of the 16-game regular season. So, essentially there were six weeks of training camp because the players battled to make the team right up until the final roster was set after the last exhibition game.

I was joining a veteran group of defensive linemen, including Stan Mikawos, Doug MacIver, John Sturdivant, Tony Norman, and flamboyant leader Pete Catan. These guys were all great guys, who welcomed me into the fold and shared their knowledge with me, in spite of me being a rookie. We were coached by Bob Vespaziani, who used a calm, intellectual demeanour to bring us together within a very competitive setting.

I had trained hard in the gym getting prepared for the first thing I would face — the strength and conditioning tests. Every position had different expectations laid out for them prior to camp, and as part of testing, linemen were expected to bench press 400 lb. I had never benched that much for a one-rep max (the maximum amount of weight you can lift for one repetition), but I had trained hard and was hoping I could get it on this day. Pete Catan, the All-Star defensive lineman, was my spotter and with his encouragement, I got it. Catan was genuinely happy for me when I completed the lift, which gave me a huge adrenaline rush. So far, so good for training camp.

Testing was only the tip of the iceberg. Coach Murphy was a hard-nosed coach and, this being his first camp, all the players, even the veterans, needed to impress him to solidify their place on the roster — competition was intense. To the veteran players, I was a cocky first-round draft pick; they didn't know anything else about me. On one of the first days of practice, we were in a "live period," the highest tempo in practice. Traditionally, one of the only differences between a live period in practice and playing in a game is that there is an unwritten rule that you don't "cut" (dive at a teammate's legs and chop them down to the ground with your body) your teammates — although it's legal in a game, in practice, you don't cut. Furthermore, if they are in a vulnerable position, you let up so they don't get injured, whereas in a game, you would never let up until the whistle went, and cutting your opponent below the waist was one more legal tool in your blocking kit. However, I learned that this training camp was different.

I got a good lesson in professional football during the first live drill in camp. I guess I pissed off John Bonk, the All-Star centre, when I lined head up on him as the nose guard and bull-rushed him back to the quarterback. On my way back to the defensive huddle, I saw Bonk turn to his guards Nick Bastaja and Lyle Bauer in the offensive huddle for a short conversation before the next play. My plan had been to bull-rush him the first play, setting him up for a swim move (see Appendix A) on my next play — my favourite pass-rush move, where I would make contact with the defender, then swat him with one arm and swim over him with the other arm to the right or left.

But I didn't get to make a second move, because as soon as I came off the ball, Bonk backpedalled out of the way and Bauer and Bastaja "high-lowed" me — meaning simultaneously one of them hammered my upper body, while the other cut out my legs – which pretty much cut me in half.

This really surprised me because this type of hit is illegal in a game. Today it's known as a "chop block" and results in a 15-yard penalty — but there are no refs in practice. They had not hesitated to risk my career with a potentially serious injury to protect their centre and send a message to the rookie, "You don't bull-rush John Bonk."

After that practice, I realized this would be a cut-throat training camp, so I wore knee braces for the first time in my career just to survive. I was angry about it at the time, but in retrospect, I know they had families to support and they were fighting for their jobs during Cal Murphy's first brutal training camp, just like I was. It made the cold reality of pro football crystal clear to me, and it was never mentioned again.

Chris "Bluto" Walby and Bobby "Big Cat" Thompson were twin towers as the Bombers' starting offensive tackles. These guys were the biggest tackles in the league, and it was eye-opening for me to line up against them in one-on-one drills. They seemed huge to me as a rookie. I had to use my best lateral moves to have any success; when I got them moving up field, I could counter with an inside move. I tried not to engage them because their size and long reach was just engulfing.

Walby's nickname was Bluto after Popeye's sidekick in the cartoon. Unfortunately for him, we actually looked alike, except that he was a couple of inches taller and had about 80 pounds on me. When the club held their annual golf tournament later on in camp, I was hitting a ball out of a sand trap when a photographer from the *Winnipeg Free Press* took a photo of me. The next day, Walby was pissed because the caption below the picture said it was him hitting the ball out of the sand. From that day on, Walby called me "Baby Bluto." Chris Walby is considered one of the best offensive linemen to ever play in the CFL, yet his humility allowed him to treat me, a rookie defensive lineman, like his little brother. It was an honour to have played with him.

Dieter Brock was the Bombers' starting quarterback. Everyone marvelled at the arm strength that earned him the nickname "The Birmingham Rifle," but as players on the field, we got a front-row seat. One day in camp, there was light rain on our grass practice field. As Brock dropped back to make a pass on the wet grass, he slipped and fell on his ass. Incredibly, from his seated position, he somehow avoided the scrum of linemen battling in front of him, launched the ball forty yards down the field, and hit the intended receiver right in the numbers on his jersey for a completion. I had never witnessed a throw like it. It was amazing how strong his arm was.

"You Really Got Me," Van Halen (1978)

Long full-contact practices twice a day made camp very tough to survive — everyone scrapped for every advantage to make Murphy's team. After several days of it, legs were getting heavy and morale was getting low. Personally, having never worn knee braces before, my legs seemed heavier and slower than they'd ever been.

Pete Catan, being the positive leader that he was (not to mention crazy), had a unique way of lifting everyone's spirits. He built a special helmet with a welder's shield replacing the face mask and two wire guides attached to the crown. He made a hobby of building miniature rockets, and to entertain the team, he would load a rocket on his helmet and launch it right off his head — for the big finale he would launch two at once. They would soar up into the sky, then the parachutes would deploy and the rockets would drift back down onto the football field in old Winnipeg Stadium (later called the Canad Inns Stadium), where Catan would then collect the reusable shells of the rockets. Incidentally, this stadium, which I was hoping would soon become my home, was located just across the parking lot from the infamous Polo Park Inn, the site of the "riot" where I had previously been targeted by the Winnipeg "SWAT" team — I had now gone full circle.

Catan's antics were always a welcome break from the burdens of camp life. Having a friend like Apeman to confide in during camp was great too. However, at one point in camp, my legs felt like lead and I just couldn't get out of the mental rut I was in. Luckily, even though I wouldn't have much free time with practices and meetings, Paulette flew out from Vancouver to visit for a weekend to cheer me up. It was great to see her and she was very supportive at a time when I was physically and emotionally drained. It was remarkable how much influence Paulette had on me.

Bob Vespaziani, my defensive line coach, was a knowledgeable and detail-oriented coach, but an even better person, who cared about his players. The day before Paulette arrived, he noticed my legs were heavy in practice; he gave me a pep-talk and told me I was having a great camp and to keep working hard. The next day, I had my legs back and had a great practice. Coach Bob commented about how much better I was moving and asked me what I was doing differently. I told him the only difference was that Paulette was visiting. He gave me a wink and a laugh, understanding the nature of the heart, and how much it can change someone's mindset. It seemed that Paulette was always there when I needed her the most.

Ultimately, I made the final roster and officially became a member of the Winnipeg Blue Bombers. Very excited to be so close to reaching my goal of playing in a CFL game, I called my folks and Paulette to tell them the news. Then, I called Mr. Chappell to finalize our deal for the car. Paulette arranged everything at the bank for the purchase. Next, I needed to get it to Winnipeg, so I asked Paulette's father, Peter, to drive the car out from Vancouver. He enjoyed driving and would use it as a vacation to visit relatives in Saskatchewan on the way to Winnipeg, after which I would provide a flight for him to get home.

Tyrone Jones and I came into the 1983 Bombers' camp together as rookies on the defensive side of the ball, he as a linebacker, me as a defensive end. We got to know each other through defensive meetings and sharing team drills in practice. We were both on special teams too, which is where most rookies solidify a roster spot. Jones and I got along well playing for the same defence and striving to make the team in a tough, physical, camp.

Jones was an amazing athlete, with speed, agility, and power emanating from his oversized glutes and quads — he could run all day long.

He also had good sense of humour, and we shared a positive relationship on the field. Once the roster was set, we shared duties on the punt team. As the season went on, his confidence in his physical skills grew — as did his vocal abilities (a.k.a. trash-talking), which was fine as long as you were not the target. During our shared Blue Bombers time, I was not in his trash-talking sights; later in our career paths is another story.

"Rebel Yell," Billy Idol (1983)

On August 7, 1983, we travelled to play the Montreal Concordes (previously and again now called the Montreal Alouettes) in an afternoon game at Olympic Stadium. It was a hot day and the afternoon sun was beaming down through the unfinished open roof of "The Big O" onto the artificial turf. The turf absorbed the heat and radiated it back into the stadium, so it acted like a convection oven for the players, who got the heat from the sun and heat rising off the turf. Everyone was hot and dehydrated as the game went on.

I was Jones' backup at right guard on the punt team and sometime in the third quarter, Tyrone was tired from a long defensive series. After a short two-and-out offensive series, he asked me to give him a break on the punt team. I thought it was great, I got an opportunity to make a play on "specials."

Inexplicably, the Concordes didn't block me on their punt return scheme. So, after Bob Cameron's punt, I was given a free-release; unhindered, I sprinted as fast as I could to cover the kick. Now, I was no speed-demon, but I had what is known in the game as "want-to speed." Fortunately, my pace happened to coincide perfectly with the trajectory of Cameron's kick, because when the kick returner caught the ball, I was going full speed exactly at the five-yard radius, where it was legal to hit the returner. I didn't have to break down and wait for him to catch the ball, so without missing a stride, I ran right through the returner with my left shoulder, hammering his chest and putting him on his back, resulting in zero net yards on the return. I was filled with the adrenaline and excitement that always accompanies a great defensive play.

Unfortunately, as I launched my body through the tackle, I felt a pop in my left foot on impact, accompanied by searing pain. When team trainer Pat Clayton helped me off the field and took my low-cut cleat off, the top of my foot swelled up like half a grapefruit. He put ice on it and told me I was done for the game — my fourth professional game and I was already out with an injury. I hoped it was just a sprain and I'd be back soon.

Back in Winnipeg, after the x-rays, the radiologist diagnosed it as a soft-tissue injury. The report said it was not fractured. I was hopeful that it would heal up soon so I could get back on the field. Pat treated it as the doctor prescribed. Soft tissue injuries are treated with ultrasound sessions, massage, and exercise to strengthen the injured tissue. However, these same treatments are harmful for new fractures.

After three weeks of this treatment, including stationary cycling to strengthen the foot, the swelling was only getting worse and Pat and I were getting frustrated. He sent me for another x-ray. Sure enough, the second x-ray revealed that the cuboid bone in my foot had been snapped in two. Three weeks of soft tissue treatment was the worst thing I could have been doing and it set me back even further. Now, I was likely dealing with a season ending injury.

In the meantime, Paulette's father Peter delivered my 280Z. When he arrived and pulled my new car into the driveway, I almost cried in a combination of joy for my new ride, and disgust from its condition. As I stood there with crutches and a cast on my foot, I saw that the entire front half of my car was covered with a thick layer of green-yellow grasshopper guts! 1983 was such a bad year for grasshoppers in the Canadian Prairies that they had to spray pesticides so the insects wouldn't destroy all the crops. These were not your garden-variety grasshoppers, either; they were huge. I used a brush and a bucket of soap and water to get all the guts off the car. I made sure I cleaned the brush well before I returned it to our kitchen sink.

Mr. Chappell's 1975 Datsun 280Z, Hamilton, 2021: Jason Riley photo

Incidentally, ownership of this car has paid dividends ever since because the Z-car fraternity is almost as tight as the football fraternity. Two guys in particular, Steve Karniej and Rick Scott, are now close friends because the car brought us together years ago, either networking for parts at a swap meet, or at one of the annual Z-car shows.

As the season went on, I continued training the best I could with a walking cast on my left foot, so I wouldn't lose any of that hard-earned weight I had put on. I was now 6′ 4″ and weighed in at 270 lb.

Six weeks later, the cast came off, and although the bone had healed, I was still dealing with torn ligaments and couldn't practice. I remember Cal Murphy saying to me, "Jason, how's that foot coming along? You know, you can't make the club in the tub!" That was his polite way of saying, "Don't be such a fucking baby and get back on the field."

Eventually, my foot healed up enough to test it out, with a heavy tape job for support. Before my first practice, however, I decided I wanted to come back with a bang. After the disappointing injury, I wanted everyone in Blue Bomber Nation to know that Jason Riley was back, true-blue, through and through. In this, I was inspired by Nick Hebeler, my old friend from Simon Fraser, when he shaved his head down to a strip in the middle of his head while with the B.C. Lions. It drew a lot of attention. So, I asked a hairdresser to shave a large "W" for Winnipeg in my hair. Thus, for my first practice back, I had a "W" on the back of my head, with the rest of my melon shaved bald. It was now October, late in the season, going into the stretch drive before playoffs.

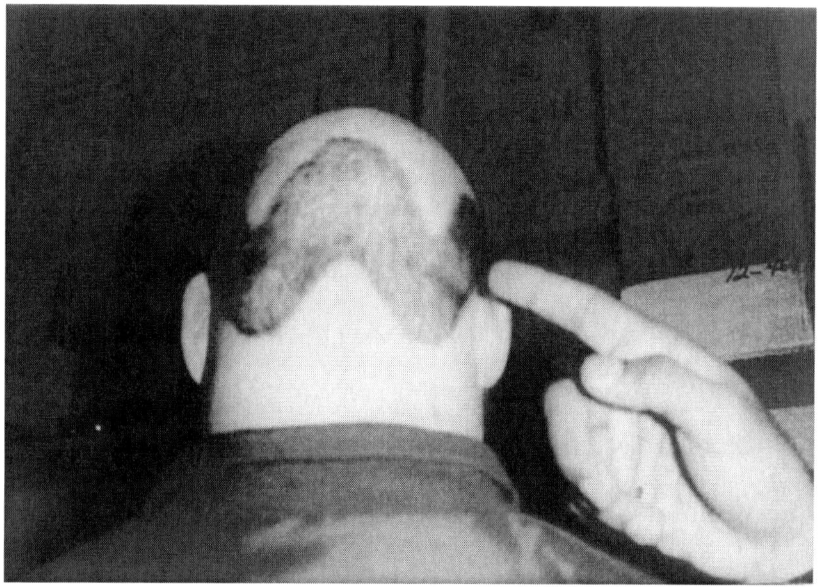

Winnipeg Blue Bomber through and through, 1983: Rick Paulitsch photo

Unfortunately, things didn't work out as I thought they would. Although I had exceeded my goal of playing one game in the CFL to prove my naysayers wrong, now that I had a taste of it, I wanted more.

Just prior to my new haircut, in a swap of two future Hall of Fame quarterbacks, Winnipeg had traded Dieter Brock to the Hamilton Tiger-Cats for Tom Clements. It was after this trade that Brock was vilified by Blue Bomber fans for making a comment about the zoo in Winnipeg. After many years as the Bombers' starter, setting club records along the way, he was trying to get out of his contract so he could play south of the border in the NFL. Frustrated by his inability to get his release from his contract with the Bombers, he made the comment to the press, "How many times can you go to the zoo?" referring to the small-town nature of the city. Unfortunately, this comment would come back to haunt Brock when he returned to play against Winnipeg.

Shortly afterwards, the same week I was cleared for practice, Tom Clements suffered an injury. Now the team needed a proven starter to replace him for the stretch run in our fight for the playoffs.

Luckily for the team it was our bye week, during which there was no game. This was a welcome break for a team that had been battling in Cal Murphy's boot camp since the start of training camp. Me and my roommates, Pat Cantner, Pieter Vanden Bos (who joined us mid-season from Edmonton), and running back Rick Paulitsch, decided to drive across the southern border to Pembina, North Dakota, for a boys' night out. Pembina is a small town a little more than 100 kilometres due south of Winnipeg, on the Pembina Highway just south of the U.S. border. The following day, we planned to use the precious day off to go fishing at the southern tip of Lake Winnipeg.

"American Woman," Guess Who (1970)

I was driving my car with Rick in the passenger seat, and Pat rode with Pieter in his little brown Toyota Celica. We played cat and mouse on the two-lane highway all the way down to the border crossing.

Geographically, football fans in Pembina are closer to Winnipeg than any major American city so they have adopted the Blue Bombers as their team. The patrons of the pub on this Friday night recognized us as Bombers as soon as we walked in the door. The "W" on my head was a dead giveaway. The hairstyle paid off because I don't remember paying for a drink the entire night. We were talking football with the local fans, eating chicken wings and pizza, and pounding beers — a football player's dream.

The next thing you know, the local sheriff walked in, dressed in full uniform. He walked right over and we thought, "Did someone make a complaint? We're just having a good time here."

The sheriff of Pembina said, "I heard you guys were in here. Thanks for coming to our town. We come up and watch your games all the time. Can I buy you a round?"

We were all compliant with the peace officer, "Sure, the night is young."

After a couple of pints, and lots of great football talk, the sheriff invited us back to his house to see his gun collection. Naturally, we said, "Yes," so as not to be rude to our host. I had never in my life seen a personal gun collection. Normally guns scared me. When you think about it, isn't it odd that we had been drinking and now this guy wants to show us his gun collection? I guess it was a testosterone thing.

When we entered the house, he offered us another beer, which we declined because we needed to get home soon and it was getting foggy out. He took us into his den, and three walls of the room were covered with guns of all shapes and sizes. I remember him telling us to help ourselves and pick up any gun we wanted to see the weight and balance of the weapon, as he proudly explained the history of each weapon. The one that caught my eye was a shiny revolver, pure stainless steel. He told me to twirl it in my hand like a gunfighter in an old Western. It really was impressive and felt well-balanced in my hand. A real work of art, except for its intended purpose.

Before we left the sheriff's place, we had agreed that Rick and I would go straight through the border so we could get a head start and pack for the fishing trip, while Pieter and Pat would stop at the duty-free shop to stock up the cooler with beverages. After we left the house, the highway was pitch black and a temperature inversion was churning up a thick blanket of fog. The drive home would take even longer with reduced visibility.

As planned, Rick and I went ahead at the border crossing on Pembina Highway, starting the trek north. The tunes were cranked on the tape deck, but I was driving slowly because it was hard to see the road in the fog. Then I noticed some headlights coming up behind us in the wrong lane. I said to Rick, "Look at these crazy bastards driving on the wrong side of the road in the fog!"

As they pulled up beside us, we realized it was Pieter and Pat. Pat had the window down with a crazed look in his eyes. He began yelling at us.

I rolled down the manual window, as Rick turned down the stereo. Pat yelled, "You've been traded to Saskatchewan!"

Assuming that the boys were just busting my balls, I told him to get serious, rolled the window back up, and cranked the stereo. I wasn't falling for that old trick. If you really wanted to piss someone off, you'd tell them they were traded — in the middle of the night, in the fog, after shaving a "W" in their hair no less. With no communication from the team, right?

I had heard that the Roughriders were becoming a model franchise in the CFL. Regina was blossoming into a vibrant city, the province had low unemployment, and they sold out every game with fans travelling, often long distances, to cheer on their team. And I knew players loved playing in that exciting sports climate, being the only major sports franchise in town.

But I was a proud Blue Bomber so I thought that these guys were messing with my head.

Rick and I continued on our way, trying to feel our way home in the fog, enjoying the tunes, when Pieter pulled up beside us again, honking the horn. This time, Pat hung halfway out the window and yelled again, "You've been traded to Saskatchewan, put on the radio and listen to the news!"

We put the radio on, even though I was still convinced that they were just pulling our legs. Suddenly, it felt like a movie scene: as soon as we switched from the cassette deck to the radio, we heard the announcer say, "There was a blockbuster trade in the CFL today. Saskatchewan traded quarterback John Hufnagel and defensive end J.C. Pelusi to Winnipeg, in exchange for quarterback Nickie Hall, receiver Nate Johnson, and defensive lineman Jason Riley."

I heard nothing after that. I pulled over to the shoulder of the road and turned the stereo off. I sat there, in the middle of nowhere, with a "W" shaved on my head and my whole world crashing down on me. Rick was speechless. I was in shock.

Pieter and Pat pulled over and told us they had heard it on the radio at the border crossing and everyone was talking about the big trade. The border guards were amused when the boys told them that one of those guys who just got traded had just drove through their border crossing.

It was the middle of the night, so I wasn't about to call Cal Murphy to confirm the trade. I was in denial. I also decided that, if it was true, because he didn't have the courtesy to tell me before we left the stadium that day, I may not call him at all. Why should I? It was like a punch in the face.

We made our way slowly back to Winnipeg and the first thing I did was ask Pat to make an "S" out of the "W" with our clippers. He couldn't, so he shaved my melon completely bald. (In retrospect, that was a mistake because it has never grown back.)

The next morning, I was still in disbelief when we packed up to go fishing. After a few hours of fishing, I went to the bait shop to get more worms. I decided I'd better get it over with and call Cal. There was a pay phone on the wall in the bait shop. Cal answered the phone right away.

I said to him, "Hey Coach, I just heard on the radio of my car that I've been traded to Saskatchewan. Please tell me it's not true!"

He said, in a very uncharacteristically sheepish tone, "Jason, I'm so sorry, I couldn't tell you yesterday before you left the stadium because it hadn't been confirmed yet. I called you at home as soon as it was official, but you had left town and we couldn't get in touch with you."

He had a point, but that didn't take away any of the anger and disappointment I had harboured all night in my gut. I hadn't come to terms with my situation yet. I had worked so hard for so long to play this game and had become a Blue Bomber at heart, so I could not grasp the fact that I had been traded away — like a stock on the stock market that has lost its value. Life seemed so unfair.

When I got back to Winnipeg, I went to collect my things from my locker and discovered that someone had pilfered my locker and stole the leather sparring gloves I wore to protect my hands when I played. They were brand new and expensive. That definitely added insult to injury. I was wishing I knew who had stolen them because I was in the mood for a fight at that point.

Back at the house, I loaded the few possessions I owned and a bag of clothes into the hatchback of the 280Z and left for Regina. The car is made for the highway, and I loved driving fast. I planned to cover the 600 km distance on the Trans-Canada Highway, from Winnipeg to Regina, in record time. It was like I was possessed and I couldn't go fast enough. I was angry at my situation and questioned the justice of it all, so it was a white-knuckle drive all the way there.

Five hours later, I was flying through some low hills near Indian Head, about an hour from Regina. At about 90 mph on a nice open prairie highway, one of Saskatchewan's finest pulled me over. I knew he had me dead to rights. I figured it was typical for this string of bad luck.

In our conversation, after he asked me for my licence, I explained that I was trying to make it to my first meeting with the Roughriders after I had been traded — he was aware of the trade and knew I wasn't making it up.

He concluded by saying, "Jason, slow down and good luck in your career with the Riders. Take it easy so you make it in one piece."

I was relieved when he didn't give me a ticket. I felt grateful that he had some compassion for my situation, and thought that maybe this was the end of my run of bad luck. This also showed me how much the Riders are loved in Saskatchewan.

I drove straight to the stadium and met the head coach, Reuben Berry. He told me he was glad to have me as part of his defensive line and he had big plans for me. He knew that it would take time for my foot to get to 100%, so he asked me to work hard on the field and off to get ready for next year — there were only a few games left on the regular schedule at this point. But the coolest thing about the rest of that season is that my new defensive line position coach was former CFL All-Star Mike Samples, who was a great character and would later become a friend.

Before I left Regina for home at season's end, Coach Berry told me to keep training for my defensive line position because he planned on making me a part of that unit next season. This gave me hope that I would get the opportunity to play. I drove home to B.C. full of excitement, knowing that if I continued to train for power and speed, I would get to continue playing the position I loved — defensive line. I planned to come back to Regina for next camp at about 275 lb, lean and ready to run. If what Coach Berry told me was true, next season I would be in the rotation on the Riders' defensive front.

During the off-season that year, I continued my job as bouncer at the Boo Pub. One night, I was manning the entrance to the Backstage Club — the dance club that was open for an hour after the pub closed — when Glenn Leonhard, the veteran offensive lineman from the BC Lions walked in by himself and met me at the door. It was late and he just wanted to talk football. I had never met him before, but we both knew each other through the football fraternity.

He asked me how I was doing after my first year in the CFL. I told him about my experiences the past season and that I was finally looking forward to playing defensive line in Saskatchewan after what Reuben Berry had told me at the end of the year. Then Glenn gave me some of the best advice I ever got.

He said, "Jason, if they ever ask you to move to offensive line, don't fight it."

I said, "What do you mean? I've never played offence in my life."

He said, "I felt the same way when they asked me to move over, and it's the best thing I could have done for my career. I'm telling you, if they ask you, do it; you won't regret it."

He explained to me that some of the nuances of the offensive line position make it enjoyable to play. He said that offensive linemen usually have more longevity in the league because they're not getting their legs cut out from under them, or getting double-teamed by guys all the time. He told me that because of this, offensive line careers generally last longer than their counterparts on defence. I don't ever remember speaking to him again after this late-night conversation, but his words turned out to be prophetic.

I had prepared all off-season to play defensive line in the 1984 season for Coach Berry's Saskatchewan Roughriders. The opposing line positions, offensive line versus defensive line (see Appendix A), require different training regimens because they utilize different skill sets. Defensive linemen have to be able to cover the width of the field, from sideline to sideline (65 yards in the Canadian game as opposed to 50 yards in the US), so they have to be agile and able to run like a deer for four quarters of play, while still having explosive power to get off the ball and take on blockers in the trenches. Offensive linemen generally have to be heavier and stronger to complete some of the unnatural movements they are expected to execute, like moving their bodies backwards and at the same time, being physical and delivering punches forward (open-handed blows to the chest and shoulder area of the defender to slow their up-field momentum) during pass protection, while also having the mass and power to create forward movement against a powerful defender in the run game. These skills are often contrary to what the human body is designed to do, and take much practice to perfect.

Almost immediately, this training camp went off the rails. First, Reuben Berry attended a luncheon in Saskatoon at the start of camp. Driving back to Regina on the highway with the car in cruise control, he fell asleep and the car went off the road, colliding with a concrete median. No one was seriously hurt, but he had the shifter on the steering wheel column driven into his right buttock. He received a deep wound that he referred to as his "second asshole" in the middle of his right butt cheek. Consequently, he wore a large bandage around his ass as he limped around for the rest of training camp.

Next, a couple of days into camp, the team traded for veteran defensive lineman Rick Goltz. This was the writing on the wall for me. Rick Goltz was a stud defensive lineman, who had spent some time in the NFL before returning to the Lions. I once witnessed him bench over 500 pounds at the gym in Vancouver. I thought, "With Goltz in camp, they don't need a rookie like me any more." With my foot injury and the trade the previous season, I still felt like a rookie because I hadn't played much. So much for being in Coach Berry's plans for the defensive line in Saskatchewan!

Finally, our offensive line coach, Bob "Swifty" Swift, proved Glenn Leonhard's advice that winter night at the Boo, prophetic. Coach Swift was a former CFL All-Star offensive lineman who now coached the offensive line for the Roughriders. Swifty was a great guy and a well-respected coach. He approached me shortly after Goltz's arrival to ask if I'd be willing to learn the offensive line position with his unit. If I was willing to join his group for camp, he would teach me the position, and the coaches agreed that I could be a back-up at both offensive line and defensive line, since I already knew the defensive system.

I remembered my conversation with Leonhard and immediately told Swifty that I would do it. My plan was to work hard to earn special-team assignments; that, plus the increased versatility of my combined roles on offence and defence, would make my job more secure and possibly extend my career.

To be successful at the new position, I knew I would also have to change my training routine to continue putting on more size and strength. Now, I figured I'd need to get up to about 290 lb to excel as an offensive lineman. In the meantime, I would use my leaner physique to my advantage on special teams.

At the first offensive meeting of my career, Coach Swift introduced me to Tom Kudaba, a guest offensive line coach for training camp. Tom was a former CFL lineman who had suffered a serious car accident that ended his career. He took me under his wing because he knew my situation, learning a new position in training camp. Essentially, Tom became my personal offensive line coach because Swifty was so engrossed in coaching the veteran group. The next day, in my first practice at the position, Tom taught me how to get into an offensive line stance, which is completely different from the defensive side of the ball.

The Roughrider offensive line group consisted of some real characters. Lawrie Skolrood, Gerry Hornett, Bryan Illerbrun, Neil Quilter, Roger Aldag, Bob "Pole Cat" Poley, Mike Anderson, and Vic Stevenson made up the unit. Scott Redl was on the injured list. If I could learn the position, I would become a member of this elite group. Swifty had to use all his experience to deal with these veterans.

Neil Quilter was a good role model for new offensive guards like myself. He had it all: size, strength, great feet – the agility and foot quickness necessary for the position, which offensive line coaches look for – and Hollywood good looks. He was probably the most low-key character in the group, but boy, could he block. He didn't say much, but I learned much from watching him practice. Being fellow UBC grads gave us something in common.

Gerry Hornett was a 6'3"-, 320-lb offensive tackle who competed hard on the field and had good mobility for a guy his size. Off the field, he always had a smile on his face.

Bryan Illerbrun, on the other hand, didn't seem to smile much. He was all business, all the time. As a former Regina Ram, and in defence of the prairies he loved, he used to say, "Mountains are nice, but they ruin the view!" Being from Vancouver, I disagreed.

Bob "Pole Cat" Poley was a 6'4"-, 270-lb centre, with a Fu Manchu mustache. He was a grizzled veteran of the trenches. Aldag also called him "Nine-Toes" because he chopped off one of his toes while chopping wood for the fire on a hunting trip. Poley was amicable with a great sense of humour. He was always level-headed and gave wise advice. He was like having a wise sage or an elder statesman in the huddle, only in a young body. In an exhibition game after training camp, I was playing in my first ever game as an offensive guard beside him, with the honour of protecting the great Joe Paopao. After I pissed off one of the opposing defensive linemen, Bob Poley said to me, "Jason, you should calm down. You don't want to poke a sleeping bear. If you don't piss off the defensive line, it'll make your job a lot easier."

I understood what he was saying, but I told him, "I can't help it Pole Cat, I can only play this game one way, pissed off to the whistle."

Roger Aldag reminded me of one of the battle dwarves from J. R. R. Tolkien's *Lord of the Rings* trilogy — and I mean this as a great compliment because I love Tolkien's characters. At 6 feet tall, he was relatively short for the position, which he made up for with incredible strength and physicality. He had a thick, powerful body and no apparent neck: his squared shoulders seemed to narrow up into his head, and his shoulder-length blond hair hid any remaining evidence of a neck. The only thing he lacked was the double-bladed battle axe, comfortably thrown over his shoulder, as he approached the LOS ready to do battle. I'm sure any defensive lineman would rather play against a battering-ram than have to deal with Aldag. He was a perennial All-Star and after retirement, he was inducted into the CFHOF. The best thing about Roger, however, was that he was an outstanding person. He took me under his wing as soon as Swifty brought me over to his unit.

Lawrie Skolrood reminded me of Chewbacca the Wookiee from the *Star Wars* movies. He was about 6'6" and 320 lb, sporting a long, brown mullet haircut and beard. He had the temperament too. Legend has it that he once kicked in the head coach's door because he read an article in the local newspaper that said he was underperforming and was about to be traded to another club. It turned out to be a misprint and Lawrie and the coach smoothed everything over afterwards, but I would bet the coach would think twice about trading him after seeing a Wookiee crashing through his door like that! This is the reason I never read the newspaper during training camp for the rest of my career.

Sometimes this veteran group would test Coach Swift's patience. One time we were in an offensive line meeting, with Swifty at the front of the room breaking down some film of our next opponent.

Whenever you have a group of large men like this in a small room for a prolonged period of time, certain physiological things tend to happen. First, regardless of a working air-conditioning system, the room temperature starts to rise, just because of the massive amount of body heat being produced. Next, the previously-consumed meals begin moving through their respective digestive tracts. Obviously, with the offensive line pedigree of these unusually large human beings, vast quantities of food are consumed during training camp. Naturally, this process results in bodily gases. Finally, the flatulence begins, like the pressure release valve on a steam-boiler with too much heat.

In this particular meeting, the farts started as short, relatively innocuous types. First, a guy at the back let one loose. Then, someone near the front answered with a similar offering, while Swifty just continued his film analysis, knowing flatulence is not unusual in an offensive-line meeting. Normally, this "planned ignoring" tactic would work; however, not in this case. The farts became contagious, and a volley began spreading throughout the room. We all added our own tune to the chorus, with relieved grins on our faces.

Now, the already hot, muggy atmosphere in the room had a distinctly musky odour, which acted as a cloud of laughing gas. Giggles accompanied each note, which quickly turned to rib-splitting laughter. At this point, Coach Swift became agitated and stopped the meeting to try and re-focus our attention on the task at hand.

Of course, when Swifty returned to his line of thought, the farting quickly resumed. We were all sitting on those laminated wood chairs that stack up for storage. This type of chair tends to amplify and carry the sound of a fart better than most others. Then, in the midst of all the jocularity, Gerry Hornett displayed a wider smile than usual. And so began his response to the cacophony of flatulence surrounding him. Hornett let out a long staccato of a fart that continued for what seemed like minutes (but was probably only several seconds), rising to a crescendo that vibrated the wooden laminate in his chair to the point of exploding. This ultimately brought such a gush of laughter from the entire group that Swifty had no choice but to end the meeting and send us to get taped for practice.

This was the first time I had ever witnessed a fart end a meeting, but it wouldn't be the last time I experienced it in a career among behemoths.

"Free Bird," Lynyrd Skynyrd (1973)

As the season went on, I was backing up all the offensive and defensive line positions except centre. In addition to that, I managed to make my way onto every special team: kick-off, kick-off return, punt, punt-return, field goal, and field goal return. Aldag was happy for me to be subbing in for him on the field goal team; it gave him a bit of well-deserved rest.

The casual fan of the Canadian game may not realize that there is so much kicking in our game because we only have three downs, as opposed to four downs in the American game. This means that if you are playing on every special team throughout the game, it can be almost equivalent to starting at an offensive or defensive position due to the number of plays and the amount of running involved on the cover teams (the units that must sprint and "cover" the width of the field after a punt, kickoff, or missed field goal to tackle the opposing kick returner). This is why good special teams players can earn a spot on a roster, even if they never start a game.

There were games, especially on the hot, humid summer weekends, where I would be exhausted from playing special teams, and an offensive or defensive lineman would go down with an injury and I needed to play their position for the rest of the game. Those games were very physically and mentally demanding. I needed to rely on all the training I had done to prepare for this opportunity. I embraced the challenge because I was finally playing on a regular basis in the CFL.

Halfway into the season, after having my best game on special teams, Coach Berry held a special teams meeting. He had a special teams film cutup he wanted to show, including all the special teams plays from the previous game. I was surprised when a few plays in, he said, "Look at Riley on this tackle on the punt team." I had made a good hit on a punt, similar to the one I made in Montreal when I broke my foot. After I laid out the punt returner, again unabated by any blocker, I got up off the field with blood streaming down my face because my helmet had lacerated the bridge of my nose on impact. Turning to the bench, I saw Poley, Aldag, and the boys cheering me on as I returned to the sidelines — high fives all around.

"Look at Riley on this block on kick-off return," Coach Berry continued. I was happy he felt that way, but feeling really self-conscious at this point. Then he said, "I wish we had 12 Jason Rileys to play special teams for us!"

The fact that the head coach had verbalized this at a team meeting was embarrassing, but at the same time I was happy that my hard work was finally being appreciated by the coaches. I now felt like I had made it in pro football, with a promising career on special teams in front of me. That sense of fulfillment was short lived though.

"Dust in the Wind," Kansas (1977)

The next day, I had a bounce in my step when I went into the dressing room, with that feeling you get when your job is secure. I really loved the game again.

That's when the equipment manager, Normie Kwong, came to me and said that Coach Berry wanted to see me in his office. A one-on-one meeting request with the head coach usually meant that you were being cut (released from your contract) or traded, but after yesterday's meeting, I was certain that I had nothing to worry about. When I sat in his office, I knew something was up. Unlike the look I saw on his face the day before, today he was stern.

He said in a calm voice, "Jason, we have to release you."

I said, "Pardon me?" I was incredulous – if I heard him right this meant he was cutting me from the team.

He continued, "It's a numbers thing. We have to release you because we have two Canadian linemen coming off the injury reserve list: Scott Redl on the offensive line, and Brent Racette on the defensive line. We have to make room for them."

These were both talented linemen and good people, Racette had played with me his senior year at UBC, and Redl was a talented local signing for Saskatchewan, but they hadn't played all year. I had been backing up both sides of the ball and playing every special team all season long. I told him that it wasn't fair to me that he should take me off the roster for guys that hadn't contributed. I had done everything that was asked of me by the coaches, and I deserved to be on the roster. If that wasn't going to happen, then I no longer wanted to be with the team. It was another punch in the face.

Coach Berry explained, "I understand how you feel, Jason, but we want to keep you on the practice roster and pay your full salary, under-the-table." With smaller rosters in the CFL and 12 players on the field (as opposed to 11 players in the U.S.) in all three phases of the game (offence, defence, and special teams), this is how all the teams used to keep extra players around. This way they could keep a player, but it wouldn't show up on the books. It was also against league rules. Rosters are bigger now, so it's not necessary to hide players from the league this way anymore.

For me, this was the final nail in the coffin. My decision was final. I told Berry, "I am done with football."

"If that's how you truly feel," Berry continued. "You have to wait 48 hours to clear waivers [a 48-hour period, where any other team can claim a released player]. Then, if no other club claims you, you're able to leave as a free agent." In other words, I would be cut from the team.

So, for two days I watched practice in my civvies to see if anyone would claim me. It was a humiliating exercise in futility for me. I knew I would not be claimed because no other teams knew who I was. If I could have left and avoided the embarrassment of watching my former teammates practice, I would have, but Berry told me league rules prevented it. I thought this was disingenuous because, after all, it was against league rules to pay a player under the table, which he had offered to keep me around.

Thus, I stayed and absorbed another emotional roller-coaster, internalizing the anxiety it caused me once again.

The minute I cleared waivers, I repacked my suitcase and blender into the 280Z, and began the long drive home from Regina. This time, I took my time and enjoyed the ride; I was in no hurry to get home. I felt so dejected that I would never again play the game I loved. It was over, and I decided I was going to enjoy the rest of the summer.

I drove through the Rockies to Penticton, where my old high school buddy, Craig Parks, lived. He had a place on the water and he taught me how to water ski during some great days on the beach.

I took the opportunity to take a deep breath and evaluate my first year of professional football: I had experienced the thrill of being a first-round draft pick; I worked very hard to make the Blue Bombers' roster; I suffered the pain of a broken foot and incorrect treatment due to medical misdiagnosis; I was traded to the Roughriders in the John Hufnagel blockbuster deal; I was asked to learn a position I had never played before;

I backed up on both sides of the ball and played on every special team for half the season; then I got cut.

It was little compensation to me at the time that I had surpassed my original goal of playing one game in the CFL! Now that I had experienced playing in the league, I knew that I belonged, if only I had found my niche.

Upon reflection, I realized that after all the hard work, sweat, blood, and training I had done since high school to make myself bigger and stronger in order to play the game, I was no better off. I decided that if this was professional football life, I wanted nothing more to do with it. I told Craig at that point that I was quitting football and going back to UBC to get my Master's degree, in City Planning. I had learned that there are always choices in life, and I had a plan B.

That was my intention when I drove the rest of the way home through the Rockies. The 280Z, hugging every turn on the mountain highway effortlessly, gave me an exhilarating adrenaline-fueled ride.

Craig had provided great hospitality at his place at the lake: we ate, drank, and partied on the beach all weekend. It was exactly what I needed to put my football career behind me and move on emotionally from the sport I loved so much. And I wasn't in a hurry because I was free as a bird to do whatever I wanted, now that I had my life back from the rigors of battling in the trenches. So, it took me several days to get back to B.C. from Regina. In the eighties, with no access to mobile phones, I was out of touch with everyone the whole time — just what the doctor ordered.

When I finally got home, Dad was excited. He told me to call the Hamilton Tiger-Cats right away. He said, "They have been calling several times a day since you left Saskatchewan. Their head coach, Al Bruno, told me the Tiger-Cats really want to talk to you!"

When I told him my decision to quit football, he and Mom were disappointed with the situation, but they supported my decision. They understood that I had been through a very difficult year, both mentally and physically, and just wanted what was best for me and my career moving forward.

Paulette was fine with it too — she was very patient with me. It had been difficult maintaining our now long-distance relationship with my unstable career and she knew my life was in turmoil. By now, we had mutually agreed to put everything on hold for a while, until I got my life straightened out. She was still comfortable living at home and working at the bank, while my life was upside down. We knew that if it was meant to be, everything would work out for us in time.

Monte Charles, the Tiger-Cats' player personnel director, called again. I told him about my decision to quit football and move on because of the way things had gone in my first year in the league. I had learned there is no loyalty to players — the commitment players are required to make for the club is not reciprocated. It's a cold business and I had other options to pursue.

Monte asked if I would speak to Al Bruno if he called me because Al really wanted to talk to me. I told him I would speak to him, but that my mind was already made up. When Al called later in the day, he told me that the Tiger-Cats had wanted to draft me, but the Bombers got me before they could. He said that they were rebuilding their offensive line to protect Dieter Brock and he thought I would be a good fit.

He sounded sincere on the phone and it started to turn my thinking, but I repeated what I had told Monte about my decision. Then, he said, "Jason, I understand how you feel after what you've been through. We want you to play offensive line for us and we'll pay you the same contract you signed with Winnipeg. Also, as a sign of good faith, I'll guarantee you'll be on the roster within two weeks, if you agree to come."

I said, "Coach, I've never really played offensive line. I played defensive line in college and I was drafted as defensive lineman." I didn't even know how he knew I played offensive line, since I had never started a game at the position.

"That doesn't matter. We want you to play offensive line for us." He continued, "We'll have a ticket ready for you at the airport, and I'll have the contract ready to sign when you get here."

He was very persuasive and he sounded like a man I could trust. I said, "If you guarantee I'll be on the roster in two weeks, I'll come and play for you."

The next day, I was packing my bag to head out to Hamilton when the phone rang again. This time it was Bill Quinter calling, the player personnel director for the BC Lions. He said, "Jason, Nick Hebeler seriously injured his leg in the game on the weekend, and we want you to come and play defensive line for the BC Lions."

I couldn't believe it. It was a very tempting offer and I hadn't actually signed anything yet with the Ticats. I thought, "If the Lions had called a day earlier, I could stay in my hometown and play my natural position — defensive line."

Ultimately, I told Mr. Quinter that my parents had taught me to be a man of my word, so I had to honour my verbal agreement with the Ticats. He said, "I appreciate your decision, and if you are not on the roster within two weeks, we will welcome you to come play for the Lions."

"Wild Night," Van Morrison (1971)

When I arrived at the Toronto airport, Ray "Jonesy" Jones, the long-time trainer for the Hamilton Tiger-Cats, met me at Pearson Airport and brought me to Hamilton. The first thing he did when we arrived was give me a brief tour of the historic Ivor Wynne Stadium. It was the first time I had seen it and I could sense the history of the stadium the moment I stepped on the field. The first thing I noticed was the large Tiger-Cats logo painted on the turf at centre field — to me it was the most eye-catching logo I'd ever seen. When we scanned the stands, they seemed so close to the field that I could almost hear the fans screaming at great games from the past, including the last Grey Cup the Ticats won, in 1972. Looking up at the empty stadium from field level, I could see that the team honoured its past greats proudly around the press box on the Wall of Honour; some of the names displayed included John Barrow, Garney Henley, Ellison Kelly, Angelo Mosca, Vince Scott, and Joe Zuger. It gave me goose bumps to think that I was being given an opportunity to play for this great franchise. That football spark that had been nearly extinguished in Regina was now instantly reignited and burning inside me. I decided at that very moment that I was not here to simply make friends: I was here to make the team.

Then Jonesy introduced me to the team doctors for my physical. Jonesy told me Dr. Jim Charters was the head of the medical team, with Dr. Nick Siksay and Dr. David Levy as his assistants. A true gentleman, Dr. Charters was the head of occupational health and safety at Stelco, the largest steel manufacturer in Canada, employing over 25,000 people. Dr. Siksay worked at Stelco with Dr. Charters. Later, when Dr. Charters' health failed, Dr. Levy would take over as team physician of the Tiger-Cats.

Dr. Levy had founded the Athletic Injury Clinic at McMaster University (also known as Mac) in 1978. This was ground-breaking medical practice at the time. By the time he took over as the head physician for the Tiger-Cats, he was considered a pioneer of sports medicine in Ontario.[10]

After I passed my physical, Jonesy took me into the meeting room and introduced me to offensive line coach Jerry Bruner and the current members of the Tiger-Cats offensive line: Marv Allemang, Jeff Arp, Pat Brady, Ross Francis, Bill Howard, Warner Miles, Paul Palma, Ralph Scholz, Bobby Thompson (recently traded from Winnipeg to Hamilton), and Henry Waszczuk. Martin Disabatino and Tone Marrone were two good local guys on the practice roster when I arrived; they both successfully contributed in the local coaching community later on. The only familiar face to me in the whole group was Pat Brady's.

Actually, Brady was the only person I knew in the entire city of Hamilton. The Tiger-Cats had drafted him as their long snapper out of Western, after our 1982 Vanier Cup game. As Brady tells it, "Coach Bruno had complimented me on my long snapping for Western during the Yates Cup that year; he said they were interested in drafting me as a long snapper in the upcoming CFL draft."

There was one problem: Pat didn't long snap on punts for Western. Somehow there was a typo on his roster depth chart and Coach Al had the wrong jersey number. Brady did not correct him.

Attempting not to look surprised, Brady replied, "Thank you, Coach, I'd love to play for the Tiger-Cats." That Brady knew that Western's actual long snapper had no interest in continuing to play at the next level made Brady's ruse all the more humorous.

It's what Brady did afterward that allowed him to take full advantage of that typo on Coach Bruno's depth chart. When he returned home to Vancouver after graduation, he researched proper long-snapping technique and fastened an old car tire to his parents' backyard fence to use as a target. Every day, he snapped the ball at the bulls-eye of that tire from fifteen yards away, until he perfected his snap. He attended training camp

---

[10] Sports Medicine. 2015. *Dr. David Levy returns to McMaster*. Marauders, McMaster University. Url: marauders.ca (accessed May 4, 2023).

in 1983, and earned the long snapper's job, successfully snapping to kicking greats Bernie Ruoff, then Paul Osbaldiston, for five years. During his time as the Tiger-Cats long snapper, Brady was considered one of the most consistent snappers in the CFL. Brady was a bit undersized for his offensive line position at this level, but he is a good example of a guy who made it on 'specials,' while backing up centre on the OL.

"The Weight," The Band (1968)

During my first two weeks in Hamilton, the Club put me up in a hotel called the City Motor Hotel, right beside the Queenston traffic-circle. Everyone called it the "City Morgue," but I didn't mind it. There was a roof over my head, a clean bed to sleep in, and the greasy-spoon restaurant served good home-cooked meals.

However, I welcomed the solitude I had at the hotel while I was there because I was in Hamilton to take care of business and I didn't want any distractions from my new goal. Al Bruno had somehow seen my potential as an offensive lineman, even though I had never started or played a full game at the position. I knew I had only a small window of opportunity to prove him right – it would be very difficult to come in and establish myself on a new team at mid-season. Additionally, I knew I would not be a popular guy in the dressing room, with the players knowing I was brought in to take a teammate's job.

Consequently, I went to practice every day with my game face on and frankly didn't care who I offended, because I didn't know anyone besides Brady. The guys on the offensive line knew why I was there, so they weren't about to embrace me as a friend, at least at first. I didn't know anyone on the defensive side of the ball, either, other than some players' names from games I'd seen on television; even that was limited because up until now I had been too busy with my university career to watch much TV. Suffice it to say that I wasn't concerned with hurting anyone's feeling because to achieve my goal of making the roster without the benefit of training camp, I had to kick ass in practice. If I didn't prove to all the coaches that I could play offensive line in the first few practices, I would become a failed Al Bruno experiment. I was going to do everything in my power to prevent that from happening.

Initially, I know I was seen as the bald-headed asshole to everyone on the field except the coaches. The important thing was that the coaches embraced my physicality, which the offensive line seemed to lack. In every drill I did, I tried to be as physical as possible and knock people down. I was able to incorporate my aggressive defensive line mentality into offensive line play. I still needed to learn all the subtleties of the position and the playbook, but as long as I was physical, I knew I would be given time to do that.

Coach Bruno inserted me at right tackle on the offensive line. My fighting experience helped me at my new position because I had quick hands and feet, which are a prerequisite on the offensive line. In fact, boxing and martial arts have become excellent off-season training tools for linemen on both sides of the ball. And as I had been doing for as long as I'd been playing football, I could summon that inner rage I stored deep inside whenever I needed it. Now, I needed it: I had to treat every practice like a game and be ready to fight if I hoped to make the team.

At that point, I even treated my fellow offensive linemen poorly. One day, Henry Waszczuk was a victim of my callous attitude. He was the somewhat-undersized starting centre, playing in the league for a decade. I didn't know him at all.

We were both kneeling on one knee, between reps in a drill. Waszczuk said to me, "So, what's with the head?" referring to my bald, shaved head — not too many men shaved their heads back then.

The hair went up on my neck, I looked him in the eye, and replied, "What's it to you?" He never mentioned it again.

Waszczuk had been the recipient of the instantly-defensive response I had developed because of my insecurities as a bullying victim; as I write this, I'm still unpacking some of these issues now.

Ultimately, he understood my situation, coming into a new team. After we got to know each other better, we put it in the past and became friends.

In teaching, there's an old saying, "You can't smile for the first two weeks of a new semester," because you need to set the tone for the new class, or the kids will walk all over you. Multiply that by a million and you'll understand why I had to be an asshole on the field to make the Hamilton

Tiger-Cats roster coming in midway through the season. I needed to maintain this singular focus to overcome everything I had working against me. Off the field, I could relax in my hotel room, but never on the field.

I didn't hold anything back in those first weeks of practice. I know I pissed off a lot of the guys on offence and defence, but I also knew that they would eventually appreciate my toughness and willingness to compete. I needed to prove that Coach Al was right in his gamble on me.

CFHOF linebacker Ben Zambiasi was arguably the best middle linebacker in the league at the time. He practiced like he played and although he wasn't the biggest physically, he was one of the best hitters in the game. That's undoubtedly why he is still a household name in the state of Georgia, where he cut his teeth in college with the University of Georgia Bulldogs.

He actually knocked guys out cold in practice if they got caught unprepared for one of Zambiasi's hits. He was never cheap, just very intense. You had to make sure you had your base under you whenever you went to the second level (see Appendix A) of our defence to block him. If not, you'd end up on your ass.

My first week in practice, we got to know each other during "inside run" periods, when I had to venture into his territory to block at the second level. I understood very quickly that Zambiasi had his finger on the pulse of our defence, and that he was the heart of a talented group, which included stalwarts like Mike Walker, Grover Covington, Paul Bennett, Less Browne, and Leo Ezerins.

In this light, Zambiasi had a unique perspective on my arrival in Hamilton. He put it like this:

> After 6 years in the CFL, all with the Cats, I knew[that] to become a Grey Cup contender, a team has to assess, recruit, and keep the best Canadian talent for a chance to drink from the holy grail.
>
> In 1984, at a mid-season practice, one of those Canadians showed up at Ivor Wynne. I

> didn't know anything about him, and had never heard anything about him.
>
> What I did see was a big man who did not smile or talk much, but had a neck as big as mine and as inflexible [during team stretch] as I was.
>
> Shortly after team warm up, the team breaks up to do individual work or fundamentals: offensive line, defensive line, linebackers, secondary, running backs, receivers, and kickers. During this part of practice, the individual groups begin the "contact" part of practice and I recognized, [or] rather heard, what the new guy would bring to our team... it was like the sound of two sedans colliding. As a heavy hitter myself, I know the kind of energy, strength and skill needed to put one's face and body into an opponent to create that sound...and it's not only special, it takes a lot of courage. This new guy's name was Jason Riley and I knew from the moment I watched him play and heard the popping of pads and helmets, it instantly gave me those feel-good chills. I got excited!

Coach Al kept his word and placed me on the roster within the two-week time period we had agreed on.

"Bud the Spud," Stompin' Tom Connors (1969)

Now, I would need to find a new place to live for the season. Brady told me he lived in a house full of Ticats and if I wanted to join them, they had one room available in the attic because a former roommate had been cut. Since I didn't know anyone else in the city, I didn't have many options, so I took his offer and moved in.

It was a big brick century home with a nice yard. The house was on Kensington Avenue, about 5 minutes from the stadium. I could walk to practice, which was important because my car was still in B.C. — if I made the team, I'd have it shipped out on the train. My room wasn't very big, but I only needed to sleep in it. Now the place was fully occupied with five of us: Brady, me, Ralph Scholz, Steve Jackson, and Bill Howard. I had no idea what was in store for us living together in that house during the second half of that 1984 season.

Ralph "Giant Opie" Scholz was a freckle-faced, red-headed, 6'5", big strapping rookie. He looked like he just stepped off a Hollywood set filming the sequel to the television show *The Andy Griffith Show* because he looked just like Opie, only huge. Naturally, we gave him the nickname Giant Opie. His personality was similar to the character too; he was a hard-working, humble, and intelligent guy, who came off as being somewhat naïve and innocent. He had just graduated from Cornell University in civil engineering, and was a territorial exemption pick for the Tiger-Cats in 1984. Like me, he played defensive line in college, and the coaches asked him to move over to the offensive side of the ball early in his first year. It's noteworthy that because Scholz and I both had defensive line experience and could run, we were both on the Ticats' punt team for a couple of seasons. We had the biggest punt team in the league for a while and returners really got punished in some of those games.

Steve "Action" Jackson was a former Guelph Gryphon All-Star slotback, who also played some fullback, but excelled on special teams in his career with the Tiger-Cats. He had California-surfer good looks with his blonde mullet hairstyle. He also enjoyed partying as much as the rest of us.

Bill "Hooch" Howard was proudly Indigenous and a Western graduate. He was built like a brick shithouse, at 6'1" and 320 lb. He had great straight-ahead power, but his build made it hard for him to move laterally at times. He developed a technique where he would dive down on the ground and roll toward the defender. When he did the "roll technique," everyone had to be aware, including his own offensive linemen, or he'd knock everybody down!

Bill's nickname was Hooch because he could pound beer with the best of them. He was also very generous, had a great sense of humour, and was very gregarious. Everyone loved hanging out with Hooch. Some nights we would sit on the front porch and Hooch, beer in hand, would start humming to himself. Then, one of us would say, "Sing it, Hooch!" He would start singing the song "Bud the Spud," by Stompin' Tom Connors:

"Well, it's Bud the Spud, from the bright red mud
Rollin' down the highway smilin'.
The spuds are big on the back of Bud's rig
Cause they're from Prince Edward Island!
They're from Prince Edward Island!"

Then we'd say, "Sing it again, Hooch. Sing it louder!" Hooch would sing it louder and louder, until the whole neighbourhood could hear it. We would laugh and sing with Hooch until the wee hours. He loved the attention, and would acknowledge us with his catchphrase, "Thanks, Dad."

The first week we were living together, Hooch and I were on the practice roster, so we were the only ones in the house who didn't go on a road trip with the team when they had an away-game. I didn't know Hamilton at all, so I asked Hooch what he wanted to do Friday night. He said, "Let's go to the Rat. It's a popular pub on campus at McMaster University with a great selection of beers and lots of chicks."

I said, "I'm in," and we ordered a cab.

When we got to the Rat, there was a long staircase leading down to the bar from the front door. The bouncers were stationed at the front door at the top of the stairs, so they had a great view of the pub floor below. We chatted with them when we arrived and learned that they played for the Mac football team, so it was good to know we were all in the football fraternity.

Hooch and I went downstairs to the bar for some beer and enjoyed the great campus atmosphere. Then Hooch noticed that some of the Mac students were staring at us, apparently because of our size. Hooch said to me, "Dad, it's like we're elephants on display at the zoo. They should feed us some peanuts!"

Laughing, I put my arm around him and said, "Hooch, I'm hungry, let's go get something to eat at the Bright Spot." The Bright Spot was a restaurant on Main Street, just down the street from our house. It stayed open twenty-four hours a day and became our dining room away from home. All the staff knew us and sat us in "our" regular booth whenever we went. They had a broad menu with great food. We could eat breakfast any time of the day or night.

Hooch turned to me, smiling, and replied, "Okay, Dad!" We walked toward the stairs, arm in arm. As we negotiated the stairs up to the front door, Hooch yelled, "Feed me a peanut!"

When the cab arrived at the corner in front of the restaurant, I realized I had spent all my cash on beer at the pub. Hooch always carried a roll of cash with an elastic band around it – he called it his "wad" — in his left shirt pocket. He offered to pay for the cab, so he searched his pockets for his wad, but couldn't find it. The cabby's eyes widened when he heard these two hulking clients had no money.

I asked Hooch if he checked his left shirt pocket, where he usually kept it. "Oh, there it is, Dad," he said, as he patted his pocket. The driver's face was relieved when Hooch pulled out his wad and paid him.

Then we went into the restaurant and made the waitress's night by ordering "the entire left side of the menu" to tide us over till breakfast. Since Hooch paid for the cab, I asked the waitress to put the food on my credit card, but Hooch wouldn't let me pay and paid the bill from his wad. Hooch's generosity had no limit.

This was just one of many nights Hooch, me, and our other "room-dogs," as we called each other, had together. There was always something happening in that house, and we often felt like we were living the real-life version of John Belushi's *Animal House*, but with athletes.

Remarkably, my first start at offensive line after being reunited with quarterback Dieter Brock in Hamilton was against our old team, the Blue Bombers, on their home turf in Winnipeg. I was motivated for this one for a plethora of reasons; first, I was fired up because it was my first start at offensive tackle and I had something to prove against guys who I respected in my old unit; plus, I was still stinging because of the way I had departed the club last season, hearing about it on the radio of my car; and finally, because I wanted our team, especially Dieter, to have success against the team that traded us both.

However, this game was made even more interesting because of the fallout from Brock's previous comments about the zoo in Winnipeg.

When we arrived for our first game back in Winnipeg, the fans went all out to show their displeasure with Brock's comment, which was really blown out of proportion by the local media by now. On game day, every fan in the stadium and their dog was dressed as a zoo animal. There were countless handmade signs held high by people referencing the zoo comment, like "Welcome to Winnipeg, we're a two-zoo town!" They turned the entire stadium into a zoo just to piss off Brock. The fans were on him right from the kickoff and the game didn't go well for us. The Bombers kicked our ass, and we left town with our tail between our legs. I felt worse for Dieter than I did for myself.

Back in Hamilton, all five of us roommates at the Kensington house loved to play football, and we loved to party after the game was over, win or lose; we were young and single at the time and celebrating life. We would go to a local pub, then invite a bunch of people in the bar back to the house to party.

During one of these parties, there were so many girls dancing in high heels on the hardwood dining room floor that the landlord had to buff the marks out of it. Other times we would be in the back yard partying in the cool night air. This might happen any night of the week after a game.

Another time, we overflowed into the back yard, and I ended up dancing on top of the old wooden picnic table to raucous cheers. Then, slowly, the legs of the table began to spread on the slippery grass, like opening a pair of scissors. Slowly they spread further and my platform dropped lower, until I was dancing at grass level. It was not a pretty sight the next morning. I was soundly mocked for destroying our only picnic table.

We would party to celebrate a win, and we would party to drown a loss. Worse, we were oblivious to the fact that we drove the neighbours nuts. We found out when one (or more) of them contacted Harold Ballard, the owner of the team, and complained that we partied after games into the wee hours, even after we lost.

Well, old Harold didn't take this well. The next week in the *Hamilton Spectator* newspaper there was an article in which Ballard was quoted, "Those boys party all night, even when they lose! They are a bunch of over-paid bums!"

Boy, did Coach Al ever give it to us at the team meeting after that article was published. He said, "If you're going to party, you'd better earn it and start winning!"

Al's words apparently did the trick because we started winning. Although our 1984 season record was a mediocre 6–9–1, we went 5–2 in the last seven games. We finished the season hot down the stretch, well enough to make the Eastern playoffs with some momentum. We knocked off the Montreal Concordes 17–11 in the Eastern Semi-Final, then snuck past the Argos with a 14–13 overtime win in the Eastern Final, which earned us the right to travel to Edmonton for the Grey Cup. Going into the Grey Cup against the Winnipeg Blue Bombers, we were on a five-game winning streak.

Now I had gone from a first-round draft pick of the Bombers as a defensive lineman to starting at right offensive tackle against them in the biggest game of my life, just a year later. Coach Al had kept his word that I would be on the roster within 14 days, and I had kept my word to come to Hamilton, in spite of the BC Lions offer that would have allowed me to play at home. This honour among men bound us together forever.

Dieter and I celebrating after winning the Eastern Final, Toronto, 1984: photographer unknown

"Don't Bring Me Down," ELO (1979)

Our starting offensive line for the 1984 Grey Cup was Ralph Scholz (LT), Ross Francis (LG) Henry Waszczuk (C), Marv Allemang (RG), and myself (RT).

Again, Dieter Brock and I were in the same boat, but at least this game wasn't in Winnipeg. The entire team was highly motivated to win the game, especially for Dieter Brock.

The temperature for kick-off was around -15ºC, but with the windchill it felt colder — the coldest game I ever played in. The groundskeepers tried their best to keep the grass clear for the game. They covered the field with tarps, weighted them down every 10 yards across the field, then positioned large hot-air blowers on both sides of the field to blow hot air under the tarps, keeping the field warm for game day. Unfortunately, the condensation built up under the tarps and pooled on the grass wherever it was weighted down. As soon as they removed the tarps on game day morning, the water froze on the field. This resulted in strips of ice across the field, alternating with snow-covered grass, as flurries fell throughout the day. The end result was an inconsistent surface, for which no footwear was well-suited. We tried everything from regular cleats, molded Nike Sharks, to broomball shoes. Nothing really provided consistent traction on the inconsistent field conditions.

One specific play early in the game shows how crazy the footing was that day. Linebacker Tyrone Jones knocked the ball out of our receiver's hands near the sideline and his partner Frank Robinson scooped up the fumble, running towards our goal line. My defensive training kicked in and I turned and sprinted on an angle to stop Robinson before he scored a touchdown. I knew I had the perfect line to make the tackle, but as soon as I got to him, I hit a sheet of ice and my feet slid right out from under me. I fell right on my ass on national television as he ran for a touchdown. How embarrassing! My saving grace was that the referees had blown the play dead, due to forward motion being stopped before the fumble, so the play was called back and the score didn't count — what a relief that was for me!

Unfortunately, this only slowed the inevitable. After taking an early 17–3 lead in the game, the Bombers took over the scoring and we lost 47–17. With the field conditions the way they were, we just couldn't get to their running back, Sean Kehoe, when he ran swing patterns into the flat. He managed to get the first down almost whenever they needed it to keep drives going. There were many crazy plays in the game that could be attributed to the weather and field conditions, but the truth is that the Bombers were better than the Tiger-Cats that day and they beat us soundly. No excuses.

Former Tiger-Cat Tom Clements was the Most Valuable Offensive Player, Tyrone Jones was the Most Valuable Defensive Player, and Sean Kehoe was the Most Valuable Canadian in the game: all my former teammates. Pouring more salt on the wound was the fact that after essentially being traded for him, John Hufnagel threw a touchdown against us late in the game to run the score up even more. For me, it was really hard to swallow.

I spent the next few days hiding away in my room, emotionally spent, depressed, and feeling physically ill after that loss. I was pretty much out of commission, other than to attend the end-of-season team meeting for Coach Al's season-closing words, and to collect my belongings from our dressing room. It shows the importance of psychology in sport that I got physically ill and emotional depressed as a result of the biggest loss of my life.

As unfortunate as this loss was, the team knew that Coach Al had brought us together at the right time in the stretch run of the season, leading up to the playoffs. He would have team meetings when things weren't where he wanted them to be and come up with an idea to bring us together. He would say things like, "Men, don't worry about the past. We need to look ahead. Looking at the past is like looking up a dead dog's asshole. It's a waste of time, dammit!"

He would place his big receiver's hands up in front of him and intertwine his fingers, "Men, we have to come together. It's us against the world. Don't worry about what the press says, or how we're ranked. Just worry about the guys in this room; I know you guys can do it!" Coach Al believed that the team was like a family and he treated us with the understanding that the only thing more important than the team to each of us was our own family.

He reinforced this over the years by keeping the core of the team together as long as he could. He knew the value of veteran players who had the knowledge and leadership to win; and he understood that continuity among the players and coaches was important for success. This led to the fringe benefit of having players who settled in Hamilton and engaged with the community. The fans were able to get to know the roster by engaging with the players at community events, and then support those players by cheering them on at the games.

Coach Al had a fierce passion for the players and coaches on the team. In most cases, this goodwill was reciprocated by his players, too, because he and general manager, Joe Zuger, had picked most of us up after being cut, like I was, traded, or injured, giving us a second chance. Many of us on the team owed our careers to him putting his faith in us, and we wanted him to benefit from it by helping the team win. He never gave up on us, or on our ability to beat any team in any game. Whenever he was questioned about the age of his veteran team, he would say, "They may have lost a step, but at least they know where to put that step!"

It was because of this that we had such great chemistry on the team. The players liked each other on offence and defence. It was about as close as you could get to the brotherhood of university football, where everyone played for free; considering professional athletes compete for each other's jobs, we were a very close team.

It's remarkable that Coach Al was able to bring all his players together, considering our diverse backgrounds. We accepted each other as equals on the team, knowing that each of us had experienced obstacles and challenges before arriving at Ivor Wynne Stadium. The end result was that we had a team with character and resilience.

"Summer of '69," Bryan Adams (1984)

Another interesting aspect of the team was the small size of the coaching staff, as compared to contemporary coaching rosters. We had a total of six coaches: two offensive coaches, John Salavantis (who arrived in 1985 as our offensive line Guru) and Mike Faragalli; two defensive coaches, Ted Schmitz and Rich Stubler; a special teams coordinator, Frank North; and head coach,

Al Bruno. It's amazing what this small group of good men were able to accomplish when compared to the large coaching staff (CFL teams are allowed up to 11 coaches) most football teams employ today.

Case in point, Coach Schmitz was the defensive line coach and defensive coordinator. His unit consisted of a core of great American players — Mike Walker, Grover Covington, Mitch Price, and Rod Skillman — and a group of Canadian guys who rotated in without missing a beat — Leon Lyszkiewicz, Dave Sauve, and Mark Napiorkowski.

Every practice, our offensive line unit battled this powerful group of men head-to-head in one-on-one drills, then inside-run periods, followed by a full twelve-on-twelve team period, which would usually escalate into a game-like tempo. We went hard in every drill. We made each other better every day.

An example of this was my ongoing battles with my roommate Leon Lyszkiewicz. He was a 280-lb defensive tackle and veteran of the game, who took much pride in his fitness and power. He was also a heavy hitter and very stubborn against giving up any ground, even in practice.

One drill, he was lined up at defensive tackle, head-to-head with my guard position. Our offence kept screwing up this run-play and the coaches made us repeat it several times. I was on the backside of the play, which meant I had to reach-block Lyszkiewicz and cut him off at the "A" gap (see Appendix A) between me and the centre so he couldn't run the play down from behind.

The first time we ran the play, it was alright because the defence didn't know what the play was. After that, every time we ran the play, Lyszkiewicz knew he had to fire through the A-gap to defeat the play, making my reach block more difficult. This meant that we had two big boys banging heads repeatedly to do their jobs, both too determined to let up.

After practice we would go home and make dinner together with our other roommate, Giant Opie. The three of us had moved in together after training camp.

As roommates, our lives reminded us of the *Looney Toons* cartoon where Ralph Wolf (often confused with Wile E. Coyote, whose nose is black whereas Ralph's is red[11]) walks to work with Sam Sheepdog, both carrying a lunch bucket. When they arrive at work, they both punch in the clock to

[11] Lenburg, J. 1999. *The Encyclopedia of Animated Cartoons*. Facts on File, Inc.: New York.

start their shift, then proceed to beat the crap out of each other all day long, fighting over the sheep. The day ends with them checking out together after their shift, as if nothing happened.

When Coach Al brought in John Salavantis as our new offensive line coach and assistant offensive coordinator in 1985, another piece of the Tiger-Cats puzzle was filled in. He's known by his players and friends simply as Coach Sal.

Coach Sal never swore at us, no matter how much we fucked up — with one exception. It was during a game when Miles Gorrell was pissed off coming off the field because either the QB missed the throw, or the receiver dropped the ball, or the kicker missed the kick — Miles was very unforgiving on the field and that's one of the traits that put him in the CFHOF. In this particular case, he stormed off the field and did a windmill pitch of his helmet from about the hash marks, like his helmet was a bowling ball. It rolled and bounced off the field in a strait line towards the bench — and hit poor Coach Sal squarely in the shins.

That was the only time we ever heard him swear — and boy, did he lay into Gorrell. Picture a 5'6", mild-mannered offensive line coach admonishing (with expletives) a massive, 6'8" monster lineman, with the monster retreating in guilt because he hurt our favourite coach! Sal was not seriously hurt, just a few bruises, but that was a sight to behold.

Coach Sal is a little Greek guy from Kansas. He was the smallest coach on staff coaching the biggest guys on the team. Sal made up for his lack of physical size and endeared himself to his players with a vast intellect, huge heart, and great sense of humour, which was often self-deprecating. As he would say in his Kansas drawl, "I may be vertically challenged, but I have a great face for radio." Even today, Sal and our unit share a special fraternity. He's a dear friend.

With a unique way of critiquing our play during meetings, Coach Sal was more suggestive than critical. He would offer us different ways to be successful instead of rubbing our nose in our failures or being heavy-handed with criticisms, as some coaches are.

He was very respectful to his players and always maintained a calm demeanour in stressful situations. This helped us maintain our composure when the “bullets started flying” on the field during hard-fought games. He would somehow sort through the jumble of information on the sidelines — without the benefit of the technological support there is in today’s game — to help us come together as a unit and win.

Sal also taught us that having good rapport off the field helped us on the field. He and his wife, Marilyn, hosted our unit for Thanksgiving dinners at their home. This was not an easy task considering the amount we ate. Just as we learned valuable lessons from Sal about skill development drills in practice, we learned the importance of camaraderie off the field.

After he coached us to success on the field, Sal became synonymous with Ticats football for decades as the voice of the Ticats on radio broadcasts. He became very popular with the fans because of his down-home cadence and his distinct baritone voice; his knowledge of the game and experience in coaching made him the perfect source of information for fans at all levels of football I.Q.

He spoke to the average fan as if sitting in their living room and educating them on the fundamentals of the game. Just as we had as his players, football fans now benefitted from listening to Sal describe a play’s pass or run-blocking schemes, or the choice of receivers thrown to by the QB based on defensive coverage.

Broadcasting was the natural progression for Sal as a coach, educating the public about our great game on a broader scale. But before he did that, Sal was stuck coaching us blockheads up front on the offensive line!

Coach Sal was the perfect coach for the unique and eclectic offensive line unit Joe Zuger, Al Bruno, and Mike McCarthy (our player personnel director) had now assembled. This was a group who share similar characteristics: large, powerful, unselfish athletes, who are required to do physical tasks that are not natural for the human body. I already detailed the physical challenges of the position earlier, but Sal had a special way of working with this group on and off the field to help refine our craft.

The unselfishness comes in, because generally, their names are not mentioned unless they are called for a penalty. Offensive linemen get very little recognition for the job they do, yet if they fail to do it, the offence cannot be successful. Therefore, it takes a special type of person to play the position, one who is willing to work hard and get little recognition for it.

John Madden, the Super Bowl-winning head coach and former offensive line coach who later became a sportscaster on *Monday Night Football*, summed it up well when he was asked by his partner, Pat Summerall, how he would compare offensive line play to another sport. Madden said surprisingly, "The closest thing that compares to offensive line play is synchronized swimming, because all five guys need to know exactly what the others are doing and move perfectly in unison to make the play work."

Accordingly, at every level of play from high school to professional, there is a direct correlation between the success of the offensive line and the success of the team. Usually, the team with the offensive line that best controls the LOS on run and pass (plays) is the team that wins; an exception would be a team that has too many turnovers (fumbles and interceptions) to overcome.

"Won't Get Fooled Again," The Who (1971)

I consider all the boys I played with as brothers in the offensive line fraternity, though I played with too many to include them all here. I'll introduce our core Tiger-Cats group from our 1985 cup run to illustrate what Coach Sal had to deal with every day!

In addition to my former roommates Scholz and Brady, who have already been introduced, here are a few of the other guys in the unit.

Marv Allemang is a legend at Acadia University, where he played both ways, at defensive end and tight end (see Appendix A). The fact that he played university ball under head coach Bob Vespaziani, who was my first professional position coach in Winnipeg, shows how small (and tight-knit) the football fraternity is. Allemang played defensive end and was nominated for the J. P. Metras trophy in university — this gave us more in common, bringing that aggressive defensive line mentality to the offensive side of the ball. We became good friends in our three years side by side on the Cats' offensive line. I called Marv "Marvelous" because he was such a classy guy. Marv is our son's godfather.

In 1984, my first year with the Cats, Al Bruno inserted me at right tackle beside Allemang, who started at right guard. In retrospect, I feel badly for him because he had to tolerate me as the new addition who still had a steep learning curve to conquer. Allemang was a good mentor who shared his experience to help me learn the position on the fly. He was an outstanding technician, always working to improve his trade, and I learned much from him. Although he was the tall, dark, and mysterious type, we learned to communicate our play calls efficiently — you could say we were on the same page. We worked so well together that the following season Coach Sal moved Allemang to centre and me to guard.

Unfortunately, we lost Allemang to Ottawa in the expansion draft in 1987. He played 14 years in the CFL, which illustrates his skill and durability.

"Down On the Corner," Creedence Clearwater Revival (1969)

John Malinosky was a territorial exemption pick for the BC Lions, after completing a full ride at Michigan State. He joined us in Hamilton in 1985. "Johnny Mal" was a 6'5" monster of a man, who brought a ton of experience and played a physical game. He came to us from Toronto after winning a Grey Cup with the Argos in 1983.

I was at BC Place stadium in Vancouver, watching that Grey Cup game with my brothers after returning home from Saskatchewan. The Argos were playing the hometown Lions in their new state-of-the-art stadium. I remember it clearly because it was a sold-out crowd and the atmosphere was electric. I imagined how great it would be to play in a Grey Cup game in front of a passionate crowd in this stadium.

We didn't know each other at the time, but Johnny Mal battled on that field below us. Johnny and I couldn't have been more different in personality because he didn't drink or curse, while I was guilty of both.

One particular demonstration of his toughness was when during a game, Mal fractured his leg on a bone-on-bone hit, while blocking tough in the trenches — and he didn't even swear after breaking his leg! Unfortunately, the injury put John out for the rest of the season.

"Saturday Night," Bay City Rollers, 1974

Dale Sanderson is a homegrown Hamilton boy, who joined us in 1985 from the University of Tennessee. The reason I know that is because Coach Al used to give him shit for wearing his orange-striped Tennessee Volunteers game socks to our Tiger-Cats practices. Al hated those socks because they were not team-issued, but Sanderson loved them, so he'd wear them at least once a week. Coach Sal would just shrug and give him that look a father gives his kid when he does something dumb.

Sanderson's physical toughness was shown through his recovery after multiple back surgeries for herniated discs during his university career. He recovered enough to play 12 seasons in the CFL. He was about 6'4" and 280 pounds, old-school, raw-boned, and nasty on the field, the way we needed to be in the trenches.

Before one game in Ottawa, we heard through the grapevine that a player had put a bounty on Dale's head. Apparently, he had hurt one of their players in the previous game. We were a very physical unit, but we never tried to hurt anyone intentionally. When we heard about the bounty on his head, our whole group became more laser-focused when we hit the field. At one point in the game, Sanderson was pass-blocking the nose guard over him, when one of their defensive ends looped inside to blindside him. Sanderson saw it coming and, while still engaged with the nose guard, turned and head-butted the other player to the turf. That pretty much put an end to the bounty!

One road trip to B.C., we were rooming together and Sanderson stayed out later than I did the night before the game. I was sound asleep when he came into the room. Instead of sitting on the end of his bed to take his boots off, for some unknown reason he sat on the edge of the small wall-mounted nightstand between the beds, about six inches from my ear. Of course, under his weight, the entire unit snapped right off the wall, which sent the lamp, my pocket change, a glass of water, and other paraphernalia spilling to the ground in a loud crash beside my head. I almost jumped right out of my skin! I was wide awake instantly with my heart pounding in my chest, while Sanderson went to sleep immediately and began snoring like a fucking grizzly bear.

First, I tried asking him to roll over to stop his snoring — but he was oblivious to the world. Then, I progressed to yelling at him, with no response. I began throwing different objects at him, starting with a pillow, then worked my way up to pitching one of his cowboy boots off the side of his noggin. This resulted in a slight skip in his snoring pattern. After about an hour of this craziness, I became desperate for sleep and thought, "Fuck it!" I got out of bed and drove-block his bed to the far corner of the room, then flipped it over on him and arranged the mattress so that it was like a lean-to against the wall. The mattress made a great sound barrier — Sanderson's snoring was now a muffled gurgle and I got back to sleep.

When he joined us at the team breakfast in the morning, I asked him how he slept. He said, "I slept great, but I can't figure out how I ended up under my bed!"

"Minnie the Moocher," Cab Calloway (1980)

When Mike "Derksy" Derks graduated from the University of Cincinnati and joined our team, we inherited a 6'5", 330 lb offensive tackle who could not only 'knock your dick off,' but make you laugh while doing it. Derksy quickly became a stalwart member of our unit, and also the team comedian.

One day in practice, Coach Sal asked the extra guys on the OL to give him an "odd look" to run a play against in a drill. An odd look means a three-man defensive front, as opposed to an even four-man front. "Give me an odd look," Sal said. At which point, Derks made the oddest and funniest face he could conjure up, with his eyes crossed, cheeks puffed out, and his face red. We laughed so hard that Sal had trouble getting us lined up for the drill.

The morning after a game in Winnipeg, Coach Sal and some other coaches were in the lobby of our hotel all ready to go to the airport for the flight home. Derks, who had stayed out all night partying after the game, walked into the lobby hungover and disheveled, with his shirt hanging out. Knowing that he just got caught breaking curfew, he said, "Coach, it sure is hard to find a newspaper in this town!" as if he'd just got up and went looking for a paper.

We were losing badly during a game in Calgary, when Trigger the horse was doing another of his several victory laps after multiple Calgary touchdowns. It was tradition that the horse, with the rider holding the Stampeder flag, would gallop a lap around the field after each touchdown Calgary scored. At this point in the game, Derks turned to the bench and yelled, "If this game doesn't end soon, we're gonna kill that fucking horse!" The horse was looking tired already; a few more touchdowns from Calgary meant that death from exhaustion would be the likely result.

These are just a few of Derks' gems. Needless to say, Derksy is one of the funniest guys you'll ever meet.

He wasn't all comedian though. Derksy also showed toughness on the field. He was a physical player and a student of the game. His toughness is epitomized by him coming back from a herniated Achilles tendon injury after corrective surgery. Even for athletes much smaller than him, it could have been a career-ending injury, but Derks came back and played several years afterward.

"I Can't Get No Satisfaction," The Rolling Stones (1965)

Miles Gorrell is a freak of nature. When he joined us, he was 6'8"in height and the doctor's scale didn't go high enough to weigh him. At the same time, he could run like a deer. He sported a mullet-style haircut and the mustache of an 80s porn star, flavoured with a hearty dose of dry wit.

Originally from Calgary, Gorrell played defensive end with the Ottawa Gee Gees in college before signing with the Stampeders in 1978, where they moved him to the offensive line. After this, he ended up in Montreal.

Coach Al continued rebuilding our offensive line by bringing Gorrell in from the Montreal Alouettes in 1985. We played side-by-side for the better part of seven years before he was unceremoniously traded to Winnipeg for his next stint. He was inducted into the CFHOF in 2013.

Gorrell was a true character. He was one of the biggest players in the league and he played longer than any other player at his position — 19 years.

When I asked him why he never tried out for the NFL, because he had all the prerequisites to do so, Gorrell said, "I just want to have fun, Jas, and the NFL is the 'No-Fun League'!"

Unfortunately, he broke his arm in his first game with the Tiger-Cats while tackling then-Stampeder Richie Hall on the kick-off team, and this put him out for the rest of the season. Gorrell missed the 1985 Grey Cup game with us because of it.

He had so much natural size and strength that, unlike most of us who had to train constantly, he seldom lifted weights.

During one training camp, we were doing mandatory testing for bench press; after my warm-up sets, I did a set of five repetitions at 315 lb. The coach recorded the lift and told me to stop there so I didn't risk injury prior to camp. Gorrell walked into the room and said, "Can I do a set?" He walked over to the bench I had just used and, without even a warm up, he quickly rattled off a set at the same weight. The rest of us were jealous as all hell!

Plainly, different paths brought us to playing side-by-side, and in some ways we had different perspectives on the game, but we were both tough competitors who loved to win. Playing beside Miles was always a great adventure. Unfortunately, in 1991 John Gregory inexplicably traded him to Winnipeg.

Gorrell's true playing weight was always a mystery to everyone, himself included, because the scales used for training camp physicals didn't go high enough to weigh him. Gorrell says that changed when he landed in Winnipeg. "When I was traded to Winnipeg, head coach Cal Murphy wanted to know the true weight of me and Chris Walby, because the trainer's scale didn't go that high. Murphy sent us to a truck stop in our pick-up trucks to verify our weights. Walby was pissed that he outweighed me by a pound; Walby weighed in at 343 lb, while I was a mere 342 lb."

Prior to Gorrell's trade, the coaches had successfully transformed our offensive line into a big, physical unit, which became the core of the offence. Our overall average was now up to around 6'5" and well over 300 lbs. In fact, this average was bigger than some NFL offensive lines.

But there is more to the success of our unit than just size. A good offensive line needs to have the athleticism and skill set to do the things the position requires, have the intelligence to implement the game plan, and the communication skills to make it happen on the field.

Then there is the intangible: toughness is also needed. Everyone in this group had that edge to play physical football. When our group got our game faces on, we were a nasty group to play against. The fact that we had depth in Canadian (non-import) offensive linemen was also a bonus for the coaches because it allowed them to play "imports" in other positions.

In describing what it was like to coach this motley crew, Coach Salavantis puts it this way:

> While it is true that they were a varied cast of characters, what they had in common was character and a great work ethic. Coming to work every day was a joy. Each challenge was met with professional courtesy and humour. The veterans did the teaching, and all I had to do was package it and feed it back as a game plan. We made a good team because we respected each other, had a common goal, and acted honourably.

Personally, I think Coach Sal must be talking about a different group of gentlemen! I know we generally didn't show professional courtesy and humour on the field.

Stu Laird, the All-Star defensive tackle for the Calgary Stampeders, offered these thoughts about our unit:

> Back then, something happened to offensive linemen in Hamilton. Just one tough bunch. My biggest memory was of your group, Jason. Playing Hamilton, no matter who was playing at any skill position, or how good the defence was, it seemed that the offensive line set the tone for the team.

It's good to know that opposition players who we respected also felt this way about our unit.

1985 Hamilton Tiger-Cats offensive line: Back row from left: Coach John Salavantis, Marv Allemang, Ralph Scholz, Miles Gorrell, Mike Derks, Jason Riley, Brian Strong; Front row: John Malinosky, Dale Sanderson, Pat Brady, Ivor Wynne Stadium, Hamilton: Tom Bochsler photo

Personally, I had continued training hard to build myself physically, earning the right to be a part of this unit. Last season, I had survived Coach Al's experiment when in mid-season, he threw me to the wolves at starting right tackle. With little experience at the position, I had been challenged to establish myself without the benefits of a training camp. I needed to practice like I played, be desperate, establish myself through tough physical play, and out-work and out-hit everyone else at my position. Luckily, I was able to do this by utilizing my aggressive defensive line mentality on the offensive side of the ball.

With this in mind, in 1985, I was looking forward to attending my first Tiger-Cats training camp at Brock University. The first thing Coach Sal did was move me from tackle to guard on our offensive line. This was my first experience at the new position and I loved it because I learned that pulling guards are always in the middle of the action. As a fan, if you want to know where the ball is going, watch the guards, the ball will follow them — unless it's a trick play.

Once again, training camp was a six-week marathon of hits before final cuts were announced. But it allowed me to learn the philosophy, expectations, and nuances of my position under Coach Sal's watchful eye. I could study the playbook, and understand the strategy of the schemes while we reviewed in practice, without the urgency and pressure of playing a game right away, like I had experienced the previous season. This time was also very important to develop the required communication skills, appropriate calls, and the camaraderie of our unit for us to become a well-oiled machine – a "synchronized swim team!"

I continued to rely on an aggressive attitude because I feared that if I allowed myself to become complacent, a young guy would come in and take my job (I was still experiencing the insecurity and maybe some paranoia from my childhood). However, it was good to know this would be my first training camp as a bona fide offensive lineman. I sopped up Coach Sal's wisdom like a sponge. It must have been a successful formula because, one day in a subsequent training camp, Coach Al was making his pre-practice comments after warm-up when he said, "I like the pace of practice in camp so far, gentlemen. Keep up the good work, making each other better," then he added jokingly, "It will be interesting to see who Riley's going to fight in practice today."

He meant this as a compliment because he valued the toughness I injected into our offence, but it did make my life more difficult. It was like he was setting up the heavyweight champ for any and all takers — an invitation to any newcomers on the defence to impress the coaches by fighting me. It definitely made life interesting!

"Takin' Care of Business," Bachman-Turner Overdrive (1973)

It was after that 1985 training camp that Scholz, Lyszkiewicz, and I moved in together. It was a large three-bedroom place, which included a banquet hall we could book for parties —though nothing will ever live up to the party house on Kensington!

Occasionally, Ralph's girlfriend Vicky came over to the apartment to make us dinner. One time, she made a very large tray of lasagna, thinking we'd have leftovers. She also made garlic bread and a big Caesar salad. It was excellent, so we ate the whole tray in one sitting. The three of us inhaled all the food on the table so quickly that we got "high" from all the blood rushing from our brains into our stomachs to digest the food. Vicky couldn't believe how fast her hard work had disappeared.

This is just one example of the copious amounts of food we needed to eat constantly to replace the calories we burned off in our daily training and practices. Needless to say, we ate like kings!

Ken Hobart earned the starting quarterback role in training camp that year, after the departure of Dieter Brock to the NFL's Los Angeles Rams. Hobart was an outstanding athlete out of the University of Idaho. He was built like a running back and loved to run over linebackers when he got the chance. He had an incredible arm too, but his aggressive disposition behind the offensive line meant he ran as often as he could. We began to anticipate his desire to run, often blocking down field for him like a true running back. Hobart was the leading rusher for the team in 1985, with 928 yards.[12] We all admired his toughness and willingness to sacrifice his body for the team.

During the 1985 season, we once again started slow, with a 2–6 record at the midway point, but Coach Al got us going in the stretch run, where we began to build momentum. Every game had to feel like a playoff game for us to make the playoffs; in the second half of the season, our record was 6–2. We finished with an 8–8 record (the CFL still had a 16-game schedule), good for first place in the East.

One of the key games in that stretch drive was in late October in Ottawa. We put a great team game together and managed a 36–4 win. After the game, we were really pumped about our playoff hopes when we entered the locker room.

Brett MacNeil, former Blue Bomber guard and CFL All-Star, was a teenager in the dressing room after the game that day, and he recently reminded me of the post-game excitement he experienced:

---

[12] Stats Crew. n.d. *Ken Hobart*. Url: statscrew.com/football/stats/p-hobarken001 (accessed May 9, 2023).

It was way back in 1985 when I had my first opportunity to visit a CFL locker room and it was unforgettable. I was playing in my second year of Ottawa high school football after spending all of my previous years on the rink. A local head coach, Jim Scott, who ended up becoming my stepfather, invited me to the Ottawa Rough Riders vs. Hamilton Tiger-Cats game. He told me he was excited to see his friend, the Tiger-Cats' Rocky DiPietro, after the game in the dressing room.

I was an aspiring defensive lineman in my early years and was eager to meet sack master Grover Covington after the game. Hamilton won the contest and we made our way down to the visitors' locker room at Lansdowne Park to visit with Rocky. We were led into the room by security and stood next to the largest bin full of beer and ice I had ever seen!

Players, showing the wear of battle, started pouring into the locker room and I was told by a few to grab a beer right along with them. I helped myself to a Molson Export and then focused on Grover Covington, who was a huge dude, and was quietly enjoying the winning atmosphere.

Just then the locker room door blew open and the doorway filled with the massive presence of #58 Jason Riley. The offensive guard let out a loud "Woo hoo!" as he entered the winning locker room and the intensity jacked up from there. I had a quick chance to meet Rocky and Grover, but would never forget seeing what a pro offensive lineman looked like after that day.

Finishing first in the Eastern Conference with Ken Hobart at the helm meant that we got a bye into the Eastern Final, where we would face Montreal at home for the right to go to the Grey Cup for the second consecutive year. We beat Montreal 50–26 that day, at a very loud Ivor Wynne Stadium.

The Grey Cup, on November 24, 1985, was played in Montreal in front of 57,000 fans: Ticat vs. the BC Lions. It was an electric atmosphere for football. Our starting offensive line was: Mike Derks (LT), me (LG), Marv Allemang (C), Jeff Arp (RG), and Ralph Scholz (RT). As a unit, we were well-prepared to keep Hobart on his feet, and we were highly motivated after losing the championship game so miserably the previous year in Edmonton. Hobart had one of his best games that day, throwing for three touchdowns and running to keep plays alive all game.

With a minute and a half left in the first half, running back Johnny Shepherd made a great catch for a touchdown, so that we took the lead, 14–13. On the next drive, our defence stuffed them and they were forced to punt. The Lions' Lui Passaglia lined up to punt from his own 35-yard line. If all went well, we'd have possession of the ball for another score before the half. Even better, Mark Streeter and Mitch Price broke through on the punt block and had Passaglia in their sights. If they got him, we'd get the ball inside their 35-yard line with just over a minute to go. Unfortunately, that didn't happen. Passaglia ducked under their pressure and squirted down the sideline for a first down.

This was a key turning point in the game because instead of us gaining at least a field goal and maybe a touchdown to close out the half, the Lions' Roy Dewalt threw a long touchdown pass before the half ended – capitalizing on a big points turnaround and seizing game momentum. By half-time, the Lions were leading 23–14.

Later in the game, Paul "Badger" Bennett made a great play, blocking a pass and knocking it away from the intended receiver, Ned Armour, but Jim Sandusky caught the deflected ball in full stride and ran it in for a touchdown. Another unlucky bounce for the good guys!

For me, it felt like a continuation of the negative karma I experienced in that stadium my rookie year, except this time, instead of a broken foot, it broke my heart. Two years in a row, a team I could have been on beat us in the Grey Cup. It was the only game I ever cried after losing — this Grey Cup loss was even harder than the first one.

◇◆◇

The next week, then-mayor of Hamilton, Bob Morrow, held a civic dinner to honour the team for winning the Eastern Conference and appearing in the Grey Cup for the second year in a row. Mayor Morrow was a classy guy and he personally awarded all of us a gold City of Hamilton ring, with the city's coat-of-arms displayed on its face.

After the banquet, Leo Ezerins, Greg "GG" Gary, myself, and a few other guys went to a downtown pub to drown our sorrows. Later in the night, Greg came back from the bathroom with a sullen look on his face. When I asked him what happened, he told me that two assholes had made racial slurs towards him when he walked by their table. Greg was a teammate and friend and, although he was willing to turn the other cheek, I wasn't going to sit by and allow him to be treated that way. I went to the table and angrily told these racists who had insulted my friend to keep their mouths shut. These bullies showed some remorse and apologized to me, but not to GG.

When we were leaving the pub later in the night, GG and Leo went to the bathroom, while I went out the front door for some fresh air. The two guys that had harassed GG followed me out and began to apologize profusely again for their behaviour in the pub. I accepted their apology and told them that to my mind, that was the end of it. Thinking they were being genuine, and now in a benevolent mood, I turned for a moment to see if the guys were coming yet — I broke the cardinal rule of bouncing, again.

As soon as I took my eyes off them, one of these assholes smashed me under the jaw. When I shook my head and turned back to him, I saw eyes the size of billiard balls, and the glint of brass knuckles in his hand. They both backpedalled and ran when they didn't put me down.

Just then, Leo and GG emerged from the pub. I threw my leather jacket to a surprised GG, and told him I'd be back in a minute. That slight pause allowed them to get out of sight: they were gone. It's a godsend I didn't catch them, because by then, I was so angry, I wanted to kill them both.

Afterwards, knowing he'd still be up, I went to Derks' house to calm down and have a beer. He told me later that as soon as he saw me, he told his roommates, "Hide the knives, Riley's really mad."

I think I kept the boys up all night, then went to see Jonesy in his morning physio clinic at the stadium. He said he thought my jaw was fractured and that I should go for x-rays. Being as stubborn as I was, I refused to admit that the clown had hurt me, so I went home for some sleep. I figured that if I iced it for a couple days, it would be fine. I was planning to go to Toronto to watch the Vanier Cup with my roommates that weekend.

When Saturday arrived, I bit into something and I felt a crunch in my jaw — I wouldn't be going to the Vanier Cup. I went for x-rays instead. Jonesy was right, I had a broken jaw. After the doctor wired my upper and lower teeth, he bound them with tight rubber bands to prevent my jaw from moving. The x-ray showed that I had mature wisdom teeth that were embedded diagonally inside my jaw, which meant that the teeth were taking up space where there should have been bone. I had developed a case of the classic "glass jaw" — hollow and easily broken. He suggested that I have my wisdom teeth removed as soon as possible after my fracture healed, so that bone could fill in the gaps and my jaw would grow strong again.

The plot of the story thickens, because Paulette was flying in from Vancouver the next day. I had arranged for us to travel to Puerto Vallarta, Mexico, for the week. I told her when I called her from the hospital that I had broken my jaw, but I hadn't told her how it happened — she assumed I had done it in the Grey Cup game and that it was a "work related" injury.

Ralph and Vicky kindly picked Paulette up at the airport while I was having my jaw wired shut. Vicky did not know I hadn't told Paulette any of the details. By the time Paulette arrived at our apartment in Hamilton, she was totally pissed off at me and didn't want to go to Mexico.

I understood how she felt. We were both looking forward to the trip, which we had planned earlier in the season. Paulette was upset that I had put myself in a situation off the field to get injured; if it was a game injury, she would have understood. Now this could prevent us from having the fun we anticipated on our vacation. On top of that, she had additional anxiety when she found out the doctor gave me a pair of cutters so I could cut through the thick elastics and open my mouth in case of emergency!

I was able to convince Paulette that I could still travel and we could have a good time in the sun. When we arrived in Mexico, we arranged for the resort restaurants to make my meals with a blender, so I could drink them with a straw. Yummy — liquid Mexican food! I also took cans of protein supplement. In reality though, I pretty much lived on beer and tequila for the week of our trip. The most important phrase in Spanish for me was, "Cerveza y tequila por favor, senor."

We had a great time on the beach, in spite of my injury, and we were able to talk about a future together. I felt much better about my career now that I had established myself on the team and we were optimistic about the team's future. I was getting to know Hamilton beyond its steel town reputation, and I shared with Paulette that it would be a great place to live. Although we knew it would be a major transition for both of us, leaving beautiful B.C., and our families behind.

After we returned to Vancouver from our trip, Paulette and I decided to get married. Because my father was in the hospital at the time and couldn't attend the wedding, we decided to elope in North Vancouver, with a justice of the peace performing the ceremony. Only my younger brother, Jeff, and Paulette's little sister, Carla, attended as our witnesses.

A few months later, after Dad was released from hospital, we planned a reception for our friends and family to celebrate our marriage. My UBC teammates were there, and I was honoured to have both my high school and university football coaches, Coach Jones and Coach Smith, present to celebrate with Paulette and I.

After we were married, we agreed I would leave for camp in the Spring, and find a temporary place for us to live in Hamilton, where she could join me after camp. I was always motivated by my insecurities during my football career, and would never take my roster spot for granted – I had to earn it every training camp.

When Paulette had reservations at home about moving from Vancouver to Hamilton, her father Peter told her she had an obligation to join her husband. Thank God for that!

Paulette and I have been married now for 38 years, and like all successful relationships, compromise is a key skill for success. In our case though, the idiom that opposites attract couldn't be more appropriate: while Paulette is gorgeous, I'm a mug; she is patient and I am not; she's a saver and I'm a spender; she's a homebody and I'm a party animal; she's a cynic and I wear the rose-tinted glasses; Paulette hates surprises, while I love them; she is myopic and I am far-sighted; she is yin and I am yang. Yet, our love has endured in spite of these contrasts, because we have learned to appreciate each other's strengths and overlook our differences (Sorted out early on in some true cat and dog skirmishes!). We have learned that if we combine our strengths, we are stronger together. This has resulted over time with her taming the angry beast inside of me, while I have reciprocated by drawing her into a more adventurous path than she would have otherwise travelled. A final note on this - Advice to all young men in marriage, learn my two favourite words, "Yes, dear!"

Back to football in Hamilton, during that year's off-season, Coach Al and his coaching staff continued to build our team for another run at a championship in 1986. While keeping our core of players together, quarterback Mike Kerrigan was brought in. Mike McCarthy always seemed to have guys available to step in when Al needed them. Joe Zuger would negotiate the contracts.

McCarthy had football contacts all over North America, from his various positions as scout with teams from the National Collegiate Athletics Association (NCAA) to the United States Football League (USFL). He identified several of our quarterbacks over the years, including Mike Kerrigan, Ken Hobart, and Tom Porras, and had them added to our negotiations list to sign them when needed. McCarthy remembers following Kerrigan's career for several years, from Northwestern College to the New England Patriots, where he made the roster in 1983. In 1986, Zuger had all three quarterbacks signed and Kerrigan won the starting job part way into the season.

That season, Kerrigan passed for over 3,000 yards in his first season and receivers Rocky DiPietro and Tony Champion were the benefactors of his success, both with over 1000 yards receiving. Ken Hobart continued to contribute, mainly in the short yardage package. Running back Walter Bender ran for over 600 yards from the backfield. On defence, Mark

Streeter had nine interceptions, while Lance Shields and Less Browne both had eight. Our outstanding defensive line, including Mike Walker, Grover Covington, Mitch Price, Rod Skillman, and Romel Andrews accumulated a combined 57 sacks on the season, led by Walker's 21.[13]

After we tied the Roughriders in our game in Regina that season, I had another interesting experience in self-preservation – from bullying. In keeping with my father's philosophy of life, "There is a trap door around every corner in life, you just don't know if it will open or not," trouble is never that far away in this crazy world we live in, so I tried to be vigilant.

We were staying for the night after our game, so a few of us went out for some drinks at a local pub. I was having a great time dancing with a local lady on the dancefloor, while Sanderson and Scholz casually leaned on the bar enjoying their beer. As I danced, I noticed a guy I had never seen before working his way through the crowd towards me, recklessly bumping into people as he came closer. Then, he walked directly at me and shouldered me as he went by. I didn't want any problems, so I just turned away and continued to enjoy the music of the live band with my dance partner. He turned and did it again.

The music was loud and I yelled, "What the hell is your problem?"

Looking eye to eye with him, I saw pure malice in his eyes and I recognized the hatred that a bully has for his targets. This asshole wanted to fight someone, come hell or high water, and I was his next intended victim. My internal fight-response jumped way up. I wasn't going to turn my back on him again.

He pushed me with both hands in the chest, and everyone on the dance floor, including the woman I was dancing with, moved back because they saw the inevitable coming. I said, "Hey man, I'm just trying to have a good time!"

When he swung at me, I instinctively slapped his arm past me with my left hand, then used one of the wrestling moves my dad taught me so many years ago. Dad used it in wrestling, stepping behind his opponent's near leg with his right leg, then leveraging him in the chest with a right

[13] Stats Crew. n.d. *1986 Hamilton Tiger-Cats Roster*. Url: https://www.statscrew.com/football/roster/t-CFLHAM/y-1986 (accessed May 10, 2023).

forearm to put him on his back. This night, being attacked by a vicious bully required a more violent response, so I used the same move, but I hammered this thug in the face with my forearm, smashing his nose. Then I grabbed his long dark hair, and pummelled his face with several hard rights.

It happened so quickly that the bouncers didn't have time to intervene, but they knew the guy was a trouble maker; when he was incapacitated, they dragged him away while another staff member mopped up the blood from the dance floor.

When I rejoined Dale and Ralph still leaning casually at the bar, they hadn't even moved — they just handed me a beer and told me their conversation at the bar had gone something like this:

Ralph, "Jas looks like he's in a tussle. Should we step in, Dale?"

Dale, "Nah, that guy picked the wrong guy to fuck with tonight."

They just sat back and enjoyed the brawl.

The bouncer knew this prick was a local gang member who loved starting fights and beating the crap out of unsuspecting victims. He explained, "When we threw him out after he attacked you, he threatened to return with his gang to get vengeance. You guys had better leave fast because we don't want to have the bar wrecked."

We finished our beers and hailed a cab to our hotel. But it's interesting to note that bullies have no limit to their scope, territory, or walk of life. I'd experienced bullying all my life; now, even as a professional athlete in a beautiful prairie city like Regina, I couldn't escape it. I guess some people just have no common decency. I still believe that the good in people far outweighs the bad. But like Dad said, we have to be tough and ready for anything while navigating the obstacles along the challenging path that we call life.

Speaking of toughness, although I had to have that "be the toughest" mindset to play the sport I loved, I came to recognize that there were lots of guys tougher than me. When Rocky DiPietro fractured his ribs, put on a flak jacket, and continued to catch balls across the middle of opposing defences, he showed such toughness. When Paul Bennett or Less Browne, both defensive backs who were half my size, caught punts and fearlessly ran the ball into the teeth of the punt team, which was paid to take their heads off, they showed such toughness. When Ben Zambiasi shed huge offensive lineman, then hammered running backs threatening his territory up the middle of our defence, he showed unmatched fierceness.

We had that resilient toughness throughout our roster in 1986. With another slow start to our season, a record of 9–8–1 was good enough to finish second in the Eastern Conference for the right to play Toronto in the Eastern Final. The CFL changed the playoff format and we had to play a two-game total-point playoff series against Toronto for the Eastern Conference Championship. Toronto finished first overall, so we played at home in the first game, while the second game was back in Toronto to finish the series. The Argos beat us by 14 points in Hamilton, so we arrived in Toronto for the second game with a big deficit.

The day before that second game for the Eastern Division Championship in Toronto, a group of us went to watch UBC battle Western again for the Vanier Cup at Varsity Stadium. It had snowed overnight and lots of snowballs were being thrown by the fans during the game. Partway into the first quarter, the announcer, concerned about player safety, said over the PA system, "Please do not throw snowballs in the stadium. The next person who throws a snowball on the field will be ejected from the game!"

Shortly thereafter, another snowball arced high into the air and crashed onto the field a few metres away from the players. When security escorted the culprit out of the stadium, we saw that it was Mark Napiorkowski, one of our Ticats players. This was probably karma, retribution for all his pranks, like all the times he had greased rookie players' jockstraps with heat balm!

Napiorkowski was one of a kind. I don't know if he ever started a game, but he won three Grey Cup rings in his career as a special teams player, with three different teams. We hoped he wouldn't be arrested that day for throwing a snowball, because he would be an important special teams contributor in our game the next day.

The Vanier Cup game that day was a very exciting contest between two good teams. UBC was behind with less than two minutes left on the clock, when Coach Smith decided on a hunch to switch quarterbacks — he took out starter Jordan Gagner and replaced him with a cold Eric Putoto. Putoto led the team on a long drive, culminating in a short pass to my old teammate, Rob Ros, for the winning touchdown: final score 25–23 UBC. This emotional outcome reinforced my respect for Coach Smith for having the guts to make a quarterback change like that so late in the game, and it inspired me for tomorrow's battle against our arch-rivals in the face of almost impossible odds.

"I Still Haven't Found What I'm Looking For," U2 (1986)

Understandably, because the Argos won the first game by 14 points the previous week, no one thought that we had a chance to win the series. We heard rumour during the week that the Argos booked everything but their Grey Cup rings after the first game, including airline tickets to Vancouver and hotel rooms for the Grey Cup Festival for the entire team and support staff. I love being the underdog because it puts all the pressure on the other team – our underdog status was clearly established for this game.

As if the score wasn't enough to cement our status as fodder for the Argos, our starting right tackle, John Malinosky, went down with a knee injury in the warm up. His knee locked up on him due to a piece of floating cartilage in the joint that needed to be removed. Big Mal had decided to postpone surgery earlier in the season because he didn't want to miss a game; suddenly, he couldn't play in the biggest game of the year.

This meant that the coaches had a decision to make. We had only dressed six offensive linemen for the game: Malinosky (RT), Scholz (RG), Allemang (C), me (LG), Gorrell (LT), and Brady (back-up centre/guard). Brady, a career long-snapper, had never started a game, so it wouldn't be fair to throw him to the wolves in this crisis.

This is why Coach Al went to the officials to ask them if we could add a player to the roster at this late juncture. They told him that we could if the opposing coach agreed to it. In preparation, Al sent our trainer, Jonesy, to find Dale Sanderson and get him ready to play, while he waited for the Argos' head coach Bob O'Billovich to give us his answer.

Sanderson had suffered a rib injury the previous game, and was placed on the injured list for the week, making him ineligible for this game.

Due to his injured status and not being on the roster, he decided to go to the game with Derksy, who was also injured, so they could drink some beer in the stands and cheer the team on from there.

Sanderson explains what happened next this way:

> We were drinking some beers and enjoying the pre-game atmosphere in Exhibition Stadium during the team warm-up. The next thing you know, there's Jonesy waving up at us. Sitting up around row 25, we couldn't hear what he was saying, so we just waved back at him. We were chuckling at Jonesy for waving at us when the game was about to start. "What's the old buzzard up to now," I said to Derksy?
>
> Then, Jonesy pointed at me and motioned with urgency for me to come down.
>
> When I got down toward the field level, Jonesy said, "Come with me."
>
> I thought he had some cold beers in the locker room to give to Derksy and I, seeing as we weren't playing today.
>
> I said, "Where we goin', Jonesy?"
>
> He said, "Don't ask questions," as he led me into our dressing room.
>
> John Malinosky was sitting in his locker with his head down. As we made eye contact, he said to me with the look of a scolded puppy, "Sorry, Dale."
>
> I thought, "Sorry? Sorry for what?"
>
> Then I look into the training room and I see the team doctor filling a syringe with novocaine, a painkiller, that I assumed was for Malinosky. I looked at Jonesy, and he proceeds to take off his grey armpit-sweat-stained Ticat t-shirt, and throws it to me. I caught it like it was road kill and held it away from myself, as Jonesy says, "Put that on, you're playin'!"

That's when the lightbulb came on and I realized that syringe was meant for me, and not for Mal's knee!

"I can't play, I'm injured, I had no sleep last night, and I've been drinking beer in the stands," I pleaded with Jonesy.

Jonesy said, "Suck it up, if O'Billovich gives Al the green light, you're playin'."

Luckily for me, at that moment our player personnel director, Mike McCarthy, came into the room and announced, "It's not going to happen because O'Billovich said no."

I let out the biggest sigh of relief, as I felt that I narrowly slipped the hangman's noose from around my neck to rejoin Derksy for another beer!

When I got back to Derksy, he asked me if Jonesy gave us any beers. And I told him, "No, Derksy, they wanted me to play today!"

And Derks said, "Are you fucking kiddin' me?"

And that was how Pat Brady, our long snapper, started his first game at offensive guard, which allowed Coach Sal to move Scholz to the OT position as Malinosky's replacement.

To add to the mayhem, Less Browne, our All-Star defensive corner, had his knee wrecked when he was returning the opening kick-off. Terry Lehne was thrown to the wolves along with Brady, pressed into the starting role in our defensive backfield in the Eastern Championship, with only a moment's notice. Lehne had joined the Tiger-Cats in 1983 after starring for the University of Saskatchewan. We had played against each other for years in the WIFL, and now had the pleasure of playing together.

Consequently, we were down two starters before the first snap of the game. To sum it all up, we were going into the conference final game with a 14-point deficit, down a starting OT (Malinosky) on offence, and down a starting DB and kick returner (Browne). One could say it was the perfect storm for Toronto to steamroll us into the turf.

At first, it seemed that's what would happen; after all, the odds were insurmountable, right? Instead of hunkering down with an us-against-the-world attitude and taking command of the game, at first, our team seemed to question whether there really were too many odds against us to overcome. When Toronto got up 12 points in the first quarter of the game, it appeared that this was the final nail in our coffin. Now, down 26 points and two starters, we were beyond underdogs. No one in their right mind would have bet on us to win.

The psychology of sport is often misunderstood, but it can become a pivotal factor in any game. It became very important in this game. Coach Al had surrounded himself with an eclectic group of players and coaches who had a similar mindset, and we'd never quit. We were two-time Eastern Champions, losing two consecutive Grey Cups. We had a unique chemistry on this team: instead of folding up our tent, we just played harder. As lame as it may sound, we still intended to play in our third consecutive Grey Cup game the next week. On the bench, the veterans on the team began to encourage the younger players not to quit, and to reinforce the idea that we could still win the game. We were passionate about fighting for every inch on every play.

On the other hand, the Argos knew they had us down by a total of 26 combined points, and I'm sure they believed that we'd quit, the way some teams would have. The net result was a shift in psychology for both teams. For the Argos, either intentionally, by changing their game plan, or subconsciously, by backing off and playing not to lose instead of playing to win, they went into a conservative "prevent" mentality. (This is what some coaches do successfully when they have a big lead near the end of a game. But it seems to me that teams that use this "prevent" technique often pay for it because it has the reverse effect: instead of preventing the opponent from scoring, it prevents themselves from winning.) Remember, this was still the first quarter of the game, so there was a lot of football still to play.

We knew that someone on our team still needed to make a play to swing the momentum in our favour, or we needed a lucky bounce of some kind. It came when a long snap on a punt sailed over Argo Hank Ilesic's head in the second quarter that set us up for a score.

CFHOF defensive tackle Mike Walker, explains:

> I remember the first game of the two-game total-point series, and we didn't play well at all. I think, going into the second game at Toronto, we knew our backs were against the wall. So, before the game, big John [Malinosky] gets hurt and Less goes down on the first kickoff. The hole could not be any deeper at that point. But two Canadians stepped up and played their [asses] off: Terry Lehne and Pat Brady. Mike Kerrigan also got hot. The defense had [Argo] J. C. Watts on the run all game — he never got comfortable. The turning point was the snap over Ilesic's head. The rest was destiny. Talk about a confidence builder!

That first score gave us hope and inspired the whole team. We knew we had to play our best football, with reckless abandon, to overcome our disadvantage. Every player on our roster went into attack mode – like a cornered animal – and we started rolling. It continued in the second half, and now the Argos could do nothing to stop the tide that was washing over them.

Our OL unit knew Brady was playing in the first start of his CFL career against an outstanding defensive front, so we all rallied around him and he rose to the occasion. We communicated well and worked hard up front to provide the protection Mike Kerrigan needed to throw the ball to our excellent core of receivers: Tony Champion, Rocky DiPietro, Ron Ingram, and Steve Stapler. Kerrigan had one of the best games of his life that day.

Our running backs, Ken Zachary and Walter Bender, both ran the ball hard every chance they got. Bender had a career game that day, catching an amazing spin-around catch for a touchdown that inspired the whole team.

We ended up winning the two-game series by three points, 59–56 — the greatest comeback in CFL playoff history. More importantly, we won the right to get back to the Grey Cup for some unfinished business. After the game, everyone was exhausted and ecstatic — we had emptied our tanks on the field. The emotion was palpable as we shared hugs and high-fives, while the fans streamed onto the field. We were emotional and physical dishrags.

After embracing coaches, teammates, family, and friends on the field, it's remarkable that the image from that amazing victory that is most etched into my mind is Pat Brady, stripped down to his jockstrap, standing proudly on his locker stool, dancing with a bottle of champagne in each hand, singing, "We're going to the Grey Cup, we're going to the Grey Cup!" at the top of his lungs, between chugs of champagne.

He had earned the right to celebrate. He was instrumental in the team's incredible comeback win after being thrown into his role at the very last second. He proved to be a great competitor and teammate.

Terry Lehne also rose to the occasion and played a great game. He had a key interception that led to a score that kept our momentum going when we needed it.

The win galvanized our team emotionally and spiritually. You could feel the love we had for each other in that dressing room, the acceptance of everyone as a respected member of a great team. The passion lit up every crevice of the room.

And this was just the beginning. This win was transformative. Unbeknownst to the rest of the world, the core of the team and coaches had been fighting so many battles together that we were all willing to fall on our swords to get that elusive championship ring. We would not be satisfied merely playing in our third consecutive Grey Cup — we were going to win it.

Incidentally, all the airline tickets and hotel rooms that the Argos had ordered prematurely were transferred into our names for the Grey Cup trip. It was nice of the Argos to order them for us in advance!

"I firmly believe that any man's finest hour, the greatest fulfillment of all that he holds dear, is that moment when he has worked his heart out in a good cause and lies exhausted on the field of battle — victorious."

Vince Lombardi

In contrast to our team's triumphant attitude, the nation's football community was still doubtful that we could win the Grey Cup. Especially since Edmonton won their Western Conference Final so handily, some people even compared us to our NFL neighbours in Buffalo, who recently had great teams but lost four Super Bowls in a row. We did not want to be known as the Canadian equivalent.

Coach Al's mantra continued to be, "Men, it's us against the world. Goddammit, the rest of the league, their fans, and the media across the country don't believe we can do it. Ignore all that, because the only things that matter are the people in this room [our team] and our families. We brought you here for a reason and the coaches believe in you, so play for each other and have confidence that we will win!"

Our third consecutive Grey Cup occurred on November 30, 1986, at BC Place Stadium in Vancouver, in front of many of my family and friends amongst the sold-out crowd of 60,000. Being in my adopted hometown just added to my personal motivation for the game. But this game was far greater than just me. Overcoming that huge deficit in the greatest comeback of all time in our previous game against the Argos, the entire team had gained confidence and momentum.

Once we achieved that and put ourselves back in the Grey Cup, the team's mindset was concrete. The key reason we played with such determination and physicality, which Edmonton could not match that day, was that the core of the team had been together for at least three years now, and after losing the two previous Grey Cups, we were emotionally prepared to make any sacrifice necessary on the field to win this game.

Mike Walker states:

> We were so locked in when we reached Vancouver, I remember doing extra video sessions after and before meetings. When we arrived at BC Place on game day, you could hear a pin drop. Even though Edmonton was favoured to win, everyone in that locker room was stone-faced. After losing two Grey Cups in a row, I could see on everybody's face there was no way we were gonna lose that game. As a front-four, our plan was to meet at the QB [Edmonton's Matt Dunigan]; we jumped on him so fast it was scary.

> I never saw Grover [Covington] so focused. We never gave them a chance to breathe. It was our destiny.

"Gonna Fly Now," Bill Conti (1976)

On game day, the attitudes of each team were in stark contrast; you could see it when the teams were introduced. Edmonton was loosey-goosey, chirping, dancing around and making hand signals to the cameras like they were at a concert or something, whereas we were quietly confident, focused, and mentally prepared for battle.

That day, our defence may have played the most complete game of any team in a championship game. They were credited with 10 sacks at the time, but would have had more under today's definition. They chased quarterbacks — first Matt Dunigan, then Damon Allen— all over the field, all day long. Our front seven, consisting of Grover Covington, Dave Sauve, Mike Walker, and Mitch Price on the defensive line, with Frank Robinson, Leo Ezerins and Ben Zambiasi behind them at linebacker, were relentless from beginning to end.

Coach Sal had prepared our offensive line well, too. He inserted Sanderson to replace Brady at right guard, so our starting unit for this game would be: Gorrell (LT), me (LG), Allemang (C), Sanderson (RG), and Scholz (RT). As a group, we protected Kerrigan well throughout the game, as we battled with an excellent front seven in the trenches. Kerrigan was sacked only once.

Gorrell's favourite memory of the game was this:

> Sitting on top of John Mandarich, after we scored to make it 29 to zip, and asking him what his mom thought of his green Nike swoosh shaved into his hair. But in reality, we knew we had a great defence and we were good as a team, so drinking from the Grey Cup with Rocky, you and my [other] teammates, [and] my mom and dad getting to drink from the Grey Cup are really my favourite memories.

It's interesting that Gorrell mentioned John Mandarich, because he was a big, strong defensive tackle, who always played hard. I let my emotions get the better of me on one play in the game, when Mandarich grabbed the back of Marv Allemang's (our centre) horse collar after the ball was thrown, and violently threw him to the turf. Seeing this as disrespecting our veteran centre, and possibly injuring him, I reacted instinctively by drilling Mandarich hard, knocking him to the turf. Unfortunately, I hit him in the back, and got a 15-yard roughing penalty for it. But it was not my intention to injure Mandarich, it was to defend my teammate and send a message to Edmonton's defence, that they were in a war and we weren't backing down a single inch.

At half-time the score was 29–0. Leo Ezerins shared his half-time conversation with one of our teammates:

> I was debating with Dave Sauve, after a stellar defensive first half of football, about which of us deserved the Most Valuable Canadian Player Award. Then someone mentioned to us that Ozzy [our kicker, Paul Osbaldiston] already had five field goals, so it was a moot point, because we knew Ozzy's name was already on the trophy!

My only regret is that we didn't finish more of our offensive drives with touchdowns instead of field goals that day. If we had, the final score would have been more indicative of how well our team played as a whole. Nevertheless, our OL unit was proud that Kerrigan, was only sacked once in the game.

But, on the other hand, if we had ended up with more touchdowns, our rookie kicker and future CFL All-Star Osbaldiston, wouldn't have tied a record of six field goals in a Grey Cup that day. For Ozzy, it was a great start to a successful career!

After the final whistle blew, the scoreboard read Tiger-Cats 39, Eskimos (now Elks) 15. It was exhilarating to know the team had exhausted itself on the field of battle, that crowd of 60,000 cheering fans adding a surreal atmosphere, as the building echoed their roar.

During the post-game euphoria on the field, Sanderson came to me and said, "Jas, let's give Coach Al a ride to remember, on our shoulders!"

I quickly threw my helmet towards the bench and joined Dale. Shoulder to shoulder, we snuck up behind Coach Al; we picked him up proudly and paraded the surprised coach around the field, amongst our celebrating teammates. The whole team (and the Cats fans in the stands) cheered him on as head coach of the new Grey Cup champion Hamilton Tiger-Cats! At the time, I hadn't noticed that Dale had kept his helmet on. When Coach Al needed a handle to stabilize himself on his perch, he grabbed the only thing available, Dale's facemask.

The media swarm took many shots of Al being carried on our shoulders and, in Monday's edition of the *Hamilton Spectator* newspaper, our victory was commemorated nicely on the front page. Along with a classic shot of our tenacious defence, the picture of Al, Dale, and I captures the jubilation of the moment. Unfortunately, Sanderson can't be seen in the image because Al's hand is blocking his face. I give Dale full credit for this iconic shot.

Celebrating the Grey Cup win with Al Bruno, Vancouver, 1986: Kaz Novak, The Hamilton Spectator

Another memorable moment in the wake of our hard-fought win happened as soon as I entered the dressing room. Our big Sam (strong-side) linebacker Leo Ezerins and I were so excited that we actually shared a big, fat, wet kiss. This may not sound like a big deal, but after banging heads with Leo in practice for three years, both of us too stubborn to back down, in this triumphant moment, only love remained. This was made even more passionate by the fact that he's a stoic first-generation Canadian-Latvian.

Then I quickly removed my soaked-in-sweat #58 jersey and threw it to Paulette, who was waiting for it outside the dressing room, after we had shared a sweaty, emotional post-game embrace on the field. I had to move fast, before Jonesy collected the jerseys from the dressing room, because he would ream you out if he caught you taking a band aid for a blister without permission! I still cherish that jersey.

For the entire organization — from the team, coaches, and support staff to administration — this game was the affirmation of all the hard work we had done in the preceding years to reach the pinnacle of Canadian football.

Team owner Harold Ballard had planned an outstanding team party at our hotel after the game. Paulette's and my family both joined us for the celebration. The Grey Cup trophy was on display for photos and two shots we took will always be special for me: one is of Mom and Dad and I with the cup — it is heartwarming to know that my parents shared our team's success after all the sacrifices they made to support us kids and the struggles we had as a family leading to this moment; the other is of Paulette with Harold Ballard, which, to me, reflects the fact that Paulette's support was instrumental for our shared success.

Mom and Dad with the Grey Cup, Vancouver, 1986; Jason Riley photo

Harald Ballard with Paulette at Grey Cup victory party, Vancouver, 1986: Jason Riley photo

The party was special for many reasons, and obviously the sheer emotion of the team's dominating victory was on display on everyone's faces. One thing that is unforgettable was Ben Zambiasi, the All-Star middle linebacker for our incredible defence, in a new suit, shirtless, and with a tie depicting a B.C. sockeye salmon around his neck. The funny thing is, he looked great and got compliments on his attire. Ben has always been one of a kind.

The Grey Cup parade in downtown Hamilton, a couple of days after the team returned home from Vancouver, was a very emotional experience. Unmitigated joy might sum it up. A local car dealership provided a fleet of convertibles for all the players, support staff, and owner, Harold Ballard, to ride along the route through the heart of the city, which ended at the stage in front of City Hall. Thousands of fans lined up on the streets along the parade route on a frigid afternoon. The crowd waved and cheered as the players held the cup high in the air with pride.

After the parade, when we congregated on the stage in front of City Hall, Harold Ballard told Jonesy he had to piss — at his age (he was 83 years old at that point), when he had to go, he didn't have much time to waste, so there was no time to find a restroom.

Jonesy recruited the taller players to surround Ballard at the back of the stage, away from the cameras. Ballard pissed off the edge of the structure onto the City Hall grass, unbeknownst to the thousands of fans cheering and the media cameras recording the event from the front of the stage. Out of necessity, the proud owner of our franchise was again thumbing his nose at social norms, much like he had done throughout his life.

Harold Ballard was often maligned by the media for being a curmudgeon, but after we won him his championship, he treated us generously. The classy Grey Cup rings he had designed for the team included a shamrock to honour his good friend, King Clancy, who sadly passed away during training camp that year. The entire team went to honour him at his funeral in Toronto, and we wore a shamrock in his honour on our helmets the entire season. The spirit of King Clancy was with the team throughout our championship season.

On a personal note, it was very meaningful to me when Marv Allemang came to me in the locker room after he heard the announcement to tell me that he, Gorrell, and I were named Eastern Conference All-Stars together on the offensive line. This was the icing on the cake for our 1986 championship season, which bonded us together forever.

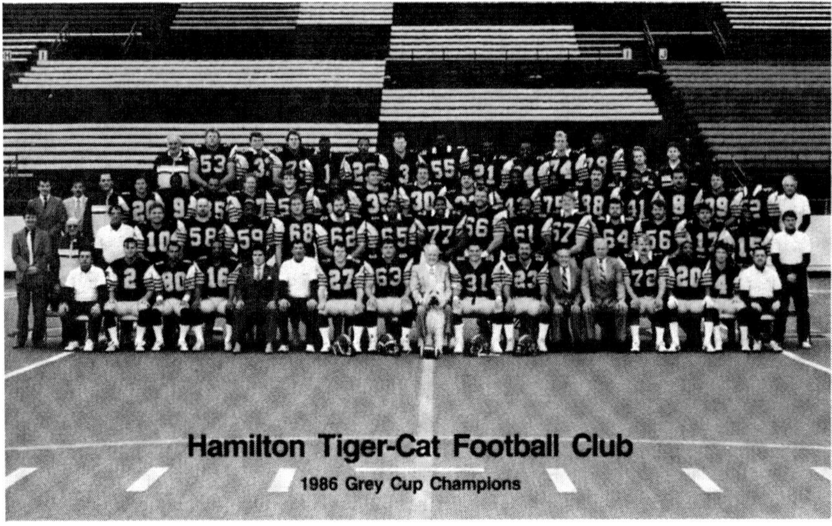

1986 Tiger-Cats Christmas Card photo

THIRD QUARTER

STREET FIGHT IN THE TRENCHES

"Can't Get Enough," Bad Company (1974)

During the years that followed our championship, Coach Al kept our offensive line mostly intact. Keeping us together to grow as a unit paid off because for two consecutive years, our unit was honoured for giving up the least sacks in the season. This isn't easy with a quarterback like Mike Kerrigan, who took the helm in 1986 as a pure drop-back passer, which meant that opposing defences knew exactly where he'd be — in the pocket directly behind the centre. Moreover, Kerrigan was never known as a fleet-footed athlete. This meant that Kerrigan got sore toes some days, having been stepped on by linemen with quick feet behind the centre. In his defence, Kerrigan had a quick release on his timing throws, but you can't throw lying on your back. We took great pride in keeping him on his feet.

This was solid recognition for our hard-working group, who developed trust in each other and worked together as a well-oiled unit. We had the size and strength to be very physical and we played with that aggressive defensive mentality.

It also meant that we relished knocking the defence off the ball on the ground game (see Appendix A) when we had the luxury of running the football. This was our chance to tee-off on guys with forward drive blocks, instead of back-pedalling in pass-blocking mode.

◇◆◇

Though we didn't win another Grey Cup while I was with the Tiger-Cats, there are still many memories — and, despite Paulette and the family managing to tame my anger off the field, still I needed that old anger during games. And it's funny — some games just stand out in my mind, like they happened recently, when I can't even remember one play from other games. One game that stands out was when the incomparable Tyrone Jones visited us in Hamilton, still with the Winnipeg Blue Bombers.

If you recall, Jones and I had a shared history because we both joined the Winnipeg defence together as rookies in 1983. That same year, I was giving him a break on the punt team in Montreal when I broke my foot to end my season. In the time since, I had moved to offensive line, and Jones developed into a CFHOF linebacker.

The only problem for me was that his development as a player brought with it a trash-talking habit that drove me nuts. I guess, in retrospect, that's the purpose of trash-talking — to try your best to get your opponent off his game. This day he started early in the game and I just wasn't in the mood for it.

Winnipeg took advantage of their depth in linebackers by running predominantly a three-man front with four linebackers on defence. Jones was lined up at the strongside inside linebacker position in their defensive scheme, which put him head-up on me at guard.

As always, the best defenders never want to be blocked, and if they are, they will make up some excuse to justify it in their mind. When I blocked him on a blitz in the first quarter, and later on a run-play in the same series, I can remember Jones' words clearly.

He told me, "You know what, Riley, I never really liked you when I played with you, and now I like you even less!" (We had always got along fine when we played together.)

"What are you trying to do, Jones, hurt my feelings?" I responded. "Just play fucking football."

Apparently, he didn't like my response, or being blocked, because his trash-talking just escalated in the game. I tried to ignore it as much as possible because I didn't want to let him get me off my game, but the more I blocked him, the more he carried on.

Finally, near the end of the third quarter, he did it. He got to me by using one of the oldest clichés in the book. "Riley, your mother wears army boots!" he yelled. As sad as it seems now, somehow in my warrior mentality in the trenches, he struck a chord with me and I snapped, "Now you've made it personal, don't ever mention my family, Jones!"

It was poetic justice that after Jones insulted my mother and sent me into a rage, our offensive coordinator called the perfect play — a reverse.

On the reverse, we showed a toss action to the strong side — Jones' side, in this case — so as usual, when I faked my pull to block the toss to my left, he instantly began to pursue to the ball. My job was to pick up any pursuit of the new ball carrier after the ball was handed off to another receiver coming in the opposite direction. I had Jones in my sights from the start and sure enough, the reverse action of the play brought him right back to me. As he was in full flight, I planted my forearm under his chin and knocked him right off his feet, onto his back. Now most of my body weight rested on my forearm, which pinned him to the turf. As he gasped for breath, I looked him square in the eyes, which grew about three sizes, and I said to him through clenched teeth, "Don't you ever fucking say anything about my mother again!"

After that scenario played out with such karma, Jones and I played many more games against each other and we both respected each other as veteran combatants of the game. Although I know his reputation as a trash-talker continued for the rest of his career, he never said another word to me in a game.

One of the best defensive linemen I ever played against was Lloyd Lewis in Ottawa. He had a motor that never quit, and a full tool kit of moves he could use at any point. I knew I had to be ready for a brawl every time I played against him and I couldn't let up for a minute or he'd be making a big play.

One play he made in one of our games still stands out in my mind. On an inside running play I got lucky and caught him off balance, pancaked him, then "splashed" him. A splash is what we offensive linemen used to relish, after knocking a guy down — we would jump on top of them, belly flop style, and flatten them into the turf, so they were completely eliminated from the play. (In today's game, splashing would likely result in an unnecessary roughness penalty.) Generally speaking, when a guy got splashed by a 290 lb lineman, they would let up knowing that they were beat and there was no point fighting it, and live to fight another day.

Not Lewis. On this particular play, he actually scrambled to his hands and knees with me on his back and bear-crawled our combined weight down the LOS to get a hand on the ball-carrier's ankle, assisting on the tackle.

I was so shocked; I couldn't believe it. How could this guy, after being knocked down and with my entire weight on his back, still manage to get in on the play? I said to him after the play, "What do I have to do to stop you, kill you?" Lewis was a man of few words, which I respected. He just shrugged with a big grin on his face, and went back to the huddle to get ready for the next play.

"Maggie May," Rod Stewart (1971)

The great Ron Lancaster was a guest quarterback coach in our training camps at Brock University for several years before he returned to coaching. Ron was between CFL coaching gigs and working as a CBC football broadcaster during this time. Because he lived locally, it was easy for him to come to our camps at Brock, where he had an open invitation from General Manager Joe Zuger and Coach Al.

Ron was always a classy guy and true gentleman of the game. Everyone respected him for his Hall of Fame playing career — he was a living legend. But he was also a great communicator, which made him a natural coach and broadcaster. His insight on everything football made him a continuous source of information. Our quarterbacks sure benefitted from having him in camp.

One morning, we were having a conversation on the field, waiting for practice to start. We were talking about coaching philosophy, and I asked him how many plays a good offence should have in its playbook. Ron chuckled, "Jason, its not rocket science, you know. There are really only 13 plays in football, and everyone runs them; it's just that everyone calls them different names!"

This has always stayed with me. By extension, the fundamentals of the game never really change; which means generally speaking, the team that keeps things simple and makes the least mistakes usually wins the game. Similarly, the team with the offensive line that plays the best usually wins the game, because they are controlling the LOS. As a former quarterback himself, Ron understood better than most the importance of protecting the "field general," so he was a strong advocate for offensive linemen.

Another wise mentor the team had the privilege of having was Bernie Custis. Bernie was the first Black quarterback in the modern era of professional football. He once told me that after he graduated from Syracuse University, he was drafted into the NFL by the Cleveland Browns. However, he was told he couldn't play quarterback, and although it wasn't said out loud, he knew it was because he was Black. Prejudice clearly existed in the NFL at the time. He was aware of the CFL, north of the border, and had some contacts up here, so he decided to come play quarterback for the Hamilton Tiger-Cats, where he won a Grey Cup in 1951, his rookie year.

After his playing career, Bernie settled in Burlington, Ontario, and began teaching and coaching. Over his coaching career — including the Burlington Braves (of the CJFL), Sheridan College Bruins (Oakville, Ontario), and McMaster University (Hamilton) programs — he coached and mentored hundreds of young men. In 1982, a season where he took the previously last-place McMaster Marauders to first place in their OUA conference, he won the Frank Tindall Trophy as CIAU (now U Sports) Coach of the Year. This brought Bernie and I full-circle, because he had received his award at the same awards banquet in Toronto, where our UBC and Western teams were honoured a few days before our Vanier Cup championship game.

Bernie, Ron Lancaster, and Angelo Mosca were fast friends and local football legends, so they pretty much had the run of Ivor Wynne Stadium when I played. During the warm up at most home games, you could find them sitting on chairs at field level, just outside the tunnel the players used to enter the field from the home dressing room.

From this perch, they could feel the excitement of the players entering the field for warm-up, then they could pass on some words of wisdom to the players as we left the field for final preparations in the locker room before kickoff. They shared encouraging words before they left the field to get to their stadium seats. If they chose to join us in the dressing room after the games, win or lose, they always had positive support for the team. They were truly local fixtures that became part of the lore of Ivor Wynne Stadium. I benefitted from knowing all of them.

Those home games were also when we got to be familiar with our team's owner and his best friend King Clancy. Ballard and Clancy were inseparable. Most of the offensive line had a game-day ritual to get to the stadium hours early to get taped and dressed in our lowers (game pants and socks). Then we'd relax, playing cards or reading books before we did the pre-game walk-about (see Appendix A) in the stadium to get focused. Like true sportsmen, for many home games, the two of them would come to the stadium early to chat with us and wish us good luck in the game, before they began the long climb up the stadium steps to the press box, where they'd watch the game. The city eventually put in an elevator to the press box because it became too high for their old legs to climb.

"Can't You See," The Marshall Tucker Band (1973)

Lee "Rooster" Knight joined the Cats directly from the Burlington Braves of the CJFL in 1986. After spending his first year on the practice roster, he earned a regular spot on our offence, playing whatever role the coaches asked of him: receiver, running back, kicker, you name it. He is one of few players to ever jump from CJFL to the Hamilton Tiger-Cats without going the university draft route.

In 1987, Knight joined the team for his first road trip and I was fortunate enough to be his roommate in the hotel in Edmonton. When we arrived at the hotel, as Knight was a receiver, I assumed that he had plans to eat dinner with his position group, so I didn't invite him to join the offensive line at the local steakhouse. You see, we had a tradition to find the best restaurants in town and spend most of our per diem on a great meal the night before games, while the receivers usually ate like birds and pocketed most of their per diem to take home. Knight, however, was not like the average receiver and had an appetite like an offensive lineman. Unfortunately, he hadn't planned to eat with the receivers, so I accidentally left him alone in the hotel to fend for himself. I really felt for the kid, when he told me that. He'll never let me forget it, either!

In spite of this early set-back, we became good friends playing together over the years. Accordingly, in the spirit of camaraderie, we began to play practical jokes on each other. For example, we both loved the *Pink Panther* movies with Peter Sellers playing Detective Clouseau, and Burt Kwouk playing his sidekick Cato. Clouseau instructed Cato to keep him sharp by attacking him at any point in time and from any location, so Cato would attack him at the most unexpected times. It was always hilarious to see Cato jump out of a closet and attack Clouseau in the movies.

Knight and I developed the same routine. Since I was around 290 lb, and Knight (being a puny receiver) was at 240 lb, he began to attack me at the most unexpected times, just to keep me on my toes. I might be sitting on the edge of the bed playing cards in the hotel room and Lee would come flying into the room from the hall and tackle me from behind, knocking a couple guys out of the way in the process. The donnybrook was on! We'd wrestle until we were both lying on the floor laughing, exhausted, in whatever corner of the room we ended up. Lee and I had officially sealed the brotherhood, wrestling just as we had with our own brothers as kids.

This went on for years. Dave Richardson joined us in 1990. As he describes it, "I never saw anything like it. Lee ran from the hotel room door, across the room, and left his feet, diving into you, knocking you clear off the bed. Then, the wrestling match began and you guys would go until you were both out of breath!"

One time, I decided to give Knight a bit of his own medicine. I had been playing cards in our hotel room, and I was in the bathroom when I heard Lee come into the room saying he needed to use the pisser. I just happened to have a brand-new cigar in the bathroom that I was planning to smoke later that night. Since I knew Knight would be the next man in the room, I bit the tip of the cigar off and placed it perfectly on the toilet seat after I flushed the toilet. I came out of the bathroom acting casual and rejoined the card game. I whispered to the guys to listen, as Knight went into the bathroom and locked the door. Suddenly, he was yelling at the top of his lungs, "Riley, you stupid motherfucker! You left shit on the fucking toilet seat! You fucking asshole!" He continued his rant, "You are the biggest fucking pig I've ever fucking met!" We were all laughing so hard when Knight came out of the bathroom that our ribs hurt. He still thought I shit on the toilet seat and his face was as red as a rooster's wattle. We still laugh about that story.

Another funny story about Rooster and I happened on the field in Vancouver. Someone must have been injured, because I was playing offensive tackle in this game against the Lions. Knight was playing slotback. On one particular play, he had to waggle in (see Appendix A), timing it perfectly with the cadence to step down and replace me at tackle to cut off the backside edge, while I slipped up field to cut off the backside linebacker — it's a routine combination block between the backside tackle and slotback as the ball is being run away from us. So, here comes Rooster, timing it perfectly, until the turf monster tripped him and he stumbled forward, causing him to go offside.

The problem was, because Knight was early when he tripped, he had no option but to brace himself on me because I hadn't moved yet, with one hand on each of my hips. At the same time, his momentum carried him into me and he knocked me forward as I tried to stay in my three-point stance prior to the snap. We were on national TV and the referee threw the flag for offside. I was about to tell Knight, "It's okay, everyone makes mistakes, buddy," when we heard the PA announcer tell the entire stadium that #58 was offside on the play! I wasn't happy that I got flagged for a penalty that wasn't my fault — shit, I got enough penalties on my own.

The funniest part of the story happened after we returned to Hamilton. At the next meeting, Coach Sal was breaking down our game film for the offensive line. That play came up, and there was Rooster just before the snap, grabbing me by the hips and thrusting me offside. Coach Sal asked with his dry Kansas drawl, "Riley, what is going on here?" before adding, "You have to stay on-side!"

"Welcome to the Jungle," Guns and Roses (1987)

In 1987, at BC Place Stadium, we played a Friday night game against the BC Lions. I always looked forward to playing there because of friends and family attending the game, and the sense that it was like a home game for me after growing up there.

Rick Klassen was an excellent defensive lineman for the Lions. The scouting report on him would read something like, "He's very athletic and has a motor that doesn't stop" — this is a high compliment, meaning that the player doesn't take plays off, and pursues the ball to the whistle every play. I knew Klassen had a motor because our teams played against each other in a couple of Shrum Bowls, the annual cross-town battle between UBC and SFU, before he was drafted by the BC Lions in 1981. Hence, we knew each other as opponents, and we had also worked together on a few weekends at the infamous Boo Pub. You always knew you were in for a game when you played against Rick. He was a great guy and a great player for the Lions for many years — the kind of guy you wanted on your team, but was really aggravating if you played against him.

This particular game was very competitive with the score going back and forth. I remember our intrepid middle linebacker, Ben Zambiasi, intercepting a Roy Dewalt pass and running it back for a touchdown late in the game.

It was ingrained in me to be relentless and go to the whistle every play, just as it was with Rick. On one play, Kerrigan threw the ball to DiPietro on a break-out pattern to the short side of the field. I made a beeline for the ball to try and spring DiPietro for more yards after the catch (YAC). I could see Klassen pursuing to the point where the ball was caught and I knew I needed to get my head in front of him to prevent him from hitting our receiver and knocking him out of bounds. My thinking was, "If I get there in time, I can spring Rocky for a big gain."

I got there just in time, and, because of my size, speed, and angle of impact, I knocked Rick head over heels — in football vernacular, it was a decleater. After the play, I started walking back to our huddle, and I heard Klassen losing it. He screamed at me all the way back to my huddle, "You clipped me, you son-of-a-bitch. Riley, that was a clip! You fucking asshole, you hit me right in the back!"

I looked around and there was no flag on the play. I said, "Hey, Klassen, calm down, it was a good hit. My head was in front! Quit your whining and play the fucking game."

He persisted in berating me all the way back to the huddle and continued his verbal assault on the LOS before the next play. He was frothing at the mouth and he gave me the middle finger salute while Kerrigan was calling the cadence just before the snap. The war of words continued for the rest of the game. In the end, we won the game 21–20.

Rick Klassen giving me the business between plays, Vancouver, 1987: photographer unknown

After the game, I went to shake his hand and explain that I didn't intend to clip him and that I thought my head was in front on the hit. He continued to insist it was a clip. I told him we would have to wait and see the film to determine who was right, but there was no flag, so that was in my favour. We agreed that if it was a clip, I owed him a beer.

In a funny twist of fate (but I believe no coincidence), after the game, my brothers met me at the Unicorn Pub, a popular place for a post-game beer near BC Place Stadium. I bought a pitcher of beer and was stretching my arm across the packed crowd to hand it to my brother. The guy next to me said, "Hey, you owe me a beer!" Klassen just happened to be right there at the pub, between me and my brothers. So, I poured him a beer and we laughed about the hit — no harm, no foul! The game is a street fight inside the white lines, and a fraternity off the field.

Many years later, Jason Quinter (the son of Bill Quinter, the former BC Lions player personnel director who called me the day I was leaving for Hamilton) contacted me on Facebook and sent me a picture of that scene. It shows Rick Klassen giving me the finger just before the next snap. I couldn't believe it; someone had taken a picture that encapsulated the emotion of that exact moment better than any words can say.

◇◆◇

"Football is many things, but mostly it's a game of passion."
Vince Lombardi

We had a back-to-back series in 1987 with the Edmonton Elks. The first game was in Hamilton. Edmonton was always tough to play against, and they had a ferocious defence that year. James Zachery played their defensive tackle position. Zachery was a big, tough, athletic guy, who I heard had a black belt in taekwondo. Since I had a black belt in street fighting, I thought it would be a fair fight.

During both games, we went head-to-head most of the game. Our home game was a close one and tempers were raw. Again, no defensive player likes being blocked, but this game Zachery was really angry with me because I had his number. I was blocking the shit out of him and the holding excuses starting flying out of his mouth.

As the game went on, I would finish my block and he would say, "Quite holding me!" then try to judo chop me in the throat after the whistle. The referees never saw it because we were behind the play and their attention was on the ball, which was up field by now. By the time the fourth quarter came around, it had evolved into an all-out street fight. We were verbally and physically combative when the game ended 36–33 for the bad guys.

The thing about back-to-back series that some fans may not know is that, even if it's not a playoff series, for the players, it is like one continuous six-hour game. All the emotion that is developed throughout the first game is continued into the second game. So, it was with Zachery and I in this series, going into Edmonton.

Consequently, right from the opening whistle in the second game, the battle continued. I was still confident in my ability to block him and he continued to accuse me of holding him and giving me judo chops in the neck after the play. By the time the third quarter came around, I was fed up with his cheap shots and I told him, "If you judo-chop me one more fucking time, you're going to pay for it!"

He responded, "Fuck you, Riley, quit fucking holding me!"

The next play I blocked him again and he judo-chopped me in the neck.

I screamed at him, "Okay, that's the last time, use a fucking move instead of what you're doing, because it's not working for you!" I was sick and tired of him judo-chopping me in the neck every time I blocked him. I had warned him.

The next play was second and long, so I expected him to make a pass rush move. Right on cue, he sunk a rip move, with his left arm to my outside hip, trying to slip past me to our quarterback. I put a hammer lock on his elbow with my left arm, and dropped my body under his, gaining leverage as I hip-tossed him into the air. It was like a suplex in wrestling, only I leveraged his arm instead of his torso. I timed it just right. The problem was that as I leveraged his arm, about halfway through my move, I heard his arm crack and he gasped in pain. This was not intentional. I was trying to toss him, not to injure him.

He jumped up off the ground holding his elbow in pain, and screamed "You son of a bitch, Riley, I'll kill you!" At that point, he tried to kick me in the balls. I turned my hips and his kick glanced off my leg, but the fight was on for real. Our teammates joined in the fracas to separate us, and next the referees got involved. They flagged Zachery for kicking me and ejected him from the game. I don't know what the injury was, but his arm wasn't broken because he played wearing a brace on his elbow for the rest of the season.

We ended up winning the second game 40–30.[14] I remember our backup quarterback, Tom Porras, had a career game, throwing for over 400 yards, making it Hamilton's first win in Edmonton since 1968.

The film session was entertaining when we returned to Hamilton. Coach Sal played the scene over and over again because you could see Zachery's feet go across my back as I tossed him in a scrum of players near the line of scrimmage. Coach Sal said, "What exactly is going on here, Jason? I never taught you to block like that." The boys all had a good laugh at that meeting.

Unfortunately, the Elks coaches saw it on film too, and they filed a formal complaint with the commissioner. They claimed that Zachery was the victim in the play, so it should have been me that was ejected from the game and fined $500 instead of him. I wrote a letter to the commissioner in

---

[14] Stats Crew. n.d. *1987 Hamilton Tiger-Cats game-by-game results.* Url: https://www.statscrew.com/football/results/t-CFLHAM/y-1987 (accessed May 12, 2023).

my appeal, explaining all the events that led up to that infamous play. They dismissed any further action in the incident. I was very relieved because $500 was a lot of money to me and Paulette, who was pregnant with twins at the time.

"I'm Gonna Drive You Out of My Mind," Charlie Major (1993)

The best birthday present I ever got was the birth of our twin girls, on October 5, 1987. They were born the day after my birthday.

We had just returned home on a red-eye flight from Winnipeg, where the Blue Bombers had laid a physical beat-down on us. Defensive back James Jefferson scored four touchdowns against us that game, and All-Star kicker Paul Osbaldiston was left in a Winnipeg hospital with a concussion. The team was in a miserable mood as we limped back home.

As soon as we arrived at the Toronto airport, Sarah Malinosky, Johnny Mal's wife, told me she had spoken to Paulette that day, and I needed to get home quickly because she thought the twins may be coming. This was unexpected because it would mean they were five weeks premature. Now I was anxious and we still had an hour-long bus ride back to the stadium before I could drive home.

When I walked in the door, I asked Paulette if she was okay. She said she felt better now that I was home. I felt relieved as I brushed my teeth before bed. Then I heard her water break.

We quickly got her in the car and rushed her down to McMaster Hospital. McMaster is renowned as an excellent hospital and school of medicine. It has an outstanding neonatal unit and sick kids focus. We knew Paulette and the twins would be in good hands.

Paulette made it clear with the nurse from the start that she wanted an epidural for the delivery. As the delivery team prepared this for Paulette, one of the nurses asked it I would like anything. I told her I felt like I had been hit by a car from the game and, having no sleep on the plane, I asked her for some painkillers. I needed to make sure, if necessary, I could stay on my feet the rest of the night to support Paulette. She left the room to get me a couple Tylenols to get me through the night.

Paulette didn't see it that way. She was so mad that the nurse had left the room to get me medication that she began crushing my hand with her grip and launching obscenities at me between breaths of the laughing gas they had already given her. For me, I was glad I asked because I stood throughout the entire night, with Paulette crushing my hands with every contraction.

In the morning, Jordan was born first. I was struck by how small and ivory (from vernix) she appeared to be. The nurse bundled her in swaddling cloth and handed her to me. Three minutes later, the doctor delivered Jessica. I handed Jordan to Paulette, so I could take Jessica from the nurse. For a few moments, I was mesmerized by these tiny porcelain dolls that had emerged into the world. They were both so small, under five pounds, and they were still covered with vernix, which is waxy white substance coating babies to protect them in the womb. It was surreal: I knew I had witnessed the "miracle of life." This was the most amazing thing I had ever seen in my life — the euphoria was beyond anything I had experienced before.

The arrival of our twins was the greatest experience of my life — an explosion of positive emotional karma! At least for me — I was doing cartwheels thinking of all the fun we'd have. To Paulette in her post-partum exhaustion, she thought of all the work she would face raising twins without the support of our moms, who both still lived in B.C. Being from hearty stock, Paulette took on the challenge successfully without any support from anyone except me. And I couldn't always be home, but she met all the challenges of being a new mom with great courage and strength. She is another example of someone much tougher than me!

Before the "Grey Cup" twins (so named for their conspicuous timing, approximately 10 months after our big win) arrived, I had become involved in the Hamilton community, doing as much as possible to support local charity events and promoting the city's beloved Hamilton Tiger-Cats. I am proud to say that I received the Charlotte Simmons Humanitarian Award, as voted by the fans, as the Tiger-Cat doing the most for his community. The award means much to me because Charlotte was such a huge fan of our team that she wore a "Tiger-Lady" costume to every home game. The Cats Claws Fan Club honoured her when she passed away by naming this award after her. Receiving this award, to me, was an extension of the positive community spirit that Paulette and I had enjoyed since moving to Hamilton, then winning the Grey Cup.

Suddenly being the father of two meant my focus had to change, though. This meant that I immediately went from the top of the food chain in our house — up till now, eating was my priority to keep my weight up — to the bottom. I had to make sure everyone else in the house was fed, including the cat, before I could eat.

This included night-time feedings. After three months of nursing the twins to strengthen their immune system and all that good stuff, Paulette couldn't keep up, so she began to bottle-feed them. This meant that during the off-season, I could share the load. Paulette and I would get up together and feed the kids side-by-side, which not all fathers get the opportunity to do. This gave me the pleasure of bonding with my girls at a very early age, which profoundly changed my perspective in life.

Instant and unconditional love accompanied the epiphany that our babies were completely dependent on us for every need. This new sense of responsibility for both Paulette and I was heightened by the fact that we had no grandparental support at all — all our support was now 3000 km away. For me in particular, it countered some of the recklessness that had characterized my life up until now.

A mysterious event occurred when the twins were just four months old, further strengthening my spiritual belief. On January 29, 1988, Paulette and I were in the basement watching television, while the kids slept upstairs. On the baby monitor, we heard one of the babies suddenly begin to cry. I went up to their room, where our tiny girls shared a crib, to check on them.

When I got to the room, Jordan was crying loudly in the crib while her sister slept. I picked her up and she continued to cry no matter how I held her, so I checked her diaper. It was dry. I wrapped her in a blanket and held her to my chest to comfort her. She promptly peed through the blanket and onto my shirt. I wiped up the pee from her bottom, and switched the blanket for a dry one. Then, as I tried to console her, she emptied her bowels into the blanket. I cleaned her up again, as she continued to cry unconsolably. Next, dashing any hope that I could finally settle her down, she vomited the entire contents of her stomach onto my shoulder. She continued bawling, red all over with exasperation, while I cleaned her up for the third time. This time, after she was dressed for bed again, just as suddenly as she started, she stopped crying and mercifully went back to sleep. I had no idea why Jordan was so upset, especially when her sister was sleeping so soundly after we fed them. I couldn't understand it.

After I cleaned myself up and changed my shirt, I was on my way back downstairs to rejoin Paulette, when the phone rang. My brother Jeff was calling from Vancouver. He said three words: "He's gone, Jason!"

Dad had died of a massive heart attack, on his recliner in the den at home, while he and Mom were watching television. It happened at the exact time that Jordan went physically and emotionally hysterical. No one will ever convince me that this was a coincidence. For me, it's one of the mysteries of my life that reinforces the notion that people are connected in a spiritual sense.

In November of 1988, I attended an Italian Club Grey Cup banquet, with some teammates, including Peter Giftopoulos. "Gifto" had joined the Cats after making "The Interception," a game-winning catch of a throw by the opposition's Vinny Testaverde within the last 18 seconds of play in the previous season's Fiesta Bowl, which sealed the national championship for Penn State. He was a household name in Hamilton, but a totally down-to-earth and hard-working young teammate.

After dinner, Gifto and I were discussing off-season jobs, when local Cathedral High School coach Tom Gallagher approached us. I had never met Tom before, but he had coached Gifto and I had heard of his reputation as a great high school coach. Tom said to me, "Jason, I overheard you and Peter speaking about off-season jobs. Do you have a university degree?"

"Yes," I responded.

"Great. Have you ever considered teaching?"

I couldn't believe it. I told him that teaching was what I had originally been accepted for at UBC.

"There is a real shortage of teachers in Ontario right now and, if you have a degree and pass the interview process, you can substitute-teach with a letter of permission." He explained the application process, pointed me in the right direction, and said, "Good luck."

Over 30 years later, I still feel indebted to Tom Gallagher for the kindness he shared with me in that brief conversation. I didn't even know him, but he took the time to guide me back to the career path I always felt drawn toward. Another guardian angel.

Shortly after that conversation, I began substitute-teaching in the local school boards. I enjoyed it so much that I continued supply teaching between football seasons every year. Paulette and I decided that this would be a great career path when I retired from ball. She encouraged me in this new adventure.

"Slow Ride," Foghat (1975)

The next off-season, I also took a job in a group home for teenaged girls to expand my understanding of teen culture, and the teen perspective, to help with my teaching. At the time, I had no idea how valuable those lessons would be.

One resident of the home was a young pregnant girl who had been abandoned by her "true love" — the teenaged father of her child. I had great empathy for her and did whatever I could to accommodate her needs, acting as the father figure she didn't have. It had been explained to me that I was hired as the only male on staff to help provide this role for the girls. I took her, along with some of the other residents and staff, roller skating, to the mall, and other outings to give her some fun and hopefully give her some hope for her future as a young mother.

One day, after we spent a great day together and she got her allowance for good behaviour, she was nice as pie. In spite of this, when she was told she couldn't miss curfew that night, I became the target of her wrath. The conversation ended when she told me to fuck off.

Being confronted like this by a 15-year-old was very difficult for me at that time because I knew I had to act as a responsible guardian, regardless of the rage that built up inside me. In the past, on the football field, it meant that I'd take the guy's number and knock the snot out of him on the next play; after all, those were fighting words. But here, my hands were tied. Although my adrenaline was pumping and the hair on the back of my neck was standing up, I couldn't respond to my natural fight response as she screamed obscenities at me. I realized I didn't have the tools to deal with it. I felt emotionally helpless, unable to navigate the situation.

At the end of every shift, following effective social work practices, we had a debriefing session with the incoming shift staff and house managers. This ensured everyone was aware of any ongoing issues with residents.

Personally, these sessions were cathartic because I got to share my anxieties with experienced professionals in the field. These women had such insight into the "teenage animal" that I benefitted from every session, reducing my own angst.

Case in point, when I shared my dilemma with staff after my shift that day, I learned a valuable lesson. Their message to me was this:

> Jason, welcome to social work. Because of the hardships these kids have faced in life, they are angry at the world. As long as they get what they want from staff, they are well-behaved. But as soon as they don't, if it suits them, they'll spit in your face. In your case tonight, even if the Pope himself was standing in front of her, she would have told him to fuck off because she was blinded by her misplaced anger. So, you just have to learn not to take it personally — remember where it's coming from and it won't bother you so much.

In other words, until we walk in another person's shoes, we really can't understand the pain, from which their anger radiates indiscriminately.

This was invaluable in my teaching experience, because it taught me to build a relationship with my students, so I could understand what they brought to the classroom every day, and relate to this as much as possible to help them reach their academic potential.

I also learned from my time at the home that, after years of patient counselling, guidance, and mentoring from experienced social workers, many of the kids grow out of this angry-at-the-world mentality into successful members of society.

This also means that, although the job seems thankless at times, eventually social workers get a well-deserved sense of accomplishment from the success of their clients, albeit not instant gratification as their charges often demand.

◇◆◇

Despite the calming effect my new family responsibilities had on me off the field, I still had the rage of a bullied child within me — which I tapped into every time I played football.

Fortunately, I was blessed with a healthy dose of natural testosterone and when I combined it with the caffeine-boost I got from my two large game-day coffees, it induced a combative mood, which was the only way I could play the game.

To maximize the effect, my game-day routine consisted of the following: no sex the night before a game to enhance my testosterone levels; eating a pre-game meal of carbohydrates four hours before kick-off, filling my "boiler" with fuel for the game; four aspirins with a banana an hour before kick-off to mask my shin splints; two large coffees to peak my caffeine level for the game; then, find a quiet space to brew my anger while individually taping each knuckle in all my fingers.

I found that tearing thin strips of athletic tape and applying them in a figure-eight around individual knuckles allowed me to reinforce each knuckle but still have full movement. This was a preventative thing to reduce knuckle damage when holding jerseys in games, because sometimes when you're put in an awkward position, hanging on for dear life was the only way to stop your quarterback from getting hammered. That taping method is why my hands are in reasonably good shape compared to some guys — its not because I never held.

When I think about the damage some guys' hands took, Mike Samples comes to mind — the All-Star defensive lineman and my former defensive line coach in Saskatchewan now has fingers pointing in different directions at the same time. Chris Walby is another — his knuckles are so knobby with arthritis; I think they'll have to amputate the Hall of Famer's fingers to get all his rings off!

Finally, when I meditated in my dressing-room stall as part of my pre-game ritual, it was not to become peaceful. Yes, of course it was important for me to visualize my assignments and our "calls" on different plays, but I would always finish it by conjuring angry thoughts lurking in my subconscious. Images of the bullies I'd faced as a kid would flash through my mind. I would rekindle thoughts of assholes from the past, who treated me or my loved ones badly, simply because of their hubris — the biker spitting into my car window is a good example. This way, I could bring to the present the rage that was always streaming in the background. I'd be ready for a fight before the referee flipped the coin.

Terry Lehne, the talented Canadian defensive back, had his locker directly across from mine in the Ticats' dressing room. We were eye-to-eye on game day for years and we developed a unique rapport between two very different positions; while he prepared to fly around in open space covering the fastest guys on the field, I prepared to battle the toughest guys in the trenches.

Terry describes my pre-game ritual like this:

> On game day you changed, Jason. I've blocked the memory of how you looked before a game from my mind! The Jason from the [horror] movie had nothing on you, my friend! Your entire body somehow became bigger, and your face transformed into someone I felt I needed to apologize to for something I did [that was] horribly wrong to you! It was scary!

Thus, whether it was true or not, I went into every game I played believing that I was the toughest son-of-a-bitch on the field. That was my mindset when I stepped inside those white lines on game day — I was looking for a reason to fight.

With that in mind, one of the most memorable of these slugfests occurred in the 1988 season when I faced the Toronto Argonauts' Glenn Kulka. He was a tough bastard. He was as strong as an ox, with a motor; before joining the football trenches, he cut his teeth as an enforcer in the Western Hockey League. He also made the news when he broke the CFL bench-press record for doing the most reps at 225 pounds. It was public knowledge that he used steroids, which partly explains his incredible strength, but he also worked his ass off in the gym to enhance his natural athleticism.

Kulka and I had played against each other in the past, but this season, Coach Sal had the offensive line flipping to the strength of the field, similar to what most defenses do, so Kulka and I were head-to-head for the entire game — the battle was on.

It was always an emotion-filled game when the Argos came to Ivor Wynne Stadium. The local fans hated the Argos as much or more than the players did. To add fuel to the fire, many Argos fans would drive to Hamilton for the game wearing their colours. Some of whom arrived with the "drink till you fight" attitude, because there would inevitably be fights in the stands whenever our teams clashed.

It got so bad that sometimes I didn't even feel comfortable taking my helmet off in our own stadium because we never knew when some drunken visiting fan would throw a battery, a smuggled whiskey bottle, or a drink at the home bench. I can't even imagine what it would be like on the visitors' bench. It was made even crazier because Ivor Wynne Stadium was the only stadium I know of anywhere where both team benches were in dugouts, virtually underneath the first few rows of seats. There were three steps we had to climb up to leave the dugout. When we looked back from the field level in front of the dugout, we were almost eye-to-eye with the front-row fans.

Additionally, many of the home fans felt that as long as we beat the Argos, they were happy, it didn't matter what our overall record was. This was especially true of the annual Labour Day game, where we always played the Argos at home. This game became the mini–Grey Cup for the fans every year — they went nuts. Fights broke out throughout the stands, just because some guy was wearing the hated Argos' double-blue, or a Tiger-Cat fan yelled, "Argoooos suck!"

This was the setting in which Kulka and I were going head-to-head in the street-fight- within-the-game that day. During the second quarter, things really started to heat up between us — I guess I was snorting, holding, and banging people around more than usual. On one particular play when I was cruising down-field looking for an ear-hole shot, I crashed into a group of Argo defenders, Kulka yelled, "Get off the fucking steroids, Riley!"

I took offence to this because, of course, I had never done steroids. I responded, "Fuck you, Kulka, you get off the steroids, I'm on coffee!"

The battle intensified throughout the game, and the fur was flying. Kulka was tough as nails and neither of us were backing down. By the mid-third quarter, when we drove the field for a touchdown, he was going haywire, with verbal shots punctuating the physical shots that were exchanged on every play.

On the convert after the score, I decided I had had enough of his extracurriculars. Lined up head-to-head, both of us covered with snot, sweat, and blood, I knew he was going to try to bull-rush me back to Osbaldiston's lap, in an attempt to block the kick. I needed to shut Kulka down. After the snap, just before the kick, I jacked up his facemask with a hard left-hand shot, then drilled him in the jaw with my right.

I knew he was a hockey fighter, so I was prepared for a heavy response. After I hammered him, Kulka completely lost it and proceeded to unleash a flurry of blows to my head. Essentially, he used my helmet as a speed bag and delivered several alternating shots with both fists. As my head swung back and forth with each blow, I saw the orange flag being thrown by an official directly behind Kulka. I was no worse for wear because he was hitting my helmet and facemask. I didn't feel a thing.

The net result was that he got a fifteen-yard major penalty for unnecessary roughness. I didn't receive a penalty because it happened so fast the ref didn't see me smash him; he saw only the retaliation. Kulka was furious, as our teammates separated us.

After returning to our respective benches and while the verbal assault continued, the referees decided to eject him from the game for unsportsmanlike conduct. The ref walked past our bench to the visitors' dugout and informed their coach Bob O'Billovich that Kulka had been ejected from the game. If he was furious before, Kulka was now apoplectic.

As the ref escorted him down the near hash marks toward the visitors' dressing room, they had to pass in front of our bench. I could see Kulka scanning our dugout looking for me. I walked up the steps to the edge of the field and took my helmet off. He screamed, "I'll meet you in the parking lot after the game, Riley, you asshole!"

Pointing to my chin, I responded, "Right here, Kulka!" Now, there was smoke coming out of his ears because he was so incensed with anger, but there was nothing he could do about it. The ref grabbed his arm and directed him off the field and into the visitors' locker room, while he indignantly endured a loud chorus of boos and a shower of concession-debris confetti from the fans.

The important thing to me at the time was that we scored on the drive to take the lead, and I didn't get a penalty on the play. Ultimately, we won the game and when you win, it makes the physical demands of the game worth it. Winning builds the passion of the team, and raises the psyche of the fans in the entire city, because the destiny of the Tiger-Cats had become an important part of Hamilton's identity.

To top it all off, when I came into the dressing room the next day for our post-game rundown, Derksy had replaced my nameplate above my locker with a new title: "The Instigator."

Kulka went on to be a successful professional wrestler after his football career. Then he took up broadcasting, while raising his family. When we spoke recently, he said, "Jason, I always enjoyed playing against you because you were a warrior, and that's how the game should be played."

I appreciate Kulka's thoughts, coming from a fellow warrior in the trenches. I know he appreciates the work that goes into molding oneself for the game, physically, emotionally, and intellectually. Obviously, it is a major commitment and it becomes a huge part of a player's life. Further, this obsessive commitment doesn't end when you "make it" because training to get better is an ongoing challenge. If you let up in any way, you can be replaced by some younger, more talented player.

Personally, in spite of — and maybe because of — some of the physical challenges I'd experienced earlier in my career, my biggest issues were in my mind. Contrary to my tough exterior, I was very insecure. I was constantly worried that someone would take my job, especially during training camp. The fear of not doing enough kept me working hard my entire career.

In that vein, I'll share my thoughts on the physical rigours of the game. The game is so intense and the opposing offensive and defensive lines are so well-trained that the pure physicality of the trenches takes a toll on your body. After every game, you wake up the next day feeling like you've been hit by a car.

Every muscle in your body aches, and you can recall specific hits in the game that caused trauma to a particular area of your body, like the four distinct, deep, fingertip-sized bruises on your biceps from a defensive lineman grabbing your arm violently while attempting to get past you on pass rush to kill your quarterback; the deep-bone bruise in your forearm from a helmet hitting it like an anvil, when a defender flew in at full speed from the side to stop the gain as you drove your block into the running back for that extra yard; or the pain in your ribs when a linebacker's shoulder pad hammered your torso from behind while making a tackle, as you pulled around the corner on a toss looking to block the defensive halfback.

So, it is for the lineman every game. Every play includes a collision with another player weighing between 250 and 350 pounds, depending on your position and where your blocking scheme takes you. Whether it's pass or run, if you're not hitting someone and trying to knock them on their ass, you're not doing your job. At the professional level, this is true for every lineman in the game, on every play in the game, the end result being that when the clock reads "00," you've pushed yourself to the very limit of your physical ability.

By the end of the game, your body is so beaten up, you need several days to recover from the physical trauma. Good coaches schedule the practice week accordingly. Thus, if the game is on Saturday, Sunday is a rundown day to get the lactic acid out of your muscles; Monday is a low-contact day with film work and game planning in the classroom; and on the third day after the game — Tuesday — your body is recovered enough to begin hitting again.

When I played, there were no restrictions on hitting during practice in our collective bargaining agreement (CBA) between the league and the players' association. In our era, coaches could have the team in full gear and hitting in every practice if they wanted to. Today, though, the CBA has strict guidelines. Coaches have a limit to the number of days the team can wear full gear and hit during practice, with the intention of reducing injuries and extending playing careers.

1989 was a special year for a myriad of reasons. It began with David Braley buying the team from Harold Ballard in the off-season. After we became the apple of his eye by winning the Grey Cup in '86, Ballard had lost his infatuation with the team.

When he announced his intention to sell the team, he was impatient. No one stepped forward immediately, so he started grumbling in the media. Ballard decided to have all our football equipment loaded onto a transport truck to show the city council and the fans that he was serious; he would sell the equipment to the highest bidder and there would be no more Tiger-Cats.

That's when David Braley decided to purchase the team from Ballard. Braley and I met soon after he bought the team, when I volunteered to help unload the equipment from that transport trailer back into our dressing room at Ivor Wynne Stadium, symbolizing for the media that the Tiger-Cats weren't going anywhere. The Cats would stay.

"Time Stands Still," Rush (1987)

Two additions to our offensive line unit in 1989 were Darrell "Burly" Harle and Brian "Hutch" Hutchings. Harle was a big country boy from Saskatchewan who graduated from Michigan State, and was drafted by Saskatchewan in 1988. We gave him the nickname Burly because he was a prototypical centre, with a shorter stature, broad shoulders, and a thick, powerful build. His head was so big it had its own satellite system, and he had long, flowing brown hair. His physical stature reminded me of that other prairie great, Roger Aldag.

Burly was a good roommate on road trips. I would wake up early to shower, then watch the news on television before we went for breakfast. Without fail, when Burly woke up and went to the shower, he would be sure to stop directly in front of the television, scratching his hairy ass, just to make sure I was awake.

One time on a road trip, Harle brought his Halloween gorilla mask along for some hijinks. He went back to the room before I did to prepare. When I opened the door to our room, all the lights were out. I walked into the dark room, and the light switch didn't work. When I went to check the bulb, Burly jumped out from behind the corner, with the mask on his head, in his underwear. It scared the hell out of me, and I almost jumped out of my skin!

At home, Harle had a beautiful shepherd-collie cross named Sable. The dog loved him so much that whenever he returned home, Sable would run around in circles, with a big grin on her face, while pissing all over the linoleum floor. A lot of people would have scolded the dog for that, but

Harle reciprocated her love by giggling while he used a towel to mop up the floor.

On the field, Harle fit right in with our physical unit. He had a high football IQ, and a great work ethic. He earned a starting role after Scholz sustained a serious back injury, and played a pivotal role on our OL that iconic season.

"Panama," Van Halen (1984)

Hutch had joined us out of St. Mary's University. Hutch's dad was the famous professional wrestler Hartford Love, one of the notorious Love Brothers. As fate would have it, Hutch's dad had trained CFHOF member and Tiger-Cats great Angelo Mosca, back when Big Ang left football and began wrestling. Mosca lived with Hutch's dad in the States and wrestled against him many times. Some fans may not realize it, but Mosca wrestled longer than he played football. These two icons shared many wrestling stories of their rivalry over the years.

Hutchings must have inherited his athletic talent from his dad. When he first came into our dressing room, the one thing we noticed was the size of his calves. He actually had full-grown cows, not calves!

Hutch was a great addition to our group, on and off the field. Unfortunately for him, he was thrown to the wolves early because of circumstances involving me.

In our first exhibition game, I took some skin off my right elbow sliding on the iconic leaping tiger logo at centre field in Ivor Wynne Stadium. This logo was ancient and every spring, the grounds crew would paint it to bring it back to life. Over the years, the grit was locked into the paint, so although it looked impressive from the stands, it was like sandpaper on the turf.

My elbow became infected and I was put on oral antibiotics. This seemed to do the trick and the infection was lessening throughout the week, so I was cleared to play in our second exhibition game in Winnipeg.

I woke up the next day with a hot red tomato protruding from my right elbow, with a red line running up from my elbow towards my shoulder: I had blood poisoning. When we got back to Hamilton, I was admitted to the now-closed Chedoke Hospital and put on intravenous antibiotics. The medical staff in the hospital insisted I wouldn't be playing in our next game. This was disappointing to me because it was scheduled to be the first regular season game in the brand new Skydome stadium (now Rogers Centre), the largest stadium with a retractable roof in the world at the time. It had been a source of inspiration for me in all my off-season training to play in this "first."

Still determined to play, I decided to sneak into the physiotherapy room to work out on the stationary bike. So, in the off-hours, I coaxed the custodian to unlock the physiotherapy room for me. Then, with my mobile intravenous tree at my side, I rode the stationary bike for a cardio workout. I knew I needed to maintain my fitness level for the game, so I did this several times over the days I spent in the hospital. The fact that, for some reason, the game was scheduled for a Wednesday (July 12, 1989) meant that I had a few more days to recover than I would have during a normal week, although I was missing practice in the hospital.

Sure enough, the high concentration of antibiotics in the intravenous over several days did the trick; my infection cleared up, just as the doctor ordered. However, on the other hand, lying in the hospital bed on potent drugs essentially killed my fitness level, in spite of my secret bike workouts.

In addition to this, we were playing against a formidable Argonauts defence, featuring many great athletes. Their defensive line was stacked with studs like Jerald Baylis, Harold Hallman, Rodney Harding, Branko Vincic, and my old nemesis, Glenn Kulka. At linebacker, they had guys like Willie Pless, Bruce Holmes, and my old UBC teammate, Don Moen. All these guys could play and their defensive front seven was considered one of the strengths of their team.

Needless to say, when game day came, I was very excited to be playing in the first regular season CFL game in the state-of-the-art Skydome, hoping that my endurance wasn't totally shot from the infection and drugs. Luckily, I had Hutch as my back-up to step in for me when necessary. Coach Sal said he'd keep a close eye on me considering the circumstances.

I don't really remember much of what happened after kick-off. I do remember a real sense of pride as we trotted out on the field for our first offensive huddle in the Skydome. The new stadium was an amazing sight from field level. As the game went on, Coach Sal would check in on me and I would assure him that I was fine.

The rest of the story is based on conversations with teammates, Hutchings and Gorrell, and, of course, Coach Sal. Sometime in the second quarter after a long drive, I came off the field out of breath, and Sal asked if I was okay. I responded, “I’m fine, Coach,” as I took a seat on the bench to catch my breath.

Just before the next series was about to begin, Sal looked at me and exclaimed, “Riley’s eyes are rolling back in his head! Hutch, get in there!”

Hutch went into the first game of his career facing Glenn Kulka. When Hutch entered the game, he was nervous as hell and was not prepared for what happened next; Kulka tossed him around like a rag doll. After a few plays of the drive, Gorrell stepped in and said, “Take it easy on the rookie will ya, Kulka!”

As one of the biggest men in the league who plays with that edge that’s so important in the trenches, people generally listen to Gorrell. I was glad to hear that Gorrell helped out our buddy, Hutch, in his initiation to the trenches. It gave Hutch confidence that Big Miles was there to support him. Although I felt badly that I couldn’t finish the game, Hutchings settled down and played well to finish his first game in that historic first league game in the Skydome. Looking back at it now, blinded by my stubbornness to play in that game, I really did cost Hutchings physical and mental preparation time to be more prepared to face an intense competitor like Kulka. I should have listened to the medical experts.

Hutch had the last laugh, however. The “Feed the Cats” ad campaign that was running at that time included a large, regal Bengal tiger in a cage, which was borrowed from a local zoo and displayed at Ivor Wynne Stadium for every home game.

One of these games was against the Ottawa Rough Riders on a muggy August day in Hamilton. Derksy, Hutch, and I were doing our pre-game walk-about with our lowers on, and in team-issue t-shirts. We met up with some guys from Ottawa and went to get a closer look at the tiger. It was prowling around its cage, placed just outside the west end zone, below the scoreboard. Now we were standing about 10 to 15 yards from the cage, and it was amazing to be so close to such a gorgeous animal — it gave the name of our team a whole new meaning.

I had my back to the cage as we got absorbed in a conversation about the game. Soon, I felt what seemed like raindrops and I looked up, but the sky was clear. I felt more of that warm rain shower as the boys backed away from me tentatively, with eyes wide open. I turned toward the cage to see the tiger with its leg lifted towards us, the bars of the cage the only protection. Suddenly, before I could move, it released a powerful stream of urine in my direction, which the cage bars atomized, creating a wide shower — I was being pissed on by a Bengal tiger! The boys had all backed off because they saw the big cat raise its leg before the blast, but my t-shirt got soaked.

I don't know anyone else that has been sprayed by a tiger, but I believe it can be looked at in one of two ways: one, it is just plain bad luck, being in the wrong place at the wrong time, to be pissed on by a large animal; or, two, it's a very rare honour and therefore very lucky to be pissed on by such an exotic and majestic beast. Being an eternal optimist, I chose to believe the latter. So, I went back to the locker room, changed my shirt and used it as a source of positive karma in mentally preparing for the game.

In retrospect, it turned out to be the first domino in a long list of positive events, not only for me, but for the entire team. First, we won the game 52–34 to take our season record to seven and four. Then, we finished the season in first place in the Eastern Conference, with a 12–6 record, which broke the all-time franchise single-season win record. In addition, Gorrell and I were selected as CFL All-Canadians on the offensive line, along with our teammates Tony Champion, Grover Covington, Rocky DiPietro, and Mike Walker, at their respective positions. Finally, that year, the team finished the season playing in the most exciting Grey Cup game ever played. We owed it all to that tiger!

During the week of the 1989 Grey Cup, after a midweek practice in Toronto preparing for the big game, Rooster and I went shopping at the Eaton Centre. I found some beautiful cowboy boots on sale. They were burgundy-brown in colour with brass tips on the toes — I bought them on the spot.

After meetings that night, a group of us went out to get our minds off the game and have a couple beers. Wearing my new boots, we took a cab to the pub. This turned out to be a big mistake.

The cab driver was new to the city and didn't speak English very well. We told him we were meeting friends at the Zanzibar Club and he claimed in his broken English that he knew where it was. This was pre-GPS, so when he pulled the cab over and said the pub was just down the block, we didn't question it, we just paid him and hopped out, walking in the direction he pointed.

After several blocks of walking in my new boots, my heels began to feel warm and I was conscious of the risk of blisters. By then, we were past the point of no return, so I had to make a choice to risk it by leaving my boots on, or take them off and walk barefoot the rest of the way in downtown Toronto. I thought that there was no way the cabbie could have been too far off the mark, so I decided to leave my boots on the rest of the way. After several more blocks, we finally arrived at our destination. My heels were getting sore now, but I thought we could sit down and have a couple of beers and get back to the hotel without any more walking.

Well, after several of our teammates showed up, the beer was really flowing. One round led to another and it turned into a party; I was feeling no pain. We decided to walk to another pub near by, then another. We met a bouncer at one pub who I worked with at the Boo. The boys got a little rowdy when we had to wait in line, and I told them not to fuck with this guy because I'd seen him in action — he was a big strong, fifth-degree black belt. We moved on to another pub.

The next morning, I woke up to searing pain in my heels. When I looked at them, I was alarmed to see a red hole, the size of a nickel, on each of my heels. They were far beyond blisters. The blisters I felt forming early last night were totally gone, only exposed flesh remained. My heart sank as I realized the damage the new boots had done to my feet, with the biggest game of the year only a few days away.

I went to see Jonesy right away. He just shook his head in disbelief. He said I had to come for treatment early every morning to have them taken care of or they could become infected and I may not be able to play in the Grey Cup. So, I showed up every morning for the rest of the season for him to do his treatment.

Jonesy is a good man, but I didn't know how sadistic he could be with his treatments. He asked me to lie on his padded trainer's bench face down. Then he poured friar's balsam on my open wounds that he said would seal the skin. Jonesy's cure seared the raw flesh on my heels all right, but it was excruciating. I gritted my teeth and squeezed the sides of the table as hard as I could for what seemed like forever, as Jonesy laughed out loud about how stupid I was to do this so close to the big game. I could have blamed the cab driver for this predicament, but I knew in my heart that I shouldn't have worn the new boots, and now I was paying my penance.

After the friar's balsam, Jonesy covered the wounds with a "second skin" bandage, wrapped them with gauze, then taped foam donuts on the heels, so that the raw parts wouldn't contact the back of my shoes and cause more damage. He instructed me to wear flipflops as often as I could to eliminate friction all together.

We went through this ritual every morning and every day again after practice for the rest of the week. The boys would never let me live this down, with comments like, "That's what happens when you buy boots at the dollar store," or "Don't be so cheap, Riley, you get what you pay for!" I had no one to blame but myself, so I swallowed my pride and took the heat.

On game day, Jonesy's treatment had paid off and when I put my game face on, the blisters were really a non-issue.

"While My Guitar Gently Weeps," The Jeff Healey Band (1990)

The starters on our offensive line for the 1989 Grey Cup game between us and the Saskatchewan Roughriders were: Mike Derks (LT), Darrell Harle (LG), Dale Sanderson (C), me (RG), and Miles Gorrell (RT). We played hard to protect Kerrigan and our offence moved the ball well. Coach Sal still had us flipping our offensive line to the strength of the field, so Gorrell and I were always to the wide side. This meant that we fought the same guys for most of the game and the battles got hotter as the game wore on. Sask's front seven was always tough so it was a war in the trenches again, especially with the Grey Cup ring at stake. My personal brawl in this one was with Gary Lewis, one of the steadiest defensive tackles there was.

During the game, Coach Bruno was going insane on the sidelines and after the game, he almost threw the microphone at the television camera in the press conference because he was so upset about the refereeing in the game.

On the field, during the game, we players tuned it out. I thought it was a tough game between two good teams, with the pace of an NHL playoff game: the last team with the ball won the game. However, watching the game later, the referee bias was clear.

Incidentally, on the field after Tony Champion made "The Catch," a mid-air twisting leap to catch a 13-yard pass from Kerrigan to tie up the score in the game, Gorrell and I were walking off the field after that long physical drive, when we checked the clock and saw that there were seconds left in the game. We were both confident that our defence would hold, and the game was destined for overtime. I said to him, "This could be the first overtime Grey Cup game ever played. Let's win it in overtime."

Gorrell, aside from being a physical freak, is also a walking encyclopedia of the game. "No, Jas, there has been an overtime Grey Cup game already," he responded. "In 1961, Winnipeg beat Hamilton in overtime, in Toronto." I couldn't believe that in the heat of the battle we were engaged in at the time, he remembered this piece of Grey Cup history without missing a beat. I was so jacked-up on caffeine and adrenaline I could barely calculate a tied score.

Unfortunately, as most football pundits know, the game didn't get to overtime because Saskatchewan drove the ball down the field and kicked the game-winning field goal with no time left on the clock.

But in retrospect, we were doomed before the opening kick-off. Bill "The Undertaker" Baker was the commissioner of the CFL in 1989, after being GM for the Riders the previous year. At the start of the Grey Cup festival pep rally, meant to honour both teams, Baker wore a Rider tie to the event. This is the commissioner of the league, who pays the refs and is supposed to be neutral, clearly indicating his bias for the team he had only recently managed. I'm not one to believe in conspiracy theories, and I'm not saying it was a conspiracy against our team in the '89 Grey Cup game, but when the commissioner shows bias like this, he doesn't show neutrality and fair play, as he should. When we saw the tie that he was wearing, several members of our team walked out of the event in protest.

Another factor that day was that we had just won the Grey Cup three years previously, and the Riders hadn't won it for 23 years. Well-loved players, like Aldag, Poley, Donald Narcisse, and Ray Elgaard on offence, and Vince Goldsmith, Eddie Lowe, and Gary Lewis on defence, had never won a cup with the Riders, so they had sympathy from the majority of the crowd. While we had a relatively small group of boisterous Ticat fans at the game, the majority of the crowd cheered for Saskatchewan — especially the local Argo fans who hated us with a passion. For the first Grey Cup game ever played in the Skydome (now Rogers Centre), the sold-out crowd of nearly 60 thousand was awash with green-clad fans. Shit, if I wasn't playing in the game, I would have been sentimental toward the underdog Riders, too!

I believe that the raucous atmosphere in the stadium had an influence on the referees as the game played out. A good example of this is the interception we had deep in our end zone early in the fourth quarter; our defensive back, Will Lewis, clearly had possession of the ball in bounds. The referees called pass-interference on the play, giving the ball back to the Riders. The next play resulted in a field goal. We lost by a field goal.

Rob Vanstone, the writer for the *Regina Leader-Post*, was quoted about that play later: "That looked like an interception to me. If there had been video replay back then, you may be reading a different story. That play could have and probably should have been turned over on video replay. Instead, the Riders keep the ball and kick a field goal to go up 40–33."[15]

On top of this, there were several non-calls by the refs that favoured the Riders and extended their drives — these are much easier to notice if you mute the sound on your TV to take out the crowd noise, so as to be unbiased. Consistently, especially late in the game, you'll see plays where Kerrigan's passes to DiPietro and Champion were accurate and catchable, but the defensive backs interfered with the receivers, and there's no call from the officials. If the calls had been made, our drives would have been extended and probably resulted in a different game outcome.

Coach Bruno was quoted after the game, "The defender held him by the jersey [on the video, you can clearly see the jersey being pulled back]. DiPietro would have caught that ball — I know he would've."[16]

---

[15] Zarum, D. 2012. *The greatest game: An oral history*. Sportsnet. Rogers Publishing Limited.
[16] Zarum, D. 2012. *The greatest game: An oral history*. Sportsnet. Rogers Publishing Limited.

Even my former roommate in training camp and grizzled veteran Roughrider receiver Ray Elgaard was quoted about the refing after the game, "There were lots of calls and non-calls that were a little bit questionable. ...There were three or four head-scratchers, but that's the way it goes."[17]

There is precedent for this sort of subconscious referee bias as influenced by a passionate crowd. In 1987, for example, when Marvin Hagler fought Sugar Ray Leonard for the world middleweight boxing title, Hagler should have won the fight. When I watched the fight live, I thought the refs had it wrong, so I re-watched the video recording with the volume turned off and counted the punches carefully. Objectively, Hagler landed many more punches than Leonard and clearly should have won the fight. However, the crowd favoured Leonard from the start, and when he started showboating and doing his windmill routine, they went nuts. The referees judging the fight were clearly influenced by the crowd and missed the fact that many of Leonard's punches missed the mark, while most of Hagler's punches landed.

Nonetheless, I don't begrudge the Roughrider players for winning the game. They were a good team and they played a great game. If we were going to lose, let it be to this team, for their great fans, and the core of veteran players on the team who I enjoyed playing with during my short stay in Regina.

In a final note on this incredible game, "The Catch" by Champion became iconic in the football world. Fred Scione, a high school teacher I later taught with, was at the game, sitting in the front row of the first balcony, in the same corner of the end zone where Champion made that acrobatic catch to tie the game. Fred was a true gentleman and a life-long Tiger-Cats fan. Fred was very passionate about Champion's catch. He said that the 1989 Grey Cup game was the best game he ever saw, and his favourite memory was The Catch.

Fred told me it was the most exciting thing he ever saw. When Champion caught the ball, in spite of his fractured ribs, to tie the game 40–

[17] Ibid.

40 with only 44 seconds left on the clock, Fred totally forgot where he was. He leapt into the air cheering deliriously, and without realizing it, began to go over the railing. He swore that if it wasn't for his friend beside him quickly grabbing the back of his jacket to pull him back, he would have fallen over the railing several stories above field level. He had never been so excited in his life.

Surprisingly, in 1990, after that great previous season, Coach Al was on the hot seat when we went on a six-game losing streak. However, this is the same coach who had led us to three Grey Cups in a row, with three different starting quarterbacks: Dieter Brock in 1984, Ken Hobart in 1985, and Mike Kerrigan in 1986. This had never been done before, or since. On top of that, he coached us to the best record in franchise history (12–6) and the most exciting Grey Cup game ever played, in 1989. In his eight years as head coach, Al amassed a .500 record and took us to four Grey Cups in total. Clearly, Al Bruno deserved more recognition than he received as head coach of the Hamilton Tiger-Cats.

Despite this previous stellar record, on this occasion, I believe team owner David Braley listened to the wrong people regarding Coach Bruno: Braley fired Coach Al. Braley also didn't take into consideration the fact that we had 12 starters injured at the time. Us veteran players still had confidence that Coach Al would turn the ship around and get us back into the playoffs, as he usually did in our four-team Eastern Conference.

It was a dark day for the franchise when Braley decided to fire Al, who all the players loved, and hire a guy named David Beckman. Beckman was a poser who talked a good game, and had "NFL" in small print on his resume as a player scout. Beckman turned out to be a disaster.

Just a couple of examples of his incompetence will suffice to make my point here. First, Beckman had zero understanding of the Canadian game. He didn't realize that because of our three-down system, special teams are essential. Here, coaches say there are three equally important aspects of the game: offence, defence, and special teams. The entire organization approaches it that way at every level of the game. General managers and player scouts are always on the lookout for a better kicker, or better special teams' players to shore up this aspect of their team.

Likewise, coaches and players know the importance of special teams meetings and practice time, because one big play on specials — a blocked punt, or a kick return for a touchdown — can turn the whole game in your favour. However, Beckman's ignorance of our game meant that he thought special teams meetings were a waste of time.

Beckman didn't understand the significance of goal line and short-yardage situations, either. It's common knowledge that although short-yardage plays are the least-used in an average game statistically, their outcome has far more impact than the average play to maintain possession of the ball in the open field, or to score on the goal line. When we questioned the lack of a goal line-short-yardage package during an offensive meeting, Beckman actually said, "If we have to run a short-yardage play in a game, we'll be desperate, so we'll act desperately and wing it when we need it." Consequently, the offence was totally unprepared for any short-yardage situation in a game because we hadn't practiced it.

Additionally, players often witnessed Beckman, at both home and away games, fill his Gatorade bottle with draft beer in the dressing room from the keg of beer left on ice for the players after the game.

This may explain his behaviour at half-time of an exhibition game in Ottawa at the start of the following season. We've all shed a tear after losing an important playoff game that brings a season to a crashing end, because it's an emotional sport that demands everything from us. However, during his first (and only) training camp as head coach in 1991, Beckman embarrassed himself by crying during his half-time speech to the team because we were losing. He was blubbering that we weren't playing for him, and his whole world was crashing down on him. This was during an exhibition game, which is just what the name implies: a game for new and veteran players to exhibit their skills for the coaches, meaningless to the standings, with many starters not even dressed for the game. It was very sad.

This was the guy who replaced Al Bruno, one of the most respected player-coaches there ever was. Thankfully, Braley fired Beckman partway through that 1991 season, but the damage had been done: the team was in great turmoil. After having a classy guy like Al Bruno being replaced by a clown like Beckman, this was inevitable.

Beckman was replaced by John Gregory, which was a major upgrade at face value. Unfortunately, he came to Hamilton like a little peacock, his ego primped by Saskatchewan's victory over Hamilton in the '89 Grey Cup game — a game that, in my opinion, we should never have lost. The team's combined 1991 season record under Beckman and Gregory was 3–15.

This brings us to what I think of as the "white shoes story," an amusing inside story, which illustrates how important communication is on the offensive line — though it wasn't funny to me at the time.

Coach Sal was preparing us for our upcoming game in Winnipeg. Sal had identified a tricky front where they shifted from a 3–4 defence, which they usually ran, to a 4–3 front with the middle linebacker, Paul Randolph, lined up on the LOS on the wide side of the field. Coach Sal wanted a big man blocking Randolph as opposed to one of our running backs, because he was a great athlete and a good pass rusher. If they lined up in this front, we had to slide our line laterally to the strong side, to get our tackle blocking Randolph.

Sal had installed this adjustment using all the appropriate player numbers and expected us to communicate accordingly, sliding to their personnel based on number recognition. However, Dale Sanderson, who at centre would make the call in the game, noticed on the film that Randolph was the only player on their defence who wore white cleats. "Coach, that's easy for me to identify," he said. "Randolph has the only white shoes on the defence, so I'll just call the slide to the guy in the white shoes. Fellas, to help clarify the read when this situation occurs, they only do it to the wide side, with white shoes out there rushing off the edge. I'll call "slide" and we'll all slide and pick up one man over to the slide side. Is that okay with you, Coach?"

To be clear, this meant that when Dale called "slide" on the front-side of the play, Gorrell would slide to his right to block Randolph (with his white shoes), I would slide to Gorrell's guy, and Dale would slide to my guy, the open tackle, Mike Gray. The backside guard and tackle would have to slide to the nose tackle and the BS linebacker. The RB would check the backside edge, as Kerrigan, the QB, would step to his right and throw the ball quickly to avert pressure from the blitzing front.

Coach Sal, who always allowed us input into whatever scheme he wanted, said, "Sounds easy enough to me, although I'd rather you used the proper numbers. Just don't screw it up!"

With this in our game plan, we went to Winnipeg, confident that we could pick up and block any front they threw at us. They were a talented defence and we needed to give Kerrigan the time he needed to throw the ball.

Sure enough, on a second and long situation, Sanderson saw "White Shoes" line up outside to our right. "Slide right!" he shouted.

I echoed "Slide right!" as I prepared to slide to my right to pick up the man over Gorrell, so he could pick up White Shoes, knowing Sanderson would come to pick up my man, Mike Gray.

Unfortunately, at that moment, just before snapping the ball, Sanderson saw another defender wearing white shoes in the middle of the defence; he instantly called "Off!" as he snapped the ball.

The problem was that the "off" call was so late, I was already committed to the slide call. Anticipating the snap, I was in motion to my right when Dale snapped the ball. This meant that I slid into Gorrell, who apparently didn't hear the original "slide" call, while Sanderson stayed on his own man. The net result was that everyone was blocked except my guy, Mike Gray, who came unblocked up the middle and sacked Kerrigan mercilessly. Now I was the scapegoat who almost got our QB killed on national TV!

Boy, I was mad. It's not enough that Mike Gray was a great player, and I had already gone several rounds in this brawl to keep him off our QB, but now we were giving him confidence by gifting him with the easiest sack he ever had in his life.

Sanderson explains, "Jason, when we left the field after that play, I ran off the field straight to Sal, whose eyes were as big as saucers, wondering what the hell just happened, and I told him. Then I said, 'Riley is coming over here and he's pissed! Be prepared, here he comes!' I had to get to him before you did, 'cause you were coming!"

"Mean Street," Van Halen (1981)

In 1990 we signed offensive tackle Dave "Big Irv" Richardson away from the Edmonton Elks, as part of the Mike Walker-restricted free agency deal. We were losing my friend and all time great, Mike Walker, but we needed Richardson because, we had some injuries on the offensive line.

Richardson had previously signed with the Elks as a 19-year-old out of the Edmonton Junior Wildcats program. Interestingly, Richardson tells a story from before he joined the Ticats roster that shows the impact of our great Hamilton fans on the visiting teams when they came into our hallowed old stadium. As a rookie, Richardson was starting at right offensive guard for the first time against Hamilton at Ivor Wynne Stadium. He explains a respected teammate's warning just before the game:

I was playing euchre with Hector Pothier in the visitors' dressing room before the game, on a hot muggy day with no air conditioning, when Pothier warned me about the fans.

Pothier said, 'Dave, this is a place like you've never seen before. You will be so close to the fans, they can touch you on the sidelines. Whatever you do, don't take your helmet off because the fans will throw shit at you. It is a crazy atmosphere here. Don't even turn around to acknowledge them, or they'll tear you apart!'

Although he meant well, Pothier hadn't actually built my confidence. Knowing that I'd be facing one of the best defensive fronts in the league, with the likes of Grover Covington and Mike Walker, the fact that I had to deal with the rowdy Hamilton fans on top of it made me a little nervous!

Richardson was still a young pup when he joined the Cats the following year and had some injury issues before he joined us, which made some people question his toughness. I took him under my wing because he was a great guy and a talented offensive tackle. I wanted to help him to dispel any notion of not being tough enough for our unit.

In one home game at Ivor Wynne soon after joining us in Hamilton, we were on a long drive and as I returned to the huddle, I noticed Richardson was down on one knee holding his hand. I said, "What's wrong, Dave?"

"I think I broke my fucking finger, Jas!" he responded.

I said, "That's okay, you've got nine more, get back in the damn huddle and get ready to play!" He came back to the huddle, shaking his hand, and finished the drive.

Richardson recalls what happened next:

After we scored on that drive, I went to the sideline with a broken finger and showed Jonesy that it was all bent out of shape. I asked him if he could tape it up so I could finish the game.

Jonesy said to me, ‘Okay, Dave, hold your hand still, I have to set the finger before I tape it up. I’m gonna count to three then pop it back in.

‘Ready?’

‘Yes.’

‘One…’ Pop!

‘Ow! Shit, you didn’t wait till three, Jonesy!’

Richardson finished the game and his toughness was never an issue in the locker room again after that. He developed into an outstanding offensive tackle of the same ilk as the rest of our unit. I really enjoyed playing in the trenches alongside him until I retired.

Richardson recalls, “There were times when our offensive line was so dominant that some defenders wanted to leave the game. There were a few over the years that faked injuries to get out of the game because we were beating them up so badly.”

“I Get Around,” The Beach Boys (1964)

Regardless of our win-loss record, we would find ways to enjoy our offensive line fraternity off the field between games, in spite of the administrative politics. On hot summer days, Sanderson would invite the offensive line to his place to cool down in his above-ground swimming pool. It was round, with a 24’ diameter, and about 5’ deep. After a few beers and burgers, the belly flop contest would begin. Man, they were painful. The neighbours could hear the “crack” as we took turns trying to make the most noise and the highest splash with each flop.

Inevitably, the whirlpool brigade would start. With six or eight 300 lb-bodies, first walking to build up momentum, then running in circles, we'd create a whirlpool that would suck down anyone who got stuck in the middle. When we got her going really well, buckets of water slopped over the sides of the pool onto the grass. The faster we went, the more water shot out of the pool. Come to think of it, this was actually really good mid-season "hydrotherapy" for the aches and pains of our lower bodies.

The only draw back was that when we were done, with everyone's girth removed from the pool, Sanderson would have to refill half the pool for his kids to have a decent swim!

Stu Laird was a thirteen-year veteran of the Calgary Stampeders, who played tough, consistent football. We had many battles in the trenches over the years, but the thing that stands out most about him was that he was part of my most embarrassing moment ever at Ivor Wynne Stadium.

The play was an outside screen pass to the tailback, in which, as left guard, I was supposed to give the defensive tackle (in this case, Laird) the inside lane, then pin him inside while the quarterback lobbed the ball over our heads to the tailback settled outside our left tackle. The problem was that, unbeknownst to me, the defensive end read the play and grabbed the tailback, so the quarterback couldn't throw the ball to him. Unfortunately for me, I looked like a total loser as I deposited Laird onto the lap of our quarterback, still standing in the collapsed pocket with the ball. The notoriously vocal crowd at Ivor Wynne went ballistic, seeing me gift the opposing team with a sack to end our drive. The boos rained down on me, especially from those raised voices behind the home bench. My name was mud on national television as well.

Over the decade that I plied my trade in that stadium, this was the worst feeling I ever had. Knowing that it was a broken play is no consolation because the perception was that I had let down my team and my home fans; Stu Laird was a stud! At least, until the next drive, when we managed a few first downs and I was able to redeem myself with some solid blocks. In football circles, you're only as good as your last play.

"Teach Your Children," Crosby, Stills, Nash & Young (1969)

In contrast, the best thing about 1991 was the birth of the twins' brother, Jason Jr. Being the off-season, there was no red-eye flight this time, as there was when the twins arrived; I was fully prepared with my new Reebok pumps and warm-up suit ready to go, though I had driven to D'Youville College, in Buffalo, N.Y., for my teacher's college interview with the dean of education when Junior was a couple of weeks overdue. As soon as I told Professor DiSibio the situation, he ushered me directly to the front of the long line, made up of mostly younger applicants who didn't carry a pager for their pregnant wife. Paulette and her mom, Roxine, who had flown out from Vancouver, went shopping to help bring him along and I hurried back from Buffalo.

It worked, because Paulette went into labour when they arrived home from their trip to the mall. I didn't want to cause Paulette any undue stress on the way to the hospital, so I diligently obeyed all the traffic laws. When I stopped at a red light, with no traffic in sight, she blasted me and began the endless stream of obscenities I'd face until the delivery. Her situation was all my fault (again) and she was in no mood to let me forget it.

You see, we knew the exact moment Jason was conceived. One evening, during the previous 1990 training camp, Paulette called me after dinner and told me, "If you want a boy, come home tonight after meetings and it will happen."

I clearly had no choice in the matter. After our team meetings, I flew home in the 280Z, we had our fling, then I sped back to Brock University. Luckily, I snuck back into our dorms without running into a coach, so I was never fined for missing curfew.

I have no idea how Paulette knew, not only that this was the optimum time to get pregnant, but also to predict the sex of our child. Paulette has always had an uncanny sense of women's intuition. She could always spot a fraud a mile away — in my experience, it's one more thing that makes the female sex superior to us mere males. In the delivery room, after Jason's birth, I cut the umbilical cord, and the nurse gave Junior to me, because they needed to attend to Paulette.

As I held him, Jason Jr. raised his head up and we briefly made eye-contact — then he head-butted me in the chest. The nurse was shocked, saying, "I've never seen a newborn baby with the strength to lift its head like that." I gushed with pride and bathed in the wonder of life once more. It was the most rewarding feeling in the world to know that we now had three beautiful children.

It was one of those amazing moments in life, so full of emotion it was almost incomprehensible, my mind racing through past hurdles overcome, striving for personal growth. Paulette had now fully and officially domesticated Mad Dog with this third blessing and euphoria of child birth. Parenting three children has a way of humbling a person, and rearranging one's priorities.

Soon, with Paulette's blessing, I was enrolled in teacher's college, preparing to support my family after football. I would take my first semester in January, which didn't conflict with the football season.

One of the most rewarding things from teachers' college resulted from an assignment in one of my courses on teen culture. It wasn't the assignment that excited me. It was the fact that I had a chance to reconnect with my old friend Bernie Custis. I knew Bernie's background in coaching and education was vast, so he came to mind immediately. I contacted him to arrange an interview for the assignment and he welcomed me into his home.

Bernie shared many stories that day about how important the game of football is for young men to learn the things that are important for success in any field of work. He shared stories about his career as a player and the obstacles he faced being a Black quarterback in the U.S. system. He shared stories about his time as head coach at McMaster University. But one particular story resonated with me because of my experience of being bullied in my youth.

When Bernie was head coach of the Burlington Braves Junior Football Team, a kid tried out who had a reputation as a bully. The assistant coaches told Bernie they didn't want the kid on the team because he was a bad apple and would bring a negative attitude to the team.

Bernie kept the guy on the roster anyway, taking him under his wing. This was riveting for me because I hated bullies and, up until now, I hadn't really considered the root cause of the behaviour. I listened to Bernie's story with renewed interest.

As Bernie got to know him, he became aware that the kid had a rough family life and had no connection with school, or anything else in the community. Bernie concluded that his bullying behaviour served to build himself up at the expense of smaller kids. This story really resonated with me because I'd experienced it; it gave me more insight into the causes of bullying and how to help prevent it.

Bernie said he began to build up the kid's self-confidence in practice. He continued to encourage him to be a part of the team and in turn, the kid committed himself to the team. It was the first time in his life that this young man had ever felt like he belonged to something good. He worked hard in practice and, with encouragement, began to become a solid player.

After a competitive season, this kid earned the Most Improved Player Award and actually cried tears of joy when Bernie awarded the trophy to him. The team gave him a standing ovation.

The power of football to transform boys into men was shown when that same kid became a hard-working tradesman and father, happily supporting a family of his own. The pride with which this great former coach shared the story of this young man's life was clear in his glowing face. It has helped me to be a better teacher and coach, knowing that such an icon in the field believed in the power of football to transform lives.

In fact, Bernie was such a respected educator and role model for kids during his career after his playing days were over, as teacher and high school principal, that the Hamilton Public School Board named a high school after him. Fittingly, it is right across the street from the new Tim Hortons Field, which replaced venerable old Ivor Wynne Stadium.

It turned out that my timing in entering teachers' college was perfect, given the direction the Tiger-Cats were going. The following year, in August 1992,

David Braley sold the team to a not-for-profit community group, whose investors included John Michaluk and Hamilton lawyer Roger Yachetti.[18,19]

The best thing the new ownership did that year was bring in future CFHOF quarterback Damon Allen. What a pleasure it was to play with this true gentleman of the game. I loved blocking for him, even if it was for only one season. Allen threw the ball a mile and led the team in rushing yards, too. We went 11 and 7 that season with Allen in the huddle.

In the Eastern Final, we fought hard against the Blue Bombers in Winnipeg. Sadly, we lost the game after beating the Blue Bombers twice in the regular season. With Allen at the helm of our offence, we had a great year, but our season ended there.

Unfortunately, Allen left for Edmonton after that season to play for the great Ron Lancaster. There, too, he led his team in passing and rushing, leading Edmonton to the 1993 Grey Cup championship.[20]

Contemporaneously, Joe Zuger retired as general manager of the club in 1992, ending a successful decade as GM. Zuger was the quintessential GM, going about his business of running a winning franchise with dignity and class. Under his management, we won four Eastern Championships and the 1986 Grey Cup. He had worked his way up from player scout in 1972, when they also won the Grey Cup. Zuger's playing days include a record that still stands for throwing eight touchdowns in a single game; he also holds the record for the longest pass completion in Tiger-Cats history, for a 108-yard toss and run to Dave Fleming.[21]

According to football lore, he was also one of the few quarterbacks who kicked converts for some of his own touchdown throws, and he was a league-leading punter for several years. He had a remarkable career, for which many people (including me) believe he should be in the CFHOF. I had

---

[18] Hamilton Tiger-Cats. n.d. *History of the Hamilton Tiger-Cats*. Url: https://ticats.ca/history-of-the-hamilton-tiger-cats-football-club/ (accessed May 18, 2023).

[19]Milton, S. 2006. Hamilton Tiger-Cats. *The Canadian Encyclopedia*. Url: https://www.thecanadianencyclopedia.ca (accessed May 18, 2023).

[20] Stats Crew. n.d. 1993. *Edmonton Eskimos game-by-game results*. Url: statscrew.com (accessed May 18, 2023).

[21] Snelgrove, B. 2009. *Sixties profile: Joe Zuger*. Hamilton Tiger-Cats. Url: https://ticats.ca/sixties-profile-joe-zuger/ (accessed May 18, 2023).

the pleasure of negotiating all my own player contracts with Zuger until his retirement.

Unfortunately, during the off-season after Zuger left, in addition to his head coaching role, Gregory was named general manager. Word got out that he planned on renegotiating player contracts. In spite of being named Eastern Conference All-Star and 1992 Tiger-Cats Offensive Lineman of the Year, Paulette and I were prepared for me to take a modest pay cut to help support the team. However, nothing prepared us for the shock of Gregory demanding I take a 50% pay cut!

I couldn't believe it. I refused, but ended up having to swallow a sizeable cut anyway. Gregory knew that I had a wife, three kids, and a mortgage to pay, but he had no sympathy for our family. He knew we loved the City of Hamilton and we weren't going anywhere, so he figured I'd play for peanuts. This was a foreshadowing of things to come, it was apparent to me that if Gregory had his way, I was on the way out the door, just as Walker and Gorrell were unceremoniously shipped out previously.

"Nobody Knows You When You're Down and Out," Count Basie (1936)

That year, we went from having an amazing training table at Brock University for every training camp, with all-you-can-eat buffet meals three times a day, to eating submarine sandwiches between training camp practices in the dressing room at Ivor Wynne Stadium — in wet gear because the team couldn't afford proper laundry services.

Accordingly, during the 1993 season, the club was cutting back in every department to stay in operation. My old friend, trainer Ray Jones recently said, "Things like athletic tape, pre-wrap, medical supplies, ointments, and analgesic balms for injury treatment were sorely lacking." This was making his job very difficult because he lacked what he needed to treat the players.

Lineman Bob MacDonald arrived in Hamilton from Calgary just in time for this chaos, unfortunately for him. MacDonald had played at McMaster under Bernie Custis.

MacDonald added his perspective recently when he said this:

> To my shock, disbelief, and horror, at my first rundown with the Cats, guys were [running] in street clothes, dress shoes, etc. and after having been in Calgary — no good! I was wondering, 'What the hell is going on here?' That stuff would never fly in Calgary.
>
> Gregory...was HC and GM. Greg Mohns was player personnel...I think. When I got released going into game 18, I had a note on my locker saying, 'Come see me' from Mohns. It was written on a sheet from a 'Property of Kansas City Chiefs' pad.

Unfortunately, I pulled my right hamstring in training camp that year. It wasn't even on the field, it was in our makeshift weight room on the Cybex machine, which is supposed to reduce injuries, not cause them. After the injury, I went to Jonesy's physiotherapy clinic every morning for treatment. The problem was that we had no depth at offensive line because of the financial cutbacks. In fact, I shouldn't have even been practicing, but I was actually playing games. Jonesy made sure I had enough meds to survive: I would take painkillers and anti-inflammatories to get through games and practices, and I continued to see Jonesy at least once a day for treatment.

Later in the season, Jonesy told me that John Michaluk had actually come into the training room to ask him if I was faking an injury to avoid being cut on September 1, the final cut day for veterans. (According to our collective bargaining agreement, after September 1, veteran players' salaries were guaranteed — and a veteran could not be cut if they were injured.)

To me, this was the last straw. In my decade with the Cats, I had played through chronic shin splints, blisters, lacerations, contusions, and fractures. I prided myself on toughness and would never fake an injury. Now, I was finding out that Michaluk had questioned my personal integrity.

The football club was nearing financial bankruptcy, I was playing injured (mainly because I was not given the time I needed to heal), and now administration was questioning my character. I made the best decision I could for my family: it was time to give up the game that I loved and move on to a more secure career path.

Dr. Levy and I had become close throughout our years together with the club, and he knew I was still hampered by my injury. When I announced my retirement, he was such a gentleman — he gave me his personal phone number to contact him any time I needed medical advice. Later down the road, his kindness would be greatly appreciated.

"The Wreck of the Edmund Fitzgerald," Gordon Lightfoot (1976)

By then, I had been substitute-teaching during off-seasons to gain experience for my post-football career for a couple of years and had attained my teaching degree from D'Youville College. I never could have done this without Paulette's support. She unselfishly put her own career on hold to allow me to go back to school, while she nurtured the kids.

When I was offered a full-time teaching contract, I felt like I was leaving a sinking ship for a lifeboat, because the Hamilton Tiger-Cats Football Club sank into receivership the following year. The CFL threatened to repeal the franchise unless the team sold 12,500 season tickets and have $1 million in corporate sponsorship deals by December 31.[22] The team managed to exceed these goals with about six days to spare. Garney Henley, one of the greatest Tiger-Cats of all time, and his wife Charlotte were instrumental in saving the franchise. Garney was a perennial All-Canadian at defensive back, but many of his fans may not know that when he was switched to receiver, he was also named an All-Canadian at his new position; he is one of few players ever to hold the honour at two positions. Henley was inducted into the CFHOF in 1979. But in my experience, the best thing about Henley is that he is the finest gentlemen one could meet.

Henley was on our coaching staff as receiver coach at this tumultuous time for the football club. His wife Charlotte told me about how she and Carol Rose, the president of the Cats Claws Fan Club, worked to sell season tickets to help meet the CFL deadline: "We organized the fan club to

[22] Milton, S. 2006. Hamilton Tiger-Cats. *The Canadian Encyclopedia*. Url: thecanadianencyclopedia.ca (accessed May 18, 2023).

knock on doors, greet the public at local shopping malls, and anything else we could think of to sell season tickets in the Hamilton area. We were determined to meet the league-imposed deadline and help save the embattled franchise from being revoked."

Carol Rose remembers recruiting Garney to autograph black and gold lapel ribbons volunteers had sewn together, which they sold for $5 each to raise money for the team. "It was heartwarming to see this CFHOF player, and now coach, sitting on the living room floor helping to sew, then signing these things...and they sold like hot-cakes because everyone loved Garney Henley! Not only did we help meet the deadline for season tickets, we also presented the club with a cheque for $10,000. It was a difficult time and we did everything we could to save our beloved team."

The sad reality is that the game of football is very unforgiving. Unless you're Miles Gorrell and play for 19 years, when most players are finally gaining the knowledge, understanding, and technique required to be really good, their bodies start to break down from the demands of the game. That's why the average career in professional football is only about three years.

The other part of the equation is that when players start to earn the salaries they deserve for their skill, long-term dedication, and commitment to their gridiron craft, they eventually price themselves out of the CFL market. Eventually, teams can sign two young players on entry level contracts for the price of one experienced veteran.

The net result is that most players don't leave the game on their own terms. Usually there is an acrimonious parting of the ways between the player and the club because the player isn't prepared to quit the sport that's now fixed in their blood, and has consumed every part of their lives for however long they've played. When the game is gone, it leaves a huge void in their lives, which sometimes cannot be filled by normal "civilian life," no matter how hard they try.

I have seen this cause mild to severe separation anxiety and real mental health issues for some former players. This can be compounded by the physical toll the sport takes on the player's body. Chronic pain from arthritis in damaged joints can be very debilitating, and many players from my era suffered from the effects of multiple concussions (recent advances in equipment have helped reduce player concussions).[23,24]

Inevitably, as in life, everyone faces their demons in their own way; some pour themselves into successful post-playing careers, some travel in pursuit of an elixir, others turn to drugs or alcohol to fill the void. I know former teammates and others across the league who have fallen into each of these categories.

For those that suffer from this post-career anxiety and related mental health challenges, a strong support network of family and friends is important to emerge from it. I was fortunate that I had this support. Paulette and the kids were always there when I needed them. And going directly from the football field to the challenges of running a successful classroom, full of kids starving for knowledge and a sense of emerging identity, gave me no time to dwell on the past. I soon learned that teachers' days are never boring, and it gave me the opportunity to pass on some of my hard-won knowledge as well as continue on my own path of personal growth.

"Starts with Goodbye," Carrie Underwood (2005)

Since I left the club, the team has experienced some highs and lows. They won another Grey Cup championship in 1999 under the ownership of George Grant and David Macdonald, with Ron Lancaster as head coach and record-setting Danny McManus at quarterback. On the other hand, they faced receivership again in 2003, when the league took temporary ownership of the franchise.

When Bob Young took over the team in 2003, he brought a new era of optimism to the franchise, which still embraces the team today in gleaming new Tim Hortons Field, the stadium that Young was instrumental in building to replace the aging Ivor Wynne Stadium. His business acumen has enabled him to create a diverse portfolio of successful companies and

---

[23] Kachur, T. 2015. *Scientists work to fight concussions with safer equipment, diagnostics*. CBC News. Url: cbc.ca/news (accessed May 18, 2023).
[24] Broglio, S. 2023. We can make football safer. *Scientific American*. Url: scientificamerican.com (accessed May 18, 2023).

philanthropic projects. Young is also a Hamilton native who holds deep affection for the team. He actually lets the "football guys" run the team and, in his easy-going way, calls himself the team's "caretaker." Young brought stability to a proud franchise, which is almost as old as the city itself.

While Hamilton was incorporated in 1846, the first version of the club, the Hamilton Tigers, began in 1869. In 1950, the Tigers joined with the Hamilton Wildcats to form the Tiger-Cats.[25]

I don't think there is another team in the league that reflects the character of its city more than the Tiger-Cats. The tough brand of football the team has become known for over the decades mirrors the tough reputation of Hamilton as the biggest steel-producing port in the country, giving it equally tough nicknames, like Steel Town and the Hammer. Hamilton has always been known as a tough, blue-collar city, with honest, hard-working people, who appreciate a hard-hitting game. Those same people would give you the shirt off their back if you need a helping hand.

I believe Bob Young's understanding of Hamilton has made his ownership of the Ticats so successful; the people he has hired to run the team are mostly from Hamilton and have their fingers on the economic and cultural pulse of the city. They clearly understand its people and its hidden jewels. Consequently, his humble but steady guidance provides a successful formula for the franchise here in Hamilton.

On the business side of things, although CEO Scott Mitchell is not a Hamilton native, he has a strong football background, winning the Vanier Cup with the University of Toronto in 1993 under head coach Bob Laycoe, my former mentor at UBC where he was the defensive coordinator. Scott Mitchell was also influenced by his father Doug Mitchell, a former UBC player who played in the CFL for the BC Lions and the Hamilton Tiger-Cats, and served as CFL commissioner from 1984–1988.[26] Executive vice president of the club is Doug Rye, a local Brock University graduate. Hamilton native Matt Afinec, is president and COO of business operations. Glenn Gibson, who grew up in Hamilton, is vice chairman. Fittingly, Drew and Matt Allemang, both sons of my old friend and teammate Marv Allemang, hold important roles on staff: Drew is assistant general manager

---

[25] Hamilton Tiger-Cats. n.d. *History of the Hamilton Tiger-Cats Football Club*. Url: ticats.ca (accessed May 18, 2023).

[26] Canadian Football Hall of Fame. 2021. *Doug Mitchell — Class of 2021.* Url: cfhof.ca (accessed May 26, 2023).

of Football Operations and director of Canadian scouting, and Matt is video coordinator. I have had the pleasure of working with most of these gentlemen in my role with the Hamilton Tiger-Cat Alumni Association (HTCAA), and I know first-hand the passion they hold for the success of the team, our alumni, and the local community.

On the football side of things, head coach Orlondo Steinauer is a former CFL All-Star defensive back, who brings youthful enthusiasm to the whole franchise along with cutting-edge coaching techniques. He has hired an eclectic group of coaches who share his appetite for success.

All these parties understand the value of developing partnerships in helping to grow football in the Hamilton community, all the way up from its grass roots, to ultimately bring Bob Young his elusive Grey Cup ring. In this light, the club has been close several times under the Caretaker's watch. The Tiger-Cats won the Eastern Championship in 2013 and 2014 with Kent Austin as head coach. Again in 2019, after breaking our 1989 season win record with a record of 15–3, the team won the East and appeared in the Grey Cup under current head coach Orlondo Steinauer only to lose to the Winnipeg Blue Bombers.

Unfortunately, the 2020 CFL season was cancelled due to the Covid-19 pandemic. At the time of writing, the 2021 season was under way, bringing new hope and optimism to football fans here in Hamilton; the Ticats won the East again — and again lost to the Blue Bombers in a heart-breaking over-time Grey Cup game. Then, in 2022, while I was working away on the next draft of this memoir, the Ticats made it into the East Semi-Final but lost to the Montreal Alouettes. With the Grey Cup game again scheduled to be played in Hamilton in 2023, fans are hoping Young's patience pays off this year, with the Caretaker finally being rewarded with a championship ring.

FOURTH QUARTER
MCMASTER MAKES HISTORY

I had been supply-teaching in the Halton Catholic District School Board for four years when they offered me a full-time position in 1993. Since the Tiger-Cats were in deep financial trouble and I had a family to feed, I accepted the offer. Thus began a rewarding second career in education.

Another of life's wrinkles was playing out for me now. My chance meeting with Tom Gallagher had redirected my career toward what I had intended so many years ago. I was embarking on another exciting challenge in life. Looking back, I believe it was no coincidence that I was drawn back to my vocation, it was something that was meant to be. I've been able to lean on what I learned in playing professional football and in my personal life, passing on those messages to my students — and learning from them in turn, continuing on my own journey of personal growth.

Anne Costello, an intelligent and dynamic leader in education, interviewed me for my first full-time position. During the interview, she asked what my career aspirations were. She wasn't expecting my response when I told her, "I want to be the best father I can be." I suspect she expected me to be interested in striving for some elite position within the school board. I simply wanted to enjoy making connections with kids in the classroom, and be a good dad for my three kids. Subconsciously, I think I really desired personal growth in the form of nurturing young people and moving away from my violent past. Nonetheless, a career in administration did not interest me in the least. She told me it was refreshing to hear a man have this perspective.

Anne hired me in spite of, or maybe because of, my lack of career aspirations.

For me, going from the gridiron to the classroom was a difficult transition to navigate. The violence on the field was my method of venting the anger I had built up from my early years. I had used it as fuel to motivate myself during games and now that outlet was gone. I needed to find personal growth in order to mitigate the aggression I was used to in the sport that saved me now that it was no longer available to me. Seeing the wonder in kids' eyes when they learned new things became my personal elixir.

Jim McGeragle was my first vice principal; he was another guardian angel, guiding me through my teaching apprenticeship. Jim was an excellent educator, with many years on the front lines helping kids, before he went into administration to support staff with his pedagogical wisdom. He was always there as an advisor if I had an issue in the classroom. He once told me, "It takes teachers five years of experience to properly manage a classroom, so it's unfair to assess their 'teaching ability' prior to that experience." I was fortunate that my life experiences helped me in this regard compared to a young teacher fresh out of teachers' college. I also had my physical presence to help me, so fortunately, I had few problems with classroom management. It is so impressive to me that there are so many cracker-jack teachers who are small in stature, but have perfect control in the classroom, through great classroom management skills. Conversely, it is sad to see some teachers with none, whose only recourse is to let the kids run the classroom — their path of least resistance. In my experience, kids need boundaries and they respect it when teachers are consistent in providing them.

Soon I was teaching intermediate science on rotary to four classes — two grade 7 classes and two grade 8s, in a portable classroom. Students rotated between Phys ed, social studies, history, and science. We were all in portables because the student population exceeded the size of the school. Those students got a great intermediate education with teachers full of energy, positive attitudes, and a good sense of humour. Young students feed off their teachers' energy, and we formed a good team.

My personal understanding of the impact of bullying heightened my empathy for all of my students. It's difficult to understand anything unless we experience it first-hand, so teachers who have never experienced bullying themselves may have less ability to deal with it in the classroom. My childhood experience allowed me to recognize when a student needed emotional support and when the time was right for them, they often opened up to me. I found it gratifying that my students could tell me things that they were afraid to voice to others; it was a sure sign that I was making connections with them and this allowed me to ease their anxiety and improve their learning.

The thing I enjoyed most about teaching elementary school before I moved to teaching high school was that I had my homeroom class all morning for core subjects. I was able to incorporate the material from several subjects together to create integrated studies. For one such memorable study, I used science, language, math, visual arts, and music to allow the students to transform our classroom into a model of the solar system.

The kids got deeply immersed in the project for several weeks. The culmination of all the students' work was a multi-media presentation to their parents, with lighting and music that would knock their socks off. Some parents were thrilled that their otherwise shy kids could be so passionate about a subject. Meanwhile, the students were the beneficiaries of the experience of working as a team to create and present something they were proud of. It was very gratifying for me to see the kids progress from scratch to the final presentation.

My own personal development continued throughout my teaching experiences. For example, although my size helped initially with classroom management because the kids were scared of me at first, as soon as they learned I had a heart, the honeymoon was over.

The steep learning curve about real-life child behaviours in the classroom was a crash course on the fly for me, one not offered in any teachers' college. Every day offered new and interesting challenges.

I thrived on this because my strategy was to engage every child and learn what motivated them, so I could capitalize on their learning style to help them learn.

Similarly, meeting the needs of kids with disabilities and integrating them into the regular classroom taught me patience — this is also when I learned to truly appreciate the support of educational assistants in the classroom.

Clearly, personal experience helps teachers in the classroom. A case in point for me was when I dealt with a serious case of bullying. It involved a girl who was being bullied on social media during the summer by a group of girls entering my new grade 8 class in September.

When I met with the self-proclaimed leader of this group of girls doing the bullying to try to get to the bottom of it, she told me, "Mr. Riley, we have run every class we've been in and we're going to run this class too — there's nothing you can do about it!"

It blew me away that a teenaged girl could say this to my face, but this is where my background experience came into play. I remembered what I had learned at the group home and I was determined that I could help these girls learn that they were wrong to treat people this way.

Undoubtedly, it took all my personal experience and most of my energy to manage it for the entire school year. The girls were being very cruel without realizing or caring about the damage they were doing to the victim and, indirectly, to the rest of the class. After several after-school conferences with their parents and many lunch discussions with the kids, we made steady progress.

At the end of the school year, we were able to enjoy the week-long Camp Tanamakoon retreat in Algonquin Park without incident. I think we all learned from the experience and became better people because of it.

Then another of life's trap doors opened and I spiralled into it.

Mom passed away on February 25, 1995, during my second year of teaching. She suffered a major inoperable aneurysm in her brain, and slowly lost her faculties over the following days. I spent five nights on a cot in Mom's hospital room. Seeing her tears when I spoke to her showed me that, although she couldn't open her eyes or speak to me, she could understand what I was saying to her. Staff at the Royal Columbian Hospital, in New Westminster, B.C., made sure she was comfortable and I got to spend quality time with her while my siblings were at work. In the end, the entire family surrounded her with love when her final breath was taken. I suppose, under the circumstances, her death was as peaceful as modern medicine could make it, but it was heart-wrenching to see her steady decline from the bright and loving woman she had always been.

The thing that hurts the most is that Mom was only 69 years old when she died. She was enjoying life and exploring her talents as a landscape painter in her retirement. Through all our family's struggles in our journey of life together, Mom never complained about anything personal. She always made sure that all our needs were met, even at the expense of her own comfort.

I'm also grateful to the school board for allowing me compassionate leave to spend time with my mother in the hospital; it took some pressure off my siblings knowing I was there with her around the clock.

Back home, on the first day of my return to work, Diane Rabenda, my school superintendent, placed a bible in my hand in the school parking lot before I went into the building. When I opened it, I saw that it was personalized, "In memory of Ruth Riley."

To a man feeling like a newly orphaned boy, this was the kindest gesture one could imagine. Mrs. Rabenda was responsible for hundreds of teachers and thousands of students, but she lived out her faith and took the time to personally console me in my grief.

At this low point in my life, Mrs. Rabenda hadn't simply shown professional support for me as a teacher, she had bolstered my faith. Once again, when it was most needed and least expected, I had experienced a revelation that offered me comfort and hope.

"Ahead by a Century," The Tragically Hip (1996)

Soon enough, another life-changing opportunity presented itself. After he left the Tiger-Cats, Al Bruno was hired as the Marauders' head football coach at McMaster University, in Hamilton. He called to tell me they needed help on the offensive line, and asked me if I was interested in coaching for him at McMaster.

Up to this point, I had never considered coaching football, let alone at the university level. I was already busy teaching and coaching my elementary school's teams.

True to form, however, Paulette agreed that the opportunity to give back to the game we loved so much, and at this elite level, seemed too good to pass up. We both recognized how much the game had given to us.

So it was that after much deliberation, I accepted Al's invitation to coach offensive line at McMaster University in 1996. Most athletes have no idea the time commitment required to be a good coach. I was no different. On the other hand, I also didn't anticipate the enjoyment it would provide — to me, it was the next best thing to playing, it was intoxicating.

Unfortunately, that first year we had a rough go — we didn't win a game. We had a small roster; recent recruiting efforts had not generated enough new players. And, although we had some good players sprinkled throughout, we didn't have the depth of talent to be competitive.

Case in point: that year, we only had six healthy offensive linemen in our group. Occasionally, one of the guys would have to work or another might have an exam, bringing our number down to four. Needing five offensive linemen just to run a basic offensive play, this meant that we could only run half-line drills the entire practice. We would run a play to the right, then flip the line to run the play the other way — not the most productive way to run a practice!

At the time, McMaster had poor football facilities, too; a dilapidated clubhouse and stadium, and a poorly-draining natural grass field, which became a muddy quagmire after the first rain in the fall. This lack of facilities made it more difficult to attract good young players to the program.

Coach Al, always staying positive no matter the situation, would say to the coaching staff, "Men, we didn't win a game this season, but we sure had a great time coaching the kids, didn't we!"

Unfortunately, after only one year of coaching together, Al was experiencing health issues, so he retired and returned to his home in Florida with his wife Marie. It was a true pleasure to have coached with him and learn the ropes of university coaching from a man I admired so much. He had first convinced me to come to Hamilton to play for the Tiger-Cats, and now he was responsible for ushering me into the next chapter of my football odyssey.

"Once in a Lifetime," Talking Heads (1980)

We had a major health scare of our own to overcome when Paulette began experiencing some weird physical symptoms. She was diagnosed with multiple sclerosis in 1999. Initially, we both thought the worst, because we knew how devastating the disease could be. MS is an insidious disease that can rear its ugly head in frightening ways without warning.

After the diagnosis, Paulette and I were both very upset and concerned. Paulette was also very emotional when she told me she thought that I'd leave her now that she had MS. I reassured her that I would stand by her, just as she had stood by my side supporting me throughout the obstacles I faced in my career. Paulette's diagnosis gave me a new perspective on the blessing of good health that most of us take for granted when navigating our busy lives.

After her diagnosis we learned that there are several types of MS and Paulette had the most common type — relapsing-remitting MS (RRMS). With RRMS, the doctor informed us that Paulette's symptoms should eventually go into remission, allowing her to recover between episodes. Additionally, Paulette's neurologist prescribed a drug called copaxone, which had just been cleared through clinical trials by Health Canada, and was successful in limiting further episodes. However, because MS is an autoimmune disease, her body was always fighting the disease in the background, so chronic fatigue became a constant battle for her.

Luckily, after 16 years of these injections, Paulette's MS went into full remission. Once again, Paulette proved she was way tougher than me!

Shortly after Paulette's diagnosis, I was asked to transfer to Notre Dame high school — we decided it was a good idea. First, I could be home earlier if Paulette was having a bad day or we had medical appointments. I could also support the high school football program, but in a limited way because of my responsibilities at McMaster.

I also welcomed the opportunity to engage students by exploring important issues at a higher academic level. We would incorporate current world issues into our learning, often leading to class discussions on important subjects that some students were not aware of, and others were passionate about.

I enjoyed teaching philosophy, for instance, because we could incorporate deep metaphysical concepts that the curious teenaged minds in my classes thrived on before they left for university. I thrived on the energy of my students in class. We explored questions like: What is it to be human? What is reality? What is time and space? What is consciousness? Does God exist? Do we have free will?

My students appreciated that we were on a path of mutual discovery; I learned much from them too. We often ended courses with a well-researched debate on an important social issue, judged by a panel of other teachers volunteering their valuable time to critique student thinking and ideas.

Another thing most of my students enjoyed was a form of guided-meditation (see Appendix B), which I learned one year at our annual staff religion retreat. The instructor's voice guides the class as they close their eyes and relax at their desks. It is a method of guiding students, through narration, to relax and meditate into one's core; isolating one's "self" from all the noise in the world, like grain from the chaff; focusing on positive energy; overcoming personal obstacles; and welcoming God (for my Catholic students) into one's heart. It was a skill for them to wind down, usually done on a Friday after a busy week of school.

Incidentally, I've discovered that with all the things we teach our kids, the last thing we teach them is how to truly relax. This is something that is so important to our mental health and ability to navigate the crazy world in which we live — it has become key for me in my own mental health tool kit (see Appendix B).

As previously stated, the thing I most enjoyed about teaching was developing relationships with each student as an individual, and always providing a safe place for them to learn; the bitter taste of being bullied as a student made me very diligent in creating a class environment of community, with mutual respect, where everyone's opinion was valued. Additionally, teamwork, trust, self-discipline, and the value of hard work were all lessons I had learned in my football career — now I felt compelled to share them with my students to prepare them for the real world after high school, regardless of the subject I was teaching.

Although some of my students didn't appreciate my teaching style (how does that quote go? "You can please some of the people all the time, and all the people some of the time..."), I think I connected with most of my students and had a positive impact on their learning. Teaching students who appreciate their time in the classroom, and whom we can see learning and growing up before our eyes, is what makes teaching so gratifying.

"Hard Day's Night," The Beatles (1964)

Although I was still committed to coaching university football at McMaster, I also wanted to support head coach Mike Harris, by coaching offensive line at my new high school. This was difficult because I also wanted to honour the Riley family tradition of eating dinner together as a family for the benefit of our young kids. To do this, most days Paulette would have dinner ready at 4:30PM. We'd often play highlight-lowlight, where we'd take turns sharing the best and worst part of our days, as a good way to get the kids talking, before I had to rush off again.

To be able to do this, Coach Harris would schedule my offensive line coaching periods at the start of practice, before I left for home, then went to Mac practice. To finish the day after practice at Mac in those early years, before digital video, we might stay in that dusty old cinderblock building until 11 p.m. or midnight, breaking down film on the old 8 mm projector. Those were very long days.

This schedule was physically exhausting to maintain for all the coaches, but for me, getting home for those family dinners when the kids were young was important. I knew the benefit of football for the young men we coached, but I had to be there for my kids, too. Obviously, I couldn't have done it without Paulette's support.

A few years later, I transferred to Assumption Catholic Secondary School because it was the board's closest high school to our home, and I could coach with my old friend Ivan Yurgan. Ivan and I attended teacher's college together and followed similar teaching careers, starting in elementary, then moving to high school. We also shared a similar coaching philosophy, in that we used the sport to teach kids self-discipline and to be accountable for themselves; it was never about just winning at all costs. This approach was successful because, along with other like-minded coaches (Joe Babic, Dave Gatza, Joe Jurus, Rick Little, Tony Mandalfino, Jerod McCrory, and Chris Worobec to name a few) we won two board championships, and an Ontario Federation of Schools Athletic Association (OFSAA) Bowl championship together, during my tenure there.

Ivan is renowned as a head coach who cares deeply for his players, many of whom also come back after graduation from university to coach with him (too many to name here) — he is a strong part of the local football fraternity.

Teaching and coaching at Assumption at that point in my career also offered the unique opportunity for me to retire from the same school I started at as a supply teacher, 30 years prior — this gave me an uplifting sense of completing the "full-circle" in education. The fine students and staff at Assumption made it very difficult to leave when I retired in 2019.

With Coach Bruno's departure, the Marauders program was at a crossroads. The university administration could now either decide to let the program completely fizzle out, or fully invest in the program to make it competitive again. Luckily for everyone involved, President Dr. Peter George, and Director of Athletics and Recreation Thérèse Quigley, chose the latter. With them at the helm, a whole new era of Marauder football was born, which would continue to unfold over the next decades.

Greg Marshall took over for Al Bruno at McMaster in 1997. Unfortunately, Greg inherited a team that was low on overall player numbers, had no commitment to strength training, and suffered with poor facilities — some of the worst in the conference. However, by hiring this new young coach away from his job as offensive coordinator at Western University, McMaster indicated its commitment to our program. Luckily, Greg had the work ethic of a Clydesdale, which few could match. From the start, he dedicated himself to working the long hours necessary to turn the program around.

The core of Greg's assistant coaching staff consisted of Lou Cafazzo, Marcello Campanaro, Mark Forsyth, Jack Frimeth, Carm Genovese, Frank

Gesztesi, me, and later, Ted Goveia, Larry Guarascia, Joe Sardo, Stu Smith. Although we received a small stipend for coaching, which covered some meals and gas, essentially, we were volunteers doing it for the love of the game.

The first coaches' meeting under our intense new head coach was on February 14, 1997 (I know the date was February 14 because, in fear of alienating our wives and losing his whole coaching staff after the first meeting, Greg gave us all nicely-wrapped boxes of chocolates to take home for Valentine's Day). At this meeting, the consensus was that we needed two key things to get the program to where it needed to be: one, a new focus on recruiting to increase the number and quality of athletes on our roster; and two, mandatory weight training for the athletes to get bigger, stronger, and faster — currently, most of our guys were getting thrown around like wet dishrags on the field.

However, it would be difficult to recruit elite players when the campus facilities were less than adequate. Additionally, at the time, with few designated training facilities, the coaches had to be very creative with training techniques to improve the team.

To describe the facilities objectively, the clubhouse building was so out of date that our coaches' room was only a small room on the opposite side of the building from the players' dressing room. Very inconvenient. The washroom and shower facilities were grungy, with intermittent hot water. There wasn't enough room for a full roster in the main dressing room, and not enough stalls in general, so some kids had to use benches in the back room. The field was natural grass with poor drainage, so it was usually wrecked after the first rain each year. The "spotter's booths," where I had the displeasure of spotting for the offence that season, was a mere 6' x 6' box, which was open to the elements. Inevitably, there was raccoon shit in the corners, and usually an active wasp nest to contend with before the game. It wasn't much higher than the field behind those old shaky, wooden stands, so there was little advantage to see the game. Finally, I had to navigate up to the spotters' booth carefully so that my body weight didn't break through any of the rotting old bench planks. Luckily, I only spent one season in the spotter's booth because I wasn't very good at being separated from my unit. I learned that I needed to be on the sidelines with my offensive line during the games to have the most impact on the game.

◇◆◇

Greg had a unique gift for bringing the coaches together and creating great family experiences. In so doing, he created a sense of community among the staff, which percolated through everything the team did, on and off the field.

With our new focus on recruiting and strength training, the team improved quickly. During the early part of Greg's tenure, he also took it upon himself to upgrade some aspects of the outdated facilities. For example, more wooden stalls were needed to house a larger roster. Although there was only so much he could do — like he used to say, "You can't make a silk purse out of a sow's ear." In quick order, Greg enlisted his coaching staff to help "get 'er done!"

All the coaches volunteered whatever time and talents they had for the "upgrade" and chipped in what they could. Most did more than I did, because I just didn't have the time and I didn't own any tools. Gerry Gaskell, who coached with us for a brief time, brought in his power tools and built most of the extra lockers from scratch. Then we converted an old storage area — previously a chain-link enclosure — into a coaches' room, by building walls and installing a door. Frank Guestaszi capped our new room off by installing an air-conditioning unit in the window for the hot august training camps.

Coaches painted the entire dressing room, floors and walls, in grey and maroon team colours. I added the Marauder logo on the wall above our new coaches' room door. Greg completed the room with a central carpet to cover up some concrete, adding some texture to the room. When we were done, it had been transformed from a dusty, old, grey brick room, into a clean, bright, uplifting space, an inspiring atmosphere for players and coaches to spend their time. This transformation could be seen as a symbol for the rise of the team over the next few years.

Thanks to Greg's leadership, the process also became a bonding experience for the coaching staff — we took ownership of what we did and our pride transcended into the team, who recognized our efforts to improve their clubhouse environment, which led to more pride and higher morale amongst the team.

When asked to reflect on his time at McMaster, Greg recalled, "We had great coaches. One of the special parts about the experience at Mac was the family atmosphere that we had. ...If there's one thing I did that was successful at Mac, it was keeping the group of guys (coaching staff) together for the duration. Players had told me before I started that there was no continuity in our coaching staff."[27]

It would certainly take a master recruiter to convince quality players to commit to McMaster with the existing facilities at that time. Luckily, that's what the McMaster brass got when they landed Greg Marshall. Right from his first off-season with the program, Greg enlisted all his coaches to help. During regular recruiting meetings, Greg would provide a short-list of key recruits to each position coach. These meetings predated cellphones, so they took place after hours in the athletic department offices, using staff telephones. All of us would be on the phones at the same time to do our canvassing for recruits — we became a recruiting machine. It transformed the athletic office into a stock market-like cacophony of dialogue every recruiting night.

If the kids didn't commit with us on the phone, Greg would usually have success using his ample charisma to charm the parents of the recruit at their home. If that didn't work, he would bring out the heavy artillery — a handwritten letter mailed directly to the recruit, explaining how much the program would benefit by his commitment to McMaster. This usually had the desired result. So, in spite of the poor facilities, Greg was successful in convincing great players to join our team, the epitome being Hec Crighton Trophy winners Kojo Aidoo (2000), Ben Chapdelaine (2001), and Jesse Lumsden (2004).

"Smooth," Santana (1999)

While we were building the team in every way we could in the early 2000s, it was also the perfect time for the Marauder coaches to bring our families

---

[27] Moko, L. Sept. 7, 2011. Mustangs coach returns to old stomping grounds. *The Hamilton Spectator*.

together through football, since most of the Marauder coaches had young kids of their own.

A natural byproduct of the camaraderie that the coaches shared and passed on to our team was the personal growth of our children. Just being around the team gave them experiences that helped with their development in these formative years. Unbeknownst to me at the time, coaching also became very therapeutic to exorcise my personal demons of angst, anger, and insecurity.

Soon, we developed a routine to bring the kids to practice every Friday night to give their moms a break. The moms would enjoy their favourite pastimes at home while we took the kids, dressed in their roughest play clothes, down to the old field at Mac. All the kids would play tackle football on the natural grass (or mud) end zone, while we coached special teams practice for the game the next day. The kids knew we'd take them to Harvey's on Main St. for burgers after practice. And it didn't matter how grass-stained and muddy their clothes got on this day, they had a "field-pass" from mom. The kids loved it — they bonded as a group through years of this tradition.

Another tradition Greg started was hosting the annual coaches' Christmas party in the old clubhouse dressing room. We set up hockey nets for the kids in the back room, so they could play indoor hockey to their hearts' content. Personalized gifts for the kids and moms were provided by Greg and his wife, Joan. Santa Claus (Lou Cafazzo) usually made an appearance to hand out the gifts. The food was always plentiful. Often, McMaster President Peter George and Athletic Director Thérèse Quigley would make a cameo appearance to wish everyone the best of the season and thank us for our hard work. These parties were memorable for all of us. The camaraderie we shared during these events was one of the best parts of coaching in this group — we are still friends to this day.

2016 Marauder coaches' reunion, Hamilton: back left Greg Marshall, Marcello Campanaro, me, Joe Sardo, Carm Genovese, Mark Forsyth, kneeling Lou Cafazzo, Frank Gesztesi (absent, Jack Frimeth, Ted Goveia, Larry Guarascia, Stu Smith): Jason Riley photo

Many of the coaches' kids volunteered for the football program, too. My twins became assistant equipment managers and ball girls, under the watchful eye of Stu Smith, our equipment manager. On game day, they took pride in putting on their Marauder shorts and tees, running shoes, and tight ponytails to retrieve the balls for the referees. Being identical twins, no one — not even their parents — could tell them apart.

One day in the buffet line at the post-game social, a player's dad said to me, "Your daughter is so fast, she'll be a track star, Jason! I can't believe how well she covers the entire field retrieving balls for the referees."

I said, "You know I have identical twins, right?"

His eyes lit up as he responded, "I didn't know you had twins, I thought it was one girl the whole game!" We both had a good laugh about that.

Because of their early experience with the game, football became the twins' favourite sport. They would have played football if they were boys. But since they couldn't play the game in a league (it was only in 2022 that Football Ontario announced the first girls' tackle football league, Ontario Women's Football League), they decided to be ball girls for our home games. One time a referee said to me, "Jason, your girls are the best 'ball boys' in the league. Boys their age are easily distracted, whereas your girls are totally focused on what they're doing, and always get the ball to us quickly."

When I informed the girls of this compliment, they smiled from ear to ear. They were happy to be appreciated, and this reinforced their efforts to support the team in any way they could. Here again was football teaching the value of hard work, the pride in doing a job well, and the value of volunteering to support family and others in their community, resulting in personal growth for this new generation. When Jason was old enough, he also joined his sisters in benefitting from the Marauder experience.

Jessica remembers her experience this way:

"From my earliest memory, we went to Mac football practice every Friday after school with our dad. It's all I could think about at school on Fridays. Punching out at the last school bell, I would run home from school with my sister and brother and wait for Dad to pick us up on his way home from work."

Jordan expands on the personal growth these experiences gave her, "I wouldn't give up those Friday nights for anything; they taught me so much in terms of toughness and never giving up. Watching McMaster win, all of those boys' hard work finally paying off, was the icing on the cake."

Jason's favourite time as a kid at McMaster was "attending the training camp sessions, where [Dad] would take me and the twins down every day for two weeks. It was right before school started and the big finish of the summer." These family times were a major reason he decided to play football at Mac because he grew up loving the program.

In retrospect, the skills, work ethic, and dedication that our kids developed in those formative years with McMaster were instrumental in their future success. All three of them are better for it now, enjoying successful careers in their chosen career paths.

It was rewarding for me to see the personal growth of our children through a shared experience with football. I realized that my own growth, and overcoming the anger instilled in me as a child, was now reflected in my kids' benefitting from the game I loved.

From left Jessica, Jason Jr. and Jordan getting ready for Coaches' Kids Friday Night Football, McMaster, 1997: Art Martin photo

"Just Dance," Lady Gaga (2008)

From the start, I didn't want to be one of those overbearing fathers who insists their kids follow in his footsteps, so I purposely pushed all of my kids toward soccer and hockey during their formative years. Being around it so much, however, they all developed an early love for football.

Despite Jordan's and Jessica's love for the game, because they didn't have football league to play in, they chose to focus on hockey. They experienced great success with the Stoney Creek Sabres organization, and eventually earned scholarships at Robert Morris University (RMU) in Pittsburgh, after they graduated from St. Thomas More Catholic High School. We put thousands of kilometres on our minivan to watch them play with and against some of the best players in the game, in RMU's NCAA Division 1 hockey conference.

RMU treats their student-athletes extremely well and the girls flourished in an environment that challenged them both physically and academically; Jessica was named RMU Rookie of the Year and Jordan was named Most Improved Player in her senior year.

After graduating from RMU, they pursued different career paths, but through some twin-propelled serendipity, they eventually returned back to each other in the field of first responders: Jordan as a 911 dispatcher and Jessica as a Hamilton paramedic. Paulette and I are proud to see the twins serving our community so courageously.

"Cats in the Cradle," Harry Chapin (1974)

Junior, on the other hand, hadn't expressed his interest in football until one day, he came home from school and asked if he could play football instead of soccer next summer because his friends were playing. I was so excited. I said, "Is the Pope Catholic?"

After only one season with Hamilton Minor Football's West Hamilton Roughriders, he declared that football was his favourite sport.

From then on, it was wonderful for me to be able to coach the teams he played for as he grew up; I would coach the offensive line, while he played defensive line (just like his old man). I volunteered to coach his community teams, since I had to drive him to practice anyway. I didn't coach him in high school because I was usually coaching at my own school.

Jason had an excellent high school experience, with no street fighting involved (that I'm aware of) — I don't think he's been in a fight in his life. It's a different world now. Whereas I had to literally fight through my struggles all through school, thankfully there is much more awareness and remediation with bullying now than there was then.

In his senior year, after playing offensive guard, defensive end, and long snapper, Jason was named player of the year for his high school team. Ultimately, when he was recruited for university, he chose to play at McMaster because he had fond memories growing up there, the facilities were now on par with the best in the nation, and he knew the entire coaching staff.

When Jason committed to McMaster, we enjoyed something that most father-son relationships don't experience: sharing a university football program together.

By now, he was used to his dad being on the field with him, but not coaching his position. Jason earned everything he accomplished through hard work and dedication, eventually becoming a captain on a championship team. It was the best part of my coaching career to witness his development from a boy to a man through the game we both love.

Jason Jr. and I after a game at WLU, Kitchener, 2012: Jason Riley photo

Before digital video came into use, most game film breakdown was done using 8 mm reel-to-reel film projectors. This was labour-intensive because coaches needed to watch the entire film to find the plays they wanted to evaluate. Today, in contrast, digital video allows technicians to categorize plays according to specific criteria; like all first down plays, specific offensive formations, or defensive blitzes, etc. This way, coaches can open a folder that contains only the plays they want to evaluate or share with the players at meetings. This has made film work much more efficient than it used to be.

Some nights in those early days, we'd stay as a group until 11 p.m. or later to break down film before games. Greg might stay up all night watching film, but the rest of us had regular day jobs.

There were times that I was so tired, I would be walking the hallways at school like a zombie, totally exhausted from the long days we put in at work, then coaching, meetings, and film work; we'd repeat the process again the next day. Trying to navigate the day in these times was a challenge, especially during the playoffs, and the further into the playoffs we went, the longer we needed to sustain this pace. We were all working hard as a coaching team to help turn the "Marauder ship" around — it was oddly exhilarating for me to push myself to exhaustion to help prepare our team for the next game. But I only live 15 minutes from campus. Other coaches lived further than I did. For example, Jack Frimeth lived over an hour's drive from campus. He would often have to stop the car on the way home to have a nap so he wouldn't fall asleep at the wheel.

Greg Marshall would never be accused of getting outworked. He was driven. When someone invested this much of themselves into a program, as Greg did, he also had high expectations of his players and staff. Greg had earned the reputation as one of the most intense coaches in the game — on game day, he had 10-foot porcupine quills and no one wanted to go near him. Unfortunately, his passion sometimes translated into a searing wrath directed at a player on the sidelines for missing a block, or "having a brain fart." Position coaches were then in the awkward position of soothing the player to build their confidence back up before they went back on the field for the next series.

Greg knew his intensity was over the top when the game was on the line, but there was absolutely nothing he could do to change his approach. He was wired that way, and it got results. Off the field, the players knew that it wasn't personal, it was simply a projection of Greg's intensity.

The coaches weren't immune from Greg's wrath either. If he saw something in a game that the coaches could improve, he made it known. No doubt, in the time that's passed since he left McMaster, his game demeanour has mellowed to a blast furnace, as compared to a flame thrower.

After the game, Greg was the best guy to sit down and have a beer with to revel in the glory of the game and the exploits of the players. He always made sure there was plenty of food, beverages, and stories after every game, which enhanced the camaraderie of the coaching staff.

On that note, another great coaching tradition we had in those years was our Thursday night coaches' meetings to set the final roster. By Thursday, most of the heavy lifting for the week was done, "the hay was in the barn," and all that remained was the Friday night walk-through to polish things up and go over special teams details before Saturday's game.

After practice on Thursdays, Greg would order pizza and chicken wings to be delivered and make sure the fridge was stocked with cold beer. This was important because we had a long night ahead to hammer out the final roster, which had to be posted the next day for our players to know who was dressing for the game.

Eventually our successful recruiting process had led to close to 100 players on our overall roster, but only 45 could dress for the games, so there was a constant tension between offence, defence, and special teams for game roster spots. Once the starters were set on offence and defence, based on injuries and who was available, the next priority was who could contribute the most on special teams. Offensive linemen did not usually fit the criteria for special teams, so it was a constant battle in these meetings to get an extra one of my guys on the game roster, so he could gain some playing experience. To a lesser extent, this applied to all the position groups.

These meetings were the closest things we would ever come to the boarding houses during the war that my dad used to tell us about, when boarding house rules meant those with the boarding house reach got the most food. As we wolfed down the food, the chicken wing bones would pile up on one of the empty pizza boxes, while whoever was closest to the fridge would hand out cold beer. For hours, we would enjoy each other's arguments for the next man up on offence or defence as we balanced the roster and lobbied for one more kid that needed a break to get playing time. Inevitably, we'd share stories of the week's practice, who impressed us the most in any given drill, and plans to bring our own kids down for Friday night walk-through to give the moms a night to themselves.

These Thursday night meetings, cramped as they were in the small coaches' room that we had converted from a storage locker, became an enjoyable coaching staff ritual.

Our coaching staff also had some classic "chalk talks" about game plans, strategies, and position techniques. But as Ron Lancaster said, the fundamentals of the game never really change — success in today's game is still predicated on how well a team blocks and tackles — the team that is most fundamentally sound will usually win. That being true, the best coaching staffs find a healthy balance between teaching team systems versus individual position techniques in practice.

Being an inexperienced second-year coach when Greg arrived, I learned a ton from his coaching experience, especially about the power run game, which Greg liked to run from a tight end formation. I had run the power run game as a player, but mostly in short-yardage situations. Our staple run series with the Ticats was the "search," which is usually run from a spread formation (see Appendix A). This is known as "zone run" in today's game. Because I was so familiar with running this style of play as a player, Greg asked me to install it with the Marauder offence. Ultimately, we developed a diverse running attack that opposition defences had difficulty defending. I will always appreciate the opportunity to work with Greg and the other great coaches for those years we were together.

"Change of Heart," Cyndi Lauper (1986)

Every training camp, to protect the grass in our stadium at Les Prince Field, the team would practice on our back fields, affectionately called the "back forty" — acres of grass fields at the back of campus, surrounded by old-growth forests that cascade down toward one of the Cootes Paradise inlets.

One night, I was coaching the offensive line in a drill deep in the back forty, when I saw a guy in the distance walking towards us over the steamy grass in the mist at dusk. He had a heavy fall coat on and he hunched to one side as he walked, as if compensating for arthritic joints. His gait seemed familiar. I recognized him when he got closer — it was Cal Murphy, after all those years!

I hadn't spoken to Cal since he traded me from Winnipeg to Saskatchewan in 1983; I avoided him whenever the Tiger-Cats played the Blue Bombers because I was still bitter about the trade. In the years that passed since then, Cal's health had failed him. In 1992, he had received one of the first successful heart transplants in the country.

I walked over to meet him so we could get reacquainted privately before I introduced him to our linemen as they finished their drill. When we shook hands, Cal said with genuine concern, "Jason, have you ever forgiven me for trading you, when you heard about the trade on the radio of your car? I know you were angry with me. You had every right to be."

I'd had many years to ponder what I'd say to Cal if the opportunity ever came. I responded casually, "Cal, I was angry with you for a long time, but since you've had a change of heart, I forgive you."

We shared a hearty laugh, the way only brothers from the football fraternity can laugh about the game.

Cal explained that he was currently a scout for the Indianapolis Colts of the NFL, and he wanted to learn more about our offensive line, which he'd heard good things about; it was possible that he would recommend one of our players for the upcoming NFL draft.

After I introduced him, he spent much of the practice with our unit, then went around to observe the other position groups. After practice, Cal joined us in the coaches' room for a beer and enjoyed talking about all of our players, this living legend sharing the camaraderie of our coaching staff.

"The Boys are Back in Town," Thin Lizzy (1976)

Brian Brock joined our coaching staff in 2005 as my assistant offensive line coach. Brian was a retired teacher who had played for McMaster when he got his undergrad degree, before attending teacher's college. We quickly gained respect for each other, as coaches who cared about kids. Brian respected what I brought to the table, and I appreciated his commitment to our program — he never missed a practice in all the years we coached together. Brian's low-key demeanour complemented my coaching style, and he kept me on schedule during practice when I lost track of time during a drill. We worked well in tandem, which the players in our unit appreciated.

As in teaching and in life, my favourite part of coaching was always the player-coach relationships built through the shared challenges to get better. The bond that results from these relationships lasts forever.

Regardless of the talent we had over the years at McMaster, with Brian's support, I used everything I knew to build the cohesiveness of our offensive line unit to become the tightest-knit unit on the field. Even in the years when we were thin on numbers and talent, I knew that if they played as one, we could have success. I would tell them every year at camp, that it was a process that lasted all season: "If we work hard, we'll be much better in October than we are in August." This process started off the field. Thus, I began a tradition to host an offensive line barbecue in the summer in our backyard to kick off every season. At first, Paulette and I would foot the bill for these meals. But soon, the "minister of finance" questioned the high cost of feeding 10 to 15 300 lb-monsters. These guys could eat!

With the increasing success of the team, I approached local restaurants to contribute to the annual offensive line barbeque, to help offset the costs. It's funny, I never had a restaurant say no to helping feed our Marauder offensive line at this event. Restaurants from Hamilton and Burlington donated their great food every year. We would have buffalo chicken wings from the Endzone Bar & Grill, trays of the house-special fried rice and chow mien from Le Chinois Express, spaghetti and meatballs with garlic bread from Gator Ted's Tap & Grill, sausages and freshly-baked buns from Sweet Paradise Bakery & Deli, and pizza and salad from the local Boston Pizza. The only rule for the players was "No one leaves hungry!"

The only things the boys had to bring to the barbeque were an appetite, a lawn chair, and a hockey stick. Every year at our barbeque, we held a road hockey game on the street in front of the house. We'd borrow a net from a neighbour's kid to add to my kids' net. We'd throw all the sticks in a pile and select teams by sorting them randomly. Friends, neighbours, and others in the offensive line fraternity would round out the teams, so we had rotating lines. I was the supervisor, leaning on my stick on the sidewalk. There was no body-checking and, if the ball went off the road, we used the honour system until it was back in play — we couldn't afford a twisted ankle this close to camp.

It's a shame we never invited the Guinness Book of Records because with the average size of the players, I think it was the biggest road hockey game on the planet! While kids playing our national sport on the road usually call "Car!" and scurry to the side of the road when a car approaches, most of the cars approaching our game would stop and pull a U-turn — they didn't want to have anything to do with these monsters! Through the hockey and the breaking of bread together, it was a truly unifying event for our unit.

Additionally, if I had a large yard project going on in the off-season, I'd invite the OL to come do it as a team-builder. This would save me a lot of work, and these strapping young men would complete the work in a fraction of the time it would have taken me. Their reward was all the barbecued chicken wings, sausages, and Caesar salad they could consume. The net result was real camaraderie; after all, hard work is good for the soul. In hindsight, after feeding these huge men, it probably would have been cheaper to hire a landscaper!

Similarly, we worked the boys hard during our individual periods during practice throughout the bulk of the season. I pushed them on the five-man sled during our heavy work days, Tuesdays and Wednesdays. We would drive the sled across the field and back, every group taking several turns, then finish with individual hitting drills to focus on leverage and hip explosion. Working hard and sweating together as a unit built the trust and resilience that allowed us to be formidable on the field for four quarters. Although it was hard work, my message was "Embrace the sled, because it makes us better. You'll benefit from it in the fourth quarter — visualize the pads on the sled as the jersey of your opponent and knock it off the ball!" This really helped our run game. As the playoffs approached, we might take it down a notch because most of the guys were nursing some sort of hurts — as the season goes on, the game takes a toll on the body. We had to be smart and know when to pull the reins if necessary. Coaches that don't do this end up with a team with no gas in the tank at the most important time of the season – the playoffs.

Wednesdays were our late team film nights, and rookies would bring treats like popcorn, cookies, donuts, chips, and chocolate milk to make watching hours of film more enjoyable after a long day of classes and practice. We made sure to also share some classic stories from the football fraternity archives.

In keeping with the theme of feeding the offensive line, Jesse Lumsden would invite the entire unit out for dinner at the Mandarin for the all-you-can-eat buffet, to reward them for their hard work every time he broke another rushing record. Aside from further unifying the group socially, this encouraged the boys to work even harder on the field to open holes for Jesse in the next game.

When the playoffs start, it's commonly referred to as a "new season." In the playoffs, coaches help create a heightened sense of urgency for the team because "there is no tomorrow" - the season ends suddenly with a loss, an emotional end for many senior players who may never play the game again.

To address this emotional aspect of the playoffs, I developed a visualization activity (see Appendix B), which was the last thing we would do as a unit after practice the night before each playoff game. It's based on three key psychological techniques I've learned in various areas over the years (today they might be called "mindfulness techniques"): first, controlling one's heartrate with one's mind to drop into a fully relaxed state, a technique I learned back in my first-ever psychology course; second, the guided-meditation technique I used with my students to get into a positive state of mind; and, third, using the "visualization technique" as a form of practice to improve skills, whereby athletes visualize doing drills successfully, while off the playing surface, which is now a common practice in coaching.

To begin, the boys would lie down comfortably in a darkened room, with relaxing background music, and close their eyes. Then, I would lead them with my voice on a journey into their core, lowering their heart rate. Next, I navigated them to a place of heightened relaxation, where a spiritual presence (obviously God in a Catholic setting, although in a secular setting, this could be a sense of connection with nature, or being at peace with the universe) was in their heart and their mind-set was completely positive; finally, by imagining the game in their mind, they would complete game specific tasks, visualizing themselves successfully completing blocking assignments on the field, and dominating the LOS as a unit, ultimately winning the game (see Appendix B).

◇◆◇

As another way to unite the offensive line, I would invite them to help celebrate the offensive line fraternity every Spring, by mixing them in with experienced coaching groups for our annual Up-Front Lineman Camp for the development of high school offensive linemen. We brought together the best mix of coaches anywhere, and bringing our Marauders players in to help out gave our unit exposure to skilled coaches and camaraderie with former professional players, who may inspire them to the next level.

All these things over time had the net effect of building relationships, bringing our offensive line unit closer together over the season, and through the years. Thus, our Marauder offensive line would find unity — you might say that they became a band of brothers, who trusted each other, communicated well, would fight in the trenches for each other, and ultimately control the LOS for our offence. The last thing they wanted was to let their teammates down. I'm pleased to say that throughout my coaching tenure at Mac, I have been blessed to develop close relationships with many of my OL players. I'll share stories about a few of these characters to illustrate this bond.

"Tubthumping (I Get Knocked Down)," Chumbawamba (1997)

Ryan Donnelly came to McMaster in 1997 as a walk-on tight end, at 6'5" and weighing only 195 lbs., "soaking wet." Coach Marshall looked at Ryan and said, "Well, you have a nice frame."

Ryan's story reminds me of my own, in that he was undersized but overcame it with toughness and a desire to train hard to get bigger, which he did gradually, year by year. He was also an elite lacrosse player, which added to his physicality and athleticism.

We were so short of offensive linemen at the time, we soon asked Ryan if he'd join our unit and learn the position. Luckily for us, he agreed because soon there was another injury and Ryan was starting at right tackle, weighing only 200 lbs.! Because of these circumstances he was forced to learn the position quickly under fire – he had no choice, but because he was smart and tough, he thrived.

By 2000 he had gained the weight and strength to match his great feet. Added to the toughness he arrived with; this made him a dominant offensive tackle in our unit. That year, in the OUA Semi-Final playoff game against Waterloo University, Ryan did something remarkable, which encapsulates his character and toughness. Late in the third quarter of this must-win game, deep in our own end of the field, he went down after a play. However, before the trainers could get on the field, he climbed up out of the mud and dragged himself back to the huddle. From the sideline, I couldn't tell exactly what had happened, or what the injury was. But when he returned to the huddle, I was relieved that he was okay. We needed him in this game.

Quarterback Ben Chapdelaine called the next play, and Ryan limped to the LOS and blocked his assignment well. After the play, he limped back to the huddle for the next play. This continued for the entire drive, which lasted the full length of the field, about an 80-yard drive. That drive culminated with a touchdown to take the lead in the game. After the score, Ryan went down in the end zone and waited for the trainers to arrive.

Later that night, we learned from Dr. Levy that Ryan's injury was a torn MCL and torn cartilage in his right knee. The fact that he finished the drive after sustaining such a serious injury remains the epitome of toughness for me. He was so determined to help the team win that he refused to quit until we scored.

But Ryan continued to astound us with his toughness the following week. He says, "I lied to Doc Levy when I told him my knee didn't hurt so I could play in the Yates Cup, but it was devastating. Probably another dumb move...Doc braced it up, and I didn't miss a snap in the Yates, or the Churchill [the following week]."

It didn't go unnoticed by the scouts because he was drafted in 2001 by the Tiger-Cats and played nine years in the CFL.

We hosted that Yates Cup — the OUA Championship Game — at old Les Prince Field, in front of a capacity crowd of 5000 fans, with people lined up four or five deep on the grass around the entire field because the old bleachers didn't hold half the crowd. The atmosphere was incredible for such a small venue. The crowd roared every time Ben Chapdelaine completed a pass to Ryan Janzen or Chris Rankin, the offensive line hammered an opening in the defence to spring running back Kojo Aidoo or Kyle Pyear (the best one-two punch in the league), or when Ray Mariuz made a big defensive play. The excitement of the crowd was palpable, celebrating the new-found success of their long-downtrodden team.

On November 11, 2000, we beat Laurier 48–23 for our first Yates Cup win as a staff. We had done it — in three years, under the leadership of Coach Marshall, we had taken a sad-sack program to conference champions!

As we came into a coaches' meeting a few weeks after season's end, Greg surprised us. He rewarded all of his assistant coaches with a beautiful Yates Cup bomber jacket, with maroon fabric shells and black leather sleeves, each one personalized with a coach's name and position. He handed them to us, one by one, as we entered the meeting room to commemorate the win. All the hard work we had done to accomplish the turnaround made it one of my most cherished sports mementos.

Ultimately, we were able to win a record four consecutive Yates Cup championships from 2000 to 2003. The Yates Cup is the oldest football trophy in North America, and only three other teams have reached this milestone: Toronto (1908–1911), Queens (1922–1925), and Western (1979–1982).[28]

Unfortunately, we never got past the OUA conference championship to play in the Vanier Cup. However, in three out of those four years, we lost in the national semi-final to the eventual Vanier Cup winner. Partly this was a result of the disparity between different school recruiting practices. Some schools, like McMaster, had true student-athletes just out of high school, while some teams across the country would recruit older kids from CJFL programs, or redshirted U.S. players. So, when we left our conference to play in the Mitchell Bowl or the Uteck Bowl, we would play a team with an average age that was years older than ours. Sometimes it seemed like it was men against boys.

Since then, U Sport has tried to even the playing field by instituting an age limit for players — now players have to finish their five years of

---

[28] Athletics and Recreation. Nov. 10, 2003. *McMaster captures fourth consecutive Yates Cup*. McMaster University Daily News. Url: dailynews.mcmaster.ca (accessed June 1, 2023).

eligibility by the year they turn 25, which makes it more fair for all teams across the country to compete at the highest level.

In this light, for the 2002 Yates Cup winning season, our starting offensive line unit included Matt O'Meara, Dave Forde, Jean-Paul Circelli, Andy Zaremba, and Fabio Filice. This group developed into a formidable unit that embodied our offensive line tenet: "Be relentless in out-working and out-hitting our opponents for four quarters." Every one of these young men were guys that I would welcome to my family dinner table.

They were blessed to have a very talented backfield to block for, too. Running backs Jesse Lumsden, Kyle Pyear, and Kojo Aidoo were the envy of the league. Unfortunately, Kojo broke his leg that year while filming a football commercial at Ivor Wynne Stadium, which put him out for the season. Jesse had the best acceleration from a standing start that I'd ever seen. He only needed a small crease in the defensive front to break into the next level, then no one on the defence could catch him. Jesse went on to play in the CFL, then became an Olympic bobsledder, winning gold and silver medals in the world championships.

Kyle was an incredibly talented and entertaining running back to watch. He had a very low centre of gravity, which allowed him to change direction quickly in the mud of Les Prince Field — no one could put their hands on him. As a group, these elite student-athletes were selfless and cheered each other on when they didn't have the ball in their own hands.

An example of this unselfish team attitude came at the end of that season, when Kyle gave each player on his OL and me a personalized framed picture of our unit. On the back of mine, it read: "I thank you for grooming your O-line into what they are now. I feel guilty for much of the recognition I get because they, and you, are the true unsung heroes. Thanks, Kyle Pyear #34." It is gratifying to know that one of my favourite players to watch appreciated his offensive line and took the time to acknowledge it, and to know that I had a small part in his success.

All the guys in that unit were tough, hard-working student-athletes. Matt O'Meara stands out because he had so many bad breaks, literally and figuratively, that he looked like a bionic player when he strapped on all his braces. It didn't matter how devastating the injury was, he would recover, rehabilitate, strap on another brace, then continue to play.

Matt's injuries included a broken fibula, close to the ankle, in 2001; a torn MCL in game two of the 2002 season — he wore a knee brace for the remainder of university; and a broken arm against Queen's in the 2002 Yates Cup game, a spiral fracture of the ulna and dislocated elbow, requiring surgery and a metal plate to repair — he wore an elbow brace for the remainder of his time in university.

In spite of these setbacks, Matt went third overall in the 2005 CFL draft. Matt played several years in the CFL, but he never really found his niche. I believe he could have been an All-Star, if given the chance to develop properly.

Over the years, I always appreciated it when coaches told me the hard truth, and I took that approach with my players, too, to help them understand what they needed to improve. Matt O'Meara was one player who appreciated this, even thanking me and other coaches for "always being straight with me, especially if it was something that I probably didn't want to hear but needed to — for example, that I needed to pick up my game If I wanted to keep playing, whether that was at Mac or the next level."

Kyle Koch committed to us from Kenora, Ontario, in 2003. We soon gave him the nickname Roadgrader, not because he was 6'2", 300 lb, and built like a brick shithouse, but because he knocked down everything in front of him when he got on a roll. I always gave the guys a "double plus" for pancakes when I graded their game film. Sometimes I was forced to give Kyle +4 on a single play because after pancaking the defensive tackle on the LOS, he would go downfield and pancake the linebacker or defensive halfback at the point of attack, springing the ball carrier for an even bigger gain!

In his senior year, I recommended to all CFL scouts I spoke to that he should be considered as a first-round pick in the upcoming draft. I told

Kyle this, too. I knew that he was the top interior (guard or centre) offensive lineman in the country, with the biggest heart.

That year, our team banquet fell on the day of the CFL draft. I knew as soon as I saw his face that he hadn't been drafted in the first round as I predicted. Worse than that, he hadn't been drafted at all. Apparently, the scouts decided collectively that Kyle was too short — I was astounded that not one scout saw the talent that Kyle possessed. I reassured him that if he could get an invite to camp as a free agent walk-on, he would open some eyes and have a successful pro career. Sure enough, he signed with Winnipeg as a free agent, then ended up the captain of the offensive line in Edmonton for several seasons.

I always worked hard to use the tools I learned to build the camaraderie of our offensive line unit and it is good to know it was appreciated by the players. As Kyle Koch attests, "The things I cherish most are the O-line dinners, the laughs, the beers, and the lifelong friendships. The culture of that group was already established (mostly by you) and that was [that] always no one guy was bigger than the group."

"Sweet Child of Mine," Guns and Roses (1987)

The epitome of relationship building between a player and coach in my experience was Jeremiah Brown. Jerry came to us in 2003, once again as a "project" because we were always hunting for good athletes who we could develop into offensive linemen. I could relate to an undersized kid that had the frame, toughness, and desire to succeed. Jerry was one such athlete.

But Jerry was unique in that he had never played football before he came to university. He was desperate to find his niche. When we invited him to join our offensive line unit, he quickly developed a love for the position. He had great feet and he played with an edge, but he needed to gain "good weight" to see the success he desired.

Jerry also presented me with a situation that would test all my coaching and parenting experience. He asked me if I'd stay on the field after practice one night so we could talk. In privacy, he told me he got his girlfriend pregnant and didn't know where to turn. He hadn't told anyone yet, and it was eating him up inside. I reassured him that I would be there to support him regardless of whether he decided to stay on the team or quit to support his new family. This was an opportunity for me to pass on the support I had received from previous coaches when I needed them most, to a player under my charge. Most importantly, Jerry needed to know I supported him unconditionally to help him through his time of need. This process was very emotional for both of us, and it bound us for life.

The fact that Jerry confided in me to share his personal crisis, at the young age of 19, had a profound impact on me. It validated the importance I placed on developing relationships with my players. My heart went out to him as if he were my own son.

Jerry decided to stay with the team for the rest of the season, but made the sacrifice in 2005 to leave the football team he loved to get a part-time job so he could support his family.

At some point afterwards, he participated in a rowing competition on campus with stationary rowing machines and discovered he had a knack for it — and he could row without having to put on 80 pounds of muscle. After he graduated from McMaster, he ended up in Victoria with his family, training with the national rowing team with the same determination that would have made him a professional football player under different circumstances.

Not ten years after leaving the Marauders, Paulette and I got up very early in the morning to watch Jerry's heat at the 2012 London Olympics. We were screaming at the television and filled with joy watching him win a silver medal as a member of the Canadian men's eight rowing team.

Jerry is now an author and motivational speaker. In 2018, he published his book, titled *The 4 Year Olympian*. I was thrilled when he called me from the passenger seat in his car recently to tell me his son Ethan was driving.

Unfortunately for the rest of us coaches and the Marauder program, after winning four consecutive Yates Cups at McMaster, Greg's success attracted the eye of the Tiger-Cats' brass, who hired him as head coach in 2004. Our well-respected strength and conditioning and quarterback coach, Marcello Campanaro, was hired to take over the program as head coach.

This was a compliment to Marcello, not only because he was taking over the program in the midst of unprecedented success, but also because he was expected to navigate the program through the construction of the David Braley Athletic Centre and Ron Joyce Stadium, which were completed in 2007 and 2008 respectively. These were multimillion-dollar investments in the McMaster athletics program made possible because of the generosity of their namesakes, due to the unflagging commitment of Peter George and Thérèse Quigley. During this period of construction (2005, 2006, and 2007), our home games were played at Ivor Wynne Stadium, which presented a host of logistical issues complicating these seasons.

It was a nostalgic time for me because of my affinity for my favourite old stadium, but it was a very difficult time for Marcello. The logistics of essentially being homeless for his tenure as head coach made his job especially difficult, in spite of support from his assistant coaches.

Unfortunately, Marcello's fate was sealed after the 2005 semi-final playoff loss against the Wilfred Laurier Golden Hawks. Jesse Lumsden, our best offensive player, was injured for that game, which limited our running attack, and Laurier was aided by a bounce pass that was missed by the referees late in the third quarter. Just when we were gaining some momentum, their quarterback's pass to their wide receiver was short by about a foot. The ball bounced off the turf and into the diving receiver's hands, to continue their touchdown drive, snuffing out any hope for a Marauder victory. When good fortune strikes like this for a team, there's nothing the other team can do about it, and it builds momentum for the "team of destiny." The Golden Hawks subsequently won the Vanier Cup by beating the University of Saskatchewan at our own home park, Ivor Wynne Stadium. It was a very exciting game, but I watched with mixed emotions, as we could have been playing in that game.

The head coach of that Laurier team was Gary Jeffries. Gary is a universally-respected coach who would give any of his players or staff the shirt off his back, if necessary. It's never easy to lose, but if you do, it makes it much easier to swallow if it's to a true gentleman of the game like Gary. We have become good friends over the years, sharing the football fraternity.

Stefan Ptaszek was the architect of Gary's Vanier Cup winning offence. In 2006, McMaster hired Stefan to take over our program and oversee the completion of our new state-of-the-art facilities. Stef is a slightly-built person, with all the speed and agility of a CFL receiver — he played for the Lions, Argos, and Tiger-Cats. Moreover, his physical agility is matched by his intellectual acuity. When asked a question, he tends to look at an issue from all sides — even some no one else considers relevant — reflecting on them fully, which means he seldom gives a yes or no answer, such that I affectionately call him "Confucius."

Stef's biggest strength is his empathy towards his players. For him, the players are people first, then students, then football players. He would never treat them any less, as some testosterone-filled coaches are prone to do in this ultra-competitive game. Thus, when recruiting, everything else being equal, Stef's reputation as a caring and empathetic coach can often be the difference-maker.

My son Jason recognized this when he committed to McMaster after being recruited by other schools, and I still appreciate it; when Junior was at his lowest point, during the time he suffered his back injury and subsequent surgery, Jason benefitted from Stef's empathy. While some coaches treat injured players like the plague with a condescending "What have you done for me lately?" attitude, Stef never stopped treating Jason like a player. Stefan named Jason captain of the defensive line after he recovered and returned to play.

On another note, I am also grateful to Stef for embracing my vision to launch our Up-Front Lineman Camp. I started the camp to develop high school offensive linemen because of a deficit in offensive line coaching in Ontario. Stef and I both agreed that, for unknown reasons, most high school coaches are not former offensive linemen; usually a former quarterback, running back, linebacker, or other position fills the role. As a result, through no fault of their own, they have no idea how to coach offensive line because they've never played the position, and it's very technical. Consequently, when asked about offensive line techniques or systems, many high school offensive linemen have told me they were coached to "Just block the guy in front of you!" They were frustrated because they would not be taught "how" to block.

Accordingly, in the spring of 2008, we launched the Up-Front Camp to great success. For the first two years, we had about 200 offensive linemen from all over Ontario register for the camp.

The camp is a fundamental skills camp, designed to teach the kids everything they need to know to become good offensive linemen. I learned early in my career that the most important thing for a successful block is your first step. Your first step often determines whether your block will be successful in the end, by putting you in the correct position to finish your block. For that reason, the camp emphasizes proper stance and where to put your first step on various types of blocks that may be implemented in the course of a game, though of course, we teach other essential skills as well. The kids really benefit from being taught these fundamentals by experienced coaches.

The Up-Front Lineman Camp became one of the highlights of my year — for me it was like Christmas in April. It is gratifying to see this wonderful fraternity of coaches come together to volunteer their time and share their wealth of experience — kids come from as far as Windsor, North Bay, Sudbury, Ottawa, and even from outside the province. The coaches are a mix of Tiger-Cat alumni, current CFL players, and experienced community coaches, with at least one Marauder lineman in each coaching group to demonstrate the techniques being taught. Tiger-Cat alumni who go out of their way every year to share their knowledge with the kids include Miles Gorrell, Darrell Harle, Brian Hutchings, Lee Knight, Bob MacDonald, John Malinosky, Dave Richardson, and Ralph Scholz. Many others have come when available over the years. Don Edwards was the President of the Ontario Football Alliance and coached at every Up-Front Camp for a decade before he passed.

Special mention goes to former Ticats offensive lineman Mike Filer. Mike attended the first Up-Front Camp as a high school player from Brantford in 2008. Ten years later, as the starting centre for the Cats, he volunteered to coach the camp and be our keynote speaker. In his beautiful team dressing room, at the brand-new Tim Hortons Field, the kids were blown away by their lavish surroundings and by the motivational speech that Mike gave them. Every one of them knew by the end of it that if they worked hard enough, they too could realize their dream of playing professional football.

Probably our best-known keynote speaker amongst the kids, was my old friend Chris Schultz. Even if they didn't know he was a former NFL and CFL star, the kids recognized him from his TSN broadcasting seat on the panel; always the best-prepared and most insightful analyst, he explained the blocking of opposing offensive lines especially well. Before his devastating sudden death in 2021, Chris always volunteered to coach at Up-Front, if his busy schedule allowed it. He loved fraternizing at the coaches' social afterward, mesmerizing the Marauder players who helped out at camp with endless stories from inside the game.

To this day, the kids benefit from the long experience of Coach Salavantis. At the age of 81, he was still attending every Up-Front Camp. His official title is "Senior Manager, Quality Control." (The camp is set to return after a pandemic-related hiatus, this time run by the Hamilton Tiger-Cats Alumni Association — we'll see if Coach Salavantis returns as well!)

Up Front Camp group shot, McMaster, 2012: Bob Butrym photo

I also wanted to thank my friends Tod Fryer and Luc Berardocco for volunteering their time helping behind the scenes at every Up-Front Camp and becoming honorary members of the offensive line fraternity.

The Up-Front Lineman Camp was a way for me to facilitate the teaching of fundamental football skills to young players and coaches and to celebrate the fraternity of offensive linemen, who usually don't get the coaching or recognition they deserve. It was fulfilling to get messages from players and coaches who enjoyed learning at our camp; many expressed their appreciation for the focus on teaching and learning and the elimination of competition and intimidation.

Every U Sport football team is in constant need to replenish their graduating players, and unlike the professional level, you can't draft or trade for a good player: it all comes down to recruiting the best players you can find.

We had some mediocre seasons for a couple of years at McMaster, because we were short a player here or there, and sometimes we were hit by the injury bug, but Stef continued to include us assistant coaches in recruiting, with recruiting coordinator Frank Gesztesi always hard at work.

Stef also engaged a network of local coaches in strategic areas as regional recruiters. Gerry Strong was our man in the Windsor area and he identified Kyle Quinlan as a quarterback recruit early.

Kyle says, "Gerry approached me after a high school game in Windsor, in my grade 10 year and stayed on me. I always liked that Mac was the first one to contact me." When Stef finally landed Kyle Quinlan out of the Essex Ravens program in 2008, we really didn't know how great he would become.

We also found the Up-Front Camp to be a good recruiting tool for offensive linemen. Offensive linemen are at a high premium in the recruiting process due to the large body-size requirement, which reduces the talent pool — because of the unique demands of their position, offensive linemen have to be the biggest athletes on the field — so there just aren't as many of them out there. Consequently, good offensive linemen are even rarer, creating competition from every school that recruits them. The Up-Front Camp is a great way to identify offensive linemen early, and Frank Gesztesi made sure he was at every one, to get potential recruits into our data bank.

It was a team effort, and once Stef confirmed he wanted them, Brian Brock and I would help land our offensive line recruits. This was marked the beginning of a new relationship with these high school boys, who we would continue to guide and mentor into solid players and who graduated as men. I like to look at it as "cultivating" the offensive line — the more time, effort, and passion we put into the process, the better the harvest.

Of course, McMaster's outstanding athletic facilities, thanks initially to the vision of Peter George and Thérèse Quigley so many years before, and the first-rate strength and conditioning staff at McMaster were a major part of the process. It's almost unbelievable comparing the current facilities at Mac with the facilities we started with, back when Al Bruno invited me to join his staff. This dramatic improvement helped in landing elite players at all positions, while building Stef's team, so our depth and leadership got stronger. It was very rewarding to see the fruit of our combined labour, not just by winning, but in seeing the personal development of these young student-athletes.

"I Can't Drive 55," Sammy Hagar (1984)

In 2011, we knew in training camp that we had the right mix up front to be good, with a group of starting offensive linemen who had the size, work ethic, and athleticism to protect our quarterbacks and run-block consistently. Here is a brief description of each of these "trench warriors:"

Matt Sewell was 6'8" and 340 lb coming out of his Milton, Ontario, high school. Matt started at left tackle for us from his first practice. He had been offered several Division 1 scholarships in the NCAA, but unfortunately, Matt's father suffered from cancer and couldn't travel far to see him play. It was our good fortune that Matt decided to come to McMaster so his dad could watch him play at our home games. Matt was so athletic, with such a high football IQ, that I just tried not to screw him up. He also had that edge on the field that, combined with his genetic gifts, would allow him to play at any level he chose to play — he was a natural.

Steve Schneider played left guard for us, at 6'5" and 310 lb, out of Cambridge, Ontario. He was a powerful and physical workhorse, who never complained about anything, no matter how hard I worked him.

Elliott Montag was our centre. He joined us from Georgetown, Ontario. Elliott was 6'2" and 280 lb, with great football instincts and communication skills. He had a superlative blocking technique and was able to stay low and use leverage to create movement on larger nose tackles.

Jason Medeiros was our right guard, at 6'4" and 320 lb. He came out of our backyard, St. Thomas More Catholic Secondary School in Hamilton. Jason had a great combination of size, physicality, and great feet for a big man. He loved his job as pulling guard, tracking down linebackers outside the box.

We pried Chris Pickard out of Western's territory when he joined us from London, Ontario. Chris played right tackle for us, at 6'4" and 285 lb. Chris was a smart rangy player, who overcame several injuries to become a consistent member of our unit.

We also had depth, provided by youngsters Tyler Goldsworthy, Bryce Hudson, Brad Minns, Sean Smith, and Tom Sterling.

Another ingredient in our successful Marauder football program was the medical staff. My old friend Doc Levy had now joined us as McMaster's team physician (and later, the medical staff at the David Braley Sports Medicine and Rehabilitation Centre), with Dr. Devin Peterson and Dr. David Robinson, all of them experts in their field.

One particular story from a home game against Guelph University, during the 2010 season illustrates the medical staff's importance. It's etched into the memory of most people at our packed stadium that day. The game was important for playoff standings, so it was very physical, with both teams determined to beat their conference rivals. Half our stadium was full of loud Guelph fans, dressed in yellow and red; of course, our fans would not be outdone, so the atmosphere was incredible at field level, with the rowdy crowd's noise echoing off the residence buildings, just across from the stadium.

We had the lead with a couple of minutes left on the clock and our young kicker, Tyler Crapigna, was punting from our end of the field. Guelph needed to block the kick to have any chance to win the game, so they attempted to block the punt. In so doing, two of their players collided behind our blockers and cascaded violently into Crapigna's kicking leg. From the sideline after the collision, I remember feeling nauseated when I saw the lower part of his leg fold in half like a limp jackknife, when he tried to pick it up off the turf, while still lying on his back. The crowd was now hushed into silence, because they saw the same thing I saw. Now a young player's fate was the only thing on everyone's mind.

The McMaster medical staff, led by Doc Levy, leapt into action. After about 15 minutes on the field, with the doctors huddled on their knees around Tyler, people started to question where the ambulance was, because it was obvious that Tyler had a severe injury. But I knew what the crowd didn't know: Crapigna didn't need an ambulance. He had the best sports medicine doctors setting his leg, right there on the field. Once the leg was set, they placed an inflatable cast on it to keep it in place and loaded him onto a golf cart, which delivered him to McMaster's on-campus hospital, a short distance away.

This immediate medical treatment made it possible for Tyler's leg to heal properly without surgery, and allow him to go on to a successful professional career in the CFL. Dr. Levy said about that day, "[Tyler] broke his tibia and fibula...I'm so glad that it did not end his career!"

The following off-season, Chris "Pusky" Puskas was hired as our head athletic therapist. Pusky was the final piece of the puzzle on our outstanding medical staff in 2011. He had served in the same role in the CFL for 17 years, 14 of them with the Tiger-Cats. His experience put us over the top for success, because of his intuitive ability to recognize when a player is injured (needs to stay off the field for rehabilitating treatment), as opposed to a player who is hurt (a temporary boo-boo, able to continue playing). On top of that, he gives his time selflessly to get the players back on the field — sometimes, it seems, working around the clock. His professionalism and ability to manage a training staff through the myriad challenges of the season are unmatched.

Another thing that benefitted us happened before the season even started. Coach Constantin, of the formidable Laval Rouge et Or, usually invites the team he thinks will be the best competition that season to attend his training camp in Quebec City. In 2011, Constantin invited Stef to bring his team up. Travelling together to spend part of training camp practicing against a top program like that helped set the tone for the season. In our unit drills and the full scrimmage, the Marauders saw that they could compete with Laval, and this instilled in them an often evasive, yet essential quality: confidence.

Although we had a relatively young team, we had a good mix of first year and veteran players. Hopefully, their confidence would continue to grow as the season progressed.

Our quarterbacks were Kyle Quinlan and Marshall Ferguson. Ferguson filled in admirably for Quinlan when he was suspended for two games for some off-field shenanigans. When he played, Quinlan was virtually unstoppable all season. They were coached by the young and innovative Jon Behie, who was also the offensive coordinator, and guided by Coach Stef's experience. I served as unofficial assistant offensive coordinator, supporting Behie primarily with the run game and pass protections.

Alongside our starting offensive line who were previously introduced we had great depth at receiver, with speed merchant Mike DiCroce, Ben O'Connor, Robert Babic, Brad Fochesato, and "Swiss army-knife" Matt Peressini — Matt knew every backfield and receiver position and he played them all at different times in the season, making him indispensable to the offensive. Receiver coach Al Anonech had a hand in recruiting most of them and enjoyed developing this hugely talented unit.

Our running backs were a mix of experience: Joey Nemet, Jimmy Hill, and rookie sensation, Chris Pezzetta — all outstanding athletes. Larry Guarascia was the running backs coach, pointing them in the right direction. Larry had played for Bernie Custis, and adopted his way of guiding his players like a favourite uncle, always offering subtle suggestions to help them hone their skills.

Our formidable defence consisted of warriors like Adam Dickson at nose guard, Roberto Filice, Kareem Ferreira, and Tanvir Bhangoo at defensive tackle; Mackenzie Dent, Scott Caterine, and Kevin Aleinik at defensive end (unfortunately, Jason Jr. didn't play because he was recovering from back surgery), coached by Carm Genovese, who had also been with the team since Al Bruno's time; Aram Eisho, Ryan Chmielewski, and Nick Shortill at linebacker (backed up by Trevor Gary, the son of my former teammate Greg Gary), coached by Tom Pain, who was also heavily involved in high school coaching; and finally, defensive backs Joey Cupido, Mike Daly, Stephen Dennis, Scotty Martin, and Steve Ventresca.

These defensive backs were a uniquely talented group coached by Mark Forsyth, the longest-standing coach at McMaster, who mentored them into a cohesive and dominant unit. Mark's experience and calm demeanour allowed him to teach the combination of skills and systems that allowed his unit to reach its highest potential.

In my opinion, next to the offensive line, the defensive back unit needs to be the closest-knit position group on a football team. Similar to offensive line, they are a five-man unit, and they need to know exactly what each member of their unit is doing. With the challenge of covering talented opposition receivers on a large field, one breakdown in their unit could lead to a game-changing score. The difference between these two position groups is that offensive linemen are bigger, stronger, and smarter — it's a shame about our looks! Kidding aside, in the open field, the defensive backs are spaced farther apart, so they don't have to worry about tripping each other, breaking each other's toes, or getting the quarterback killed if they make one wrong step.

Our special teams featured our now fully-recovered kicker Tyler Crapigna, coached by his one-on-one mentor, Dana Segin. Our "teams" were led by a demon on cover teams, Spencer Moore.

The season started out well, with a win over Queen's. But we hit a roadblock in our second game against Western. It was a hot summer day, and they implemented a no-huddle offence, which they hadn't shown before. Our defence got worn down by their long, physical drives that utilized the power-run game. We got our asses soundly kicked, with the final score 21–48 for the bad guys. The one positive taken from this one was that it put our feet firmly on the ground, and redoubled everyone's efforts: players, coaches, and support staff. We all sensed that we had a special group here — we just needed to right the ship. We finished the rest of the season unscathed, then handled Queen's in the OUA semi-final, 40–13.

This gave us another shot at Western in the final, which we had anticipated all season long as a test to see which team had improved the most over the season. Quinlan caught fire in the second half to complete 16 of 24 passes for four touchdowns — including a 102-yard strike to Michael

DiCroce. We knocked off our biggest rival in the Yates Cup — the oldest football trophy in existence — by a much improved 41–19 margin.[29]

It was a pivotal win for the program, demonstrating how hard the team had worked, and it earned us a trip to the Uteck Bowl, the national semi-final.

For the national semi-final Uteck Bowl, we flew from Toronto to Moncton to play Acadia, coached by Jeff Cummins, the burly and gregarious former Tiger-Cats defensive tackle and Atlantic University Sport (AUS) coach of the year.

The trip began on a rocky note. After we boarded the Porter charter prop plane and all our luggage was stored, the pilot told us we had to reduce the weight on the plane to get off the ground. After removing several items, like some of Pusky's physio gear and some player equipment bags, we could only pray that the gear would make it to Moncton in time for our game.

Our luck didn't improve at the start of the game, either. We were down 14 points to the Acadia Axemen early in the first quarter, due partly to an uncharacteristic fumble by quarterback Kyle Quinlan deep in our own end. We were all surprised when their entire team began to celebrate like they had won the Vanier Cup — and with so much of the game left to play.

Their premature celebration really motivated our players. Soon we shook off the cobwebs and started to play with the emotion and confidence we'd built over the course of the season. After taking control of the LOS on both sides of the ball, we won the game 45–21.

This was a historic victory for us, as it was the first time McMaster had won a national semi-final to earn the right to play in the Vanier Cup since the 1960s.

In retrospect, flying to Moncton for the Uteck Bowl, then a quick turnaround to Vancouver for our chance at a national championship was nostalgic for me, like a geographic reversal of my own Vanier Cup experience as a player with UBC three decades earlier. In this sense, for me, it was somewhat prophetic.

---

[29] Home the of McMaster Marauders. n.d. 2011 football schedule. Url: marauders.ca (accessed June 2, 2023).

◇◆◇

Likewise, preparing for the Vanier Cup, which was to be played on Friday, November 25, 2011, in BC Place Stadium, Vancouver, was like a homecoming for me. Except that after the multimillion-dollar upgrade the province did for the 2010 Olympics, the stadium was more gorgeous now than it was when I played. Now, with its new retractable roof, huge suspended video board, improved seating, and soft blue background lighting, it was a state-of-the-art entertainment venue. The perfect place to host the greatest university football game ever played on Canadian soil.

Being back at BC Place Stadium brought back great memories of all the games I played there in front of my friends and family, especially our 1986 Grey Cup win over the much-favoured Edmonton. This gave me a great feeling about the outcome of Friday's game, which would also be against a much-favoured team — the Laval Rouge et Or. I shared these positive thoughts with the offensive line in our ongoing practices and meetings, preparing them for their own national championship game.

Similarly, the former All-Star and broadcasting great Chris Schultz was in town covering the Grey Cup, so Coach Stef invited him to speak to our team in the dressing room after one of our practices. In a game of this magnitude, coaches can't afford to miss any opportunity to motivate the team, and Schultzy didn't disappoint. He clearly outlined why we were there, and that in a game like this, it's our team against the world because no one, except for the people in that room, thought we had a chance against the great Rouge et Or with their six championships. The entire team was filled with motivation when Chris finished his talk.

On Thursday, the night before the game, I held our last offensive line pre-game visualization session. After the guys were all comfortable in one of the hotel rooms, and before I started the relaxation activity, I asked each of the players to share with the group what was most important about tomorrow's game. It became a very emotional moment, with some of them shedding tears as they opened their hearts to their closest teammates; it was truly a binding moment for our unit, which I felt privileged to be part of. After this, I took them through a much-deserved period of complete relaxation to rest their weary bodies before the battle they would face the next night. I concluded the session with these words: "Let's show the world that we are the best offensive line in the country. Visualize yourself tomorrow after the game, bloodied, sweaty, and exhausted — victorious!"

Another source of positive karma for me took place the next morning, at the Grey Cup breakfast put on by the CFL. Because the Grey Cup was scheduled for Sunday of that weekend, the Grey Cup festival was in full swing. At this breakfast, my former coach Frank Smith was being honoured with a university scholarship in his name, to be awarded to a deserving local athlete. I made sure I was at the event to honour my old coach, before hopping into a cab back to my hotel for our last offensive line meeting. It seemed fitting that Coach Smith, one of my greatest mentors, was being honoured the same day we would be battling on the gridiron for the Vanier Cup.

"Bobcaygeon," Tragically Hip (1999)

That night, before the team left the dressing room for the biggest game of their lives, Coach Stef's last pre-game speech of the year was short and from the heart:

> Gentlemen. The biggest game of our lives is right out that door; one team, one team walks out that door. One team is my Marauder team. We can move fucking mountains! This is the best football team to ever put an 'M' on their chest. Ever! I got nothing left to say to you guys except God bless you, I love you. Let's go get em!

At this point, the head coach's words were the exclamation mark culminating a spirited week of practice, which in itself was a microcosm of a whole season of hard work, sweat, and blood — the emotion was palpable as the team stormed out of the dressing room for their last team breakdown of the season at centre field of this iconic stadium.

Meanwhile, at home in Hamilton, thousands of Marauder fans gathered on campus, in pubs, and around their home TVs and computer screens, to watch McMaster's biggest game in decades unfold before their eyes. With the three-hour time difference and the riveting game unfolding, most people didn't realize that they would be glued to their screens into the wee hours of the night.

After the kickoff, we had so many outstanding players making big plays in the game that there is not enough space here to do them all justice, so I'll focus on the key things I witnessed during the game.

Kyle Quinlan threw the ball with pinpoint accuracy for the entire game. Many of these went to Robert Babic, who tied the single game record with 12 catches, for 135 receiving yards.

Quinlan mixed in 106 yards on the ground, with one of the great rushing hurdles of all time. Some people call it "The Game When Quinlan Jumped" because of that drive-preserving leap in the second quarter. Quinlan led us to 675 yards of total offence, and 41 first downs — a second and first in Vanier Cup history, respectively.[30]

Quinlan's counterpart on our defence was Aram Eisho, who was relentless from his middle linebacker position and led all players with 11.5 tackles in the game.[31]

Nick Shortill, another outstanding linebacker, must be recognized for overcoming his sickness to play in the game, period. He woke up on game day as pale as a ghost with serious flu-like symptoms. Pusky stayed back at the hotel with him, administering his unique form of TLC, until Shortill felt well enough to travel to the stadium, let alone play. Although they arrived at the stadium in a taxi at the last possible moment, you'd never believe he was sick watching his stellar play.

Our whole team started fast and dominated the first half, with the score 23–0 at half-time. Laval battled back with a couple of quick scores to start the second half. Then, OUA Player of the Year Mike DiCroce almost put the game out of reach when he responded with a 102-yard touchdown catch from Quinlan. However, the score was negated when DiCroce was called offside by a hair, which allowed Laval some "Oh my god, that was close" momentum. From this point, both teams fought hard in a back-and-forth second half.

Our coaches on both sides of the ball were constantly guiding their units when they came off the field between series. It was a human chess match, and no one could let their guard down for a second — every detail

---

[30]Watson, A. Nov. 25, 2011. *2011 Vanier Cup: McMaster claims first Vanier Cup*. Vanier Cup History. Url: presto-en.usports.ca (accessed June 2, 2023).
[31] Ibid.

we had covered in preparation mattered and was now being applied on the field. When Laval fought back, as we knew they would under Coach Constantin, the blood pressure started to rise on the bench. My consistent message to the offensive line was, "This is why we play this game. We knew it wouldn't be easy. This is where all our training, meetings, and practice pay off. Stay the course!"

The players responded.

With about five minutes left in the fourth, Quinlan had driven us just inside the ten-yard line. Coach Behie, in concert with Coach Ptaszek, had been calling plays at a frantic pace the entire game. Behie turned to me and asked what run-play I recommended for the situation. I suggested "the Counter" to Matt Peressini, which quickly came to mind because we had been successful with it earlier in the game. Behie didn't always take my suggestions, but this time he did. Peressini took the hand off and followed his blockers, weaving through Laval's entire defence for the touchdown. He capped the drive off with a catch on the two-point convert and we had a seven-point lead again.

Later in the fourth, with the score tied at 31 and less than two minutes left on the clock, we were pinned deep in our own end, needing to get the ball at least out of field goal range to avoid a loss in regulation. On second down, Quinlan threw the ball from inside our own end zone — and Ben O'Connor rose up vertically amidst three defenders, to snatch the ball out of the air, making an astonishing fingertip catch. A miraculous play. It kept us alive and we continued the drive out of the shadow of our own goalposts, putting us in position for a game-winning field goal.

While it was a disappointment that regulation time ended with the game tied after the great start we had, if we hadn't missed that field goal, the game would not have become the classic that it is considered today.

The teams exchanged touchdowns in the first overtime period. This set the scene for the boisterous crowd of 25,000 to cheer in double overtime in a championship game — every football fan's dream.

It was at about this time that TSN's analyst Duane Forde exclaimed on national television his famous, "Best. Game. Ever!" All the fans back home went nuts, especially those on campus packing McMaster's Burridge Gym.

Then, in the second overtime period, intrepid defensive back Steve Ventresca intercepted the ball, which resulted in one of the most exciting defensive plays at any level. After the catch, Ventresca lateralled the ball to a teammate and the defence turned it into a rugby play, lateralling to each other several times, as they moved the ball down the field. The crowd was deafening as they witnessed this incredible football play. I had goose bumps, knowing our offence would get the ball back with a chance to win the game.

This set us up for another game-winning field goal, which Tyler Crapigna nailed for the win!

The entire team exploded onto the field with excitement after the historic kick, knowing the Marauders had won the first Vanier Cup in school history. Everyone was spent, both physically and emotionally. Players, coaches, and support staff formed a mosh-pit on the field; we danced, and hugged, and cried, and high-fived whoever was nearby. What a rush!

Matt Sewell and I came together in the crowd. As he knocked the Tilley hat off my bald head with his big bear hug, he cried, "Coach, you told me when I committed to Mac that we would win the Vanier Cup, and now we have!" We wept tears of pure joy together – two big tough guys balling, as the emotion of the moment took over. We had just won the first Vanier Cup in McMaster University history!

After the game, I was exhausted and stoned out of my mind on adrenaline. I felt like I was in a dream — it was surreal, my feet seemed like they were two feet off the ground and there was a haze around everything I saw, created by the fireworks in my mind. The long days preparing throughout the playoffs, with late coaches' meetings and film breakdown, team meetings, practices, travel from coast to coast through multiple times zones, hotel rooms and restaurant meals, and lack of sleep, meant we were all running on fumes by game's end. But the win made it all worth it.

2011 Vanier Cup Champion McMaster Marauders, Vancouver: Rick Zazulak photo

"Good Day Sunshine," The Beatles (1966)

Paulette and the twins had flown out for the game, and both our families living in B.C. had joined them in the stadium stands. Now somehow, we all ended up in the tunnel under the stands just outside our dressing room. Everyone was totally absorbed in the excitement of the game and basking in the glow of victory. Suddenly, Kyle Quinlan appeared with the Vanier Cup in his arms — the entire family took advantage of this unique photo opportunity with the player of the game holding the cup.

When we left the stadium to find the car, we came across Ken Welch, the long-time Hamilton T.V. sports broadcaster, wandering outside the stadium with a wide grin on his face, also delirious with excitement. Ken was an extraordinary Marauder supporter, who covered many games over the years broadcasting the *OUA Game of the Week* on CHCH TV. If he wasn't doing the game live, he was on the sidelines so he could report about it on his sports broadcast. He also generously volunteered his time to emcee sports-related events in the city, especially our football banquets. After an emotional hug, Ken joined us for the ride back to our hotel for the team victory party.

The McMaster brass had thought of everything for the team party. There was enough food and beverages to feed an army, which I guess they did. Coaches and parents shared cigars outside on the balcony of the ballroom, reliving all the spectacular plays of the best game they'd ever seen.

I had vowed that I would stay up all night partying if we won the cup. I kept my promise in Mark Alfano's room, much to his chagrin. As assistant athletic director, he had the responsibility of being "Cup Watcher," so many of us enjoyed champagne from the Vanier Cup in Mark's room. I was there until I saw the sunrise.

"Knocking at the Door," Arkells (2016)

Probably the best description of the game comes from renowned sports columnist, Steve Milton:

> Maybe there will be other national football championships but there could be none as sweet, none as excruciatingly memorable as the first. McMaster's unexpected 41–38 double-overtime win over Laval entered Hamilton folklore just seconds after its wild and redemptive conclusion in the wee eastern minutes of Saturday morning. ...And this was clearly the greatest team in Marauder history.[32]

The game was watched by thousands across the country and many in Hamilton attested it was the greatest game they ever watched — the game was transformational, uplifting the entire city. The win immediately placed our program in the midst of Hamilton's great football tradition, including that of the Tiger-Cats, the Hurricanes of the CJFL, and greats like Bernie Custis, Ron Lancaster, Russ Jackson, Ang Mosca, and Rocky DiPietro. I was proud to be a part of something great.

[32] Milton, S. Nov. 28, 2011. Marauders make history. *The Hamilton Spectator*. Url: thespec.com/sports (accessed June 5, 2023).

The best offensive lineman on the best team in the country was Matt Sewell. Matt had committed to McMaster for personal reasons, in spite of receiving multiple NCAA Division 1 scholarship offers.

Matt shared with me the beginning of his journey with McMaster:

> After calling Coach Ptaszek and informing him of my decision to play at McMaster, my next call was to Coach Riley. As soon as I told him I was going to be attending Mac, the first thing he said to me was 'Matty, we're going to win the Vanier Cup!'...Coach was right. From the coaching staff to athletic trainers to the team managers, every single one, not only helped us develop as players, but also as people...[Our offensive line] were never the most talented group, but we were the toughest and the hardest working, and most importantly, we learned to play for each other and not for ourselves. Coach Riley's emphasis on the mentality needed to be successful and play at the next level was one of the biggest benefits for me.

Matt's words illustrate his appreciation for the camaraderie, unity, and psychology of sport we used for personal growth: all these aspects of the team were important to our success. Matt was drafted 8th overall into the CFL in 2013 by the Argos, while already having signed a contract with the NFL's Tennessee Titans.

Including that Vanier Cup victory, McMaster had the longest winning streak in U Sport history, with 21 consecutive wins from 2011–2012. And all of the offensive linemen in that superlative unit have graduated to become successful contributors to their communities — all fine young men with families and careers. I am proud to be associated with them and to see their success unfold after graduating.

OVERTIME

ALUMNI FRATERNITY

"As the Years Go Passing By," The Jeff Healey Band (2013)

I began writing this book during the pandemic, after I retired from teaching. Since I started, I've seen the world turned upside down by the global pandemic and I've had a complete left knee replacement resulting from that knee injury back in grade 12. I've continued my participation in the Hamilton Tiger-Cat Alumni Association (HTCAA) and the Canadian Football League Alumni Association (CFLAA), which allows me to give back to the sport that gave me so much: an outlet for the internalized rage of my bullied younger self; a path away from street-fighting; a career; and a path towards Paulette and ultimately, the taming of the Mad Dog within me.

I was fortunate enough to join the HTCAA soon after I retired from playing. It's funny though, as active players, no one even entertains the idea of joining the Alumni Association because we're all invincible and therefore playing the game we love forever! The HTCAA is for the old farts, right?

In 2014, when my old friend Dave Richardson was president, he invited me to join him and the other alumni on the Board of Directors. It was a pleasure to team up with guys like Mark Bowden, Dave Lane, Terry Lehne, Bob Krouse, Mike McCarthy, Dave Marler and Glenn Timlock to help steer the association's growth and success.

Eventually, I was asked to run for president of the HTCAA. I set my priorities as building a closer partnership with the football club, developing a mission statement to keep us on the constitution's path, and resurrecting the Wall of Honour Dinner, which went temporarily dormant when state-of-the-art Tim Hortons Field stadium was built to replace historic Ivor Wynne. We also needed to create a gathering spot for our alumni members in the new stadium.

Our Board's creation of the Alumni Clubhouse, a unique place for alumni to celebrate our fraternity at the new Tim Horton Field stadium, is the biggest project we've undertaken and also helped to improve our relationship with the football club. Essentially, our partnership in the clubhouse build became a springboard to many opportunities for us to work together, supporting amateur football in the Greater Hamilton community. This symbiotic relationship for both parties at the top of the football food chain is crucial for the health and growth of football at the grassroots level.

Jessica (left), Jordan and I enjoy our HTCAA Clubhouse, Tim Hortons Field, 2019: Jason Riley photo

◇◆◇

After my term as president of the HTCAA, Leo Ezerins invited me to join the CFLAA board, which has a national scope, including representatives from the alumni associations of each CFL team. I appreciated the invitation to help in supporting our former players on a national level.

In this regard, the most important event on the CFLAA calendar is the Legends Luncheon. This annual event is put on at each Grey Cup Festival to generate funds for the Alumni Support Fund, which helps former CFL players who experience financial burdens due to high medical bills or other difficult circumstances. It was exciting to be involved with planning the 2021 Luncheon when the Grey Cup was held in Hamilton.

You may recall the nationally-televised brawl between Joe Kapp and Angelo Mosca, which occurred during the Legends Luncheon in Vancouver, in 2011. These two long-retired players were so competitive that they had a fistfight on the stage over a conflict they had on the football field nearly 50 years prior! This really put the Legends Luncheon on the map for football fans across the country because it went viral on social media. Mosca even accepted an invitation from Dr. Phil, to share the story of the 48-year-long conflict on national television. Kapp declined the invitation.

Mike Walker was inducted into the CFHOF in 2021, as one of the greatest defensive tackles ever to play in the CFL. It was uplifting to see so many of our teammates in town to celebrate with Mike, who has experienced devastating health issues over the past few years related to disc degeneration in his spinal column.

He brought the crowd to its feet when he got out of his wheelchair and walked with a cane across the stage to receive his award and unveil his bust. It brought a tear to the eye to witness it after all the surgeries and rehab he has endured, which have included laminectomies and discectomies on the eighth to tenth thoracic vertebrae; transforaminal lumbar interbody fusion (TLIF) surgery on the eighth to eleventh thoracic vertebrae; cervical laminoplasty of the third to seventh cervical vertebrae. Mike notes, "The surgeon reconstructed most of my spinal column." During one of the surgeries, a spinal fluid leak necessitated an additional surgery 10 days later. Mike's thyroid was also found to be massive, and his spleen lacerated, so even more surgeries were needed; he has degenerative disc disease and a rare arthritis called ankylosing spondylitis. Mike says, "Post-op, I also got blood clots in my legs and lymphoedema. ...The doctors thought I would regain much more function, but even though I swim and do therapy almost every day, it is increasingly apparent I am disabled for life and will need more surgeries — likely fusions — in the future." Mike kindly offered to include his story here to illustrate why the Alumni Support Fund is so important for former CFL players, as his medical issues have resulted in financial challenges for his family.

Additionally, the annual Legends Luncheon is well-known for recognizing a local alumnus with the Alumnus of the Year Award. The recipient is selected by the host club's alumni association each year.

This puts into context why I'm so happy that Bob Krouse and I were co-recipients of the 2021 CFLAA Alumnus of the Year Award. This was truly an unexpected honour. I was very humbled and grateful to be forever associated with Bob in this way, as he is one of the most respected Tiger-Cat alumni of all time.

Last year, the CFLAA also initiated the annual Indigenous Champion Award, in keeping with the Canadian Football League's Truth and Reconciliation initiatives. I felt fortunate to chair the first steering committee for the new award, which recognizes the contributions of local Indigenous coaches or non-Indigenous coaches who coach Indigenous players. Indigenous HTCAA board member John Macdonald acted as our Indigenous advisor and was instrumental in launching this excellent award. The co-recipients of the inaugural award were Jim Styres (posthumously) from the Deer Clan of the Cayuga Nation, and Justin Shakell, from the Tyendinaga Mohawk Territory. The new award was embraced by all the local football stakeholders and the media. It was really nice to see local Indigenous communities celebrating the recognition of their contributions to the football community.

POST-GAME ANALYSIS

"Jeremy," Pearl Jam (1991)

Throughout this journey, I've learned that the most important things in life are human relationships and the collective power of the human spirit to overcome any obstacles in life. Of course, we are all different, and we each need to discover the tools available to us to deal with these obstacles; these, plus personal inner strength, will allow us to not only overcome challenges, but also to grow as people. You've read throughout this book how for me, football was that first tool I picked up, which I used as an outlet for the inner rage I had as a result of being bullied as a child.

Football coaches often use the term, "When the bullets are flying," as a metaphor for the battles on the football field during a game, which tests the ability of a player to apply all the things they've been prepared for in meetings and practice. It is also a test of character — how does one respond under pressure? Going full circle, this illustrates that microcosm of life that football games are: each game tests the athlete's (and coaches') ability to succeed in the face of the emotional ups and downs they experience on the field. It's true football is only a game, but it gives us the tools to deal with life. All sports provide this to an extent, but football does it best.

But for kids who are victims of bullying, it doesn't have to be football. Any sport will help them develop their self-confidence, give them a sense of belonging, and get the exercise needed for their physical and mental well-being. As the saying goes, "movement is a privilege," and we tend to take it for granted until we lose it. That's why I encourage all parents to find a sport their kids enjoy, to participate in some form, to the level they are able.

It is common knowledge that bullying can have profound effects on its victims, and can lead to depression, anxiety, and other mental health issues.[33,34,35] Early intervention and a strong support network for bullied kids are crucial. As a youth, I developed anger-management issues in spite of my support network at home. Fortunately, I found football gave me a positive outlet to channel that anger.

That experience of being bullied as a child also made me an empathetic teacher to my students. I was able to recognize the most vulnerable students and provide a safe place for them to learn every day. Most of my students appreciated knowing I was in their corner, and willing to spend time with them to help them cope.

Though I was able to use my experience of being bullied in this positive way later in my life, this may not be shared by many other bullying victims. In fact, in contemporary society, the growth of social media has made bullying even more dangerous to our youth than it was when I was a child. Kids like myself could escape from it when we got home, but today's kids can be victimized around the clock unless they turn off their techno-gadgets.

In the years leading up to my retirement, I noticed this trend as a first aid provider in my school. I witnessed a steady increase in mental health issues among students. I'm not a Luddite, but I do believe social media can be catastrophic for vulnerable youth, especially those without a strong support network outside of school; recent research supports this.[36]

---

[33] Takizawa, R., Maughan, B., and Arseneault, L. 2014. Adult health outcomes of childhood bullying victimization: evidence from a five-decade longitudinal British birth cohort. *American Journal of Psychiatry* 171 (7): 777–784.

[34] Brunstein Klomek, A., Sourander, A., and Elonheimo, H. 2015. Bullying by peers in childhood and effects on psychopathology, suicidality and criminality in adulthood. Psychiatry, *The Lancet* 2 (10): P930–941.

[35] Bjereld, Y, Daneback, K., Gunnarsdóttir, H., and Petzold, M. 2015. Mental health problems and social resource factors among bullied children in the Nordic countries: a population based cross-sectional study. *Child Psychiatry & Human Development* 46: 281–288.

[36] Abi-Jaoude, E., Treurnicht Naylor, K., and Pignatiello, A. 2020. Smartphones, social media use and youth mental health. *Canadian Medical Association Journal* 192 (6): E136–E141.

Social isolation due to the pandemic has exacerbated this problem over the past few years.[37]

It's like we have created a huge social experiment with our youth as the guinea pigs, and we are just seeing the initial outcomes of the study. The final empirical data of this experiment may come too late. Though it seems that the horse is out of the barn and now we're trying to close the gate, hopefully as a society we can figure out how to mitigate the damage. I believe less screen time and investing in more sports for our kids would be a good start.

Beyond this, when we see bullying, we need to identify the aggressor, improve dialogue to uncover the cause of the toxic behaviour, and provide psychological and emotional support for both parties, especially the victim. On a higher level, we should start with legislation protecting youth on the unsupervised online bullying platforms that the big-tech companies provide.

For people like me, who are or were victims of bullying, please remember that you are not alone. There are many people in your situation, with trained professionals available for support. If it's cyber-bullying, first try turning off your device, then speak to a trusted person to get the help you need. Remember, there are always options in life and talking to someone will help you find the right option for you.

"Shine," Collective Soul (1993)

Post-football, I still need an outlet and an adrenaline fix, which I get by riding the trails on my mountain bike amid Hamilton's beautiful natural areas. I've enjoyed the Niagara Escarpment Greenbelt since Paulette and I arrived in the city (contrary to popular belief, other than the obvious industrial pockets, Hamilton is a beautiful city). Riding this amazing trail network helps

---

[37] Loades, M.E., Chatburn, E., Higson-Sweeney, N., Reynolds, S., Shafran, R., Brigden, A., Linney, C., McManus, M.N., Borwick, C., and Crawley, E. Rapid systematic review: the impact of social isolation and loneliness on the mental health of children and adolescents in the context of COVID-19. *Journal of the American Academy of Child & Adolescent Psychiatry* 59 (11): 1218–1239.e3.

maintain my physical fitness, which has become a key in my mental health regimen; as well as my adrenaline fix, it also provides an escape from the craziness enveloping our contemporary world.

Our little Yorkie-cross pup, Rambo, has become an important mental health support for both Paulette and I. He has helped to fill the void in the house when all the kids moved out and we became empty-nesters. He brings much joy to our home and Rambo's companionship was therapeutic for me during the isolation of the pandemic. He never left my side when I was bed-ridden during recovery from my knee surgery. Rambo's dedication to us is a humbling reminder of what unconditional love is.

Rambo thinking about his frisbee with Paulette and I in Hamilton, 2022: Jason Riley photo

I don't include Paulette in the "pandemic isolation" discussion above because she chose to continue to work at the bank through the worst of it. She was close to retirement and I encouraged her to do so, but being the loyal person she is, she refused to let down her colleagues at the bank and continued to put herself at risk to support them. She's one tough cookie!

It has been therapeutic to reconnect with many of my old teammates and coaches to corroborate stories from championship seasons for this book. One thing I've noticed is that the bond between us never fades and, when we talk, it's like we were never apart.

Spirituality is also important both to my mental health and, I think, in my ongoing personal growth. Though mine wasn't a particularly religious family when I was growing up, our parents taught us to respect others, appreciate the natural world, and celebrate the beauty of life. Now, contemplating my experiences, I am awed by life's unexplained mysteries. I am convinced that many of my experiences are not just coincidences or the result of sheer dumb luck, including the times I would have died as a child (the bee attack and the deep wrist laceration) if specific people weren't in the exact right place at the right time to save my life. And whenever I reminisce about my favourite summer job as park warden assistant at Buntzen Lake, I remember how my connection with the natural world gave me spiritual inner peace.

And of course, I still feel both awed and blessed that my friend and I didn't die on the way home after draft night when we were headed straight for that light post and somehow missed it by inches.

Spiritualism has become increasingly more important for me over the years, especially as a Catholic teacher, but although attending Mass or any organized religious event led by a holy person can be very comforting and emotionally therapeutic, we can be sure that the brick-and-mortar building is not "the Church." Spirituality has been part of the human condition from the beginning — so we don't even need a physical building to enjoy the benefits of our personal spiritual journey. "The Church" is the people. It's the collective human spirit that unites us all — yes, bound by the Holy Spirit in the Catholic faith, but for people who have no organized religion in their lives, this unity can still be embraced in other ways. Likewise, the best definition for the Holy Spirit is love — God is love. Everyone, all people, need and strive to attain love in their busy, often difficult lives. We cannot live without love, regardless of our sexual orientation, ethnicity, age, or any part of our personal identity. Love is love is love.

Love, the human spirit, and our connections to each other are the most striking mystery to me, illustrated by the hysterics my then-four-month-old daughter, Jordan, went into at the exact time my father died. I will never forget it and, although they were over 4,000 kilometres apart, I will always believe in my heart that I witnessed a spiritual connection between them.

Finally, what does one call it when a scrawny, undersized boy with zero self-confidence ultimately wins three national championship rings at a big man's sport? It's the ring that motivates everyone through the endless work, blood, and sweat of the game. It's the ring that we cherish for the rest of our lives as evidence of our team's greatness, which no one person can win on their own. I don't know the answer to the question, but I do know this; the human spirit, unity of purpose, and love among the players for each other on all three of my championship teams transcended any of their physical aspects.

Though football provided me first with an outlet for my rage, it gave me those other tools for personal growth — hard work, working as a team, resilience, and that love between teammates who ultimately often became more like brothers. And of course, since I met her back in university, there has been Paulette, the perfect woman for me, with the temperament, character, and sense of humour to domesticate this Mad Dog. It has been love that really saved me: love and football.

APPENDIX A

CANADIAN FOOTBALL 101: POSITIONS AND BASIC TERMINOLOGY DIAGRAM AND GLOSSARY

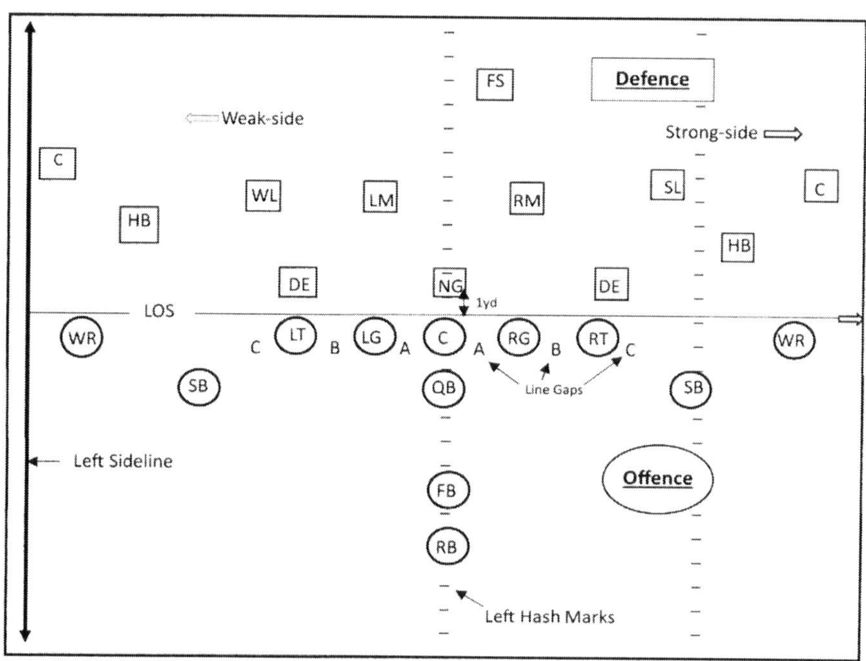

12 Offensive Positions

LT – Left Tackle
LG – Left Guard
C – Centre
RG – Right Guard
RT – Right Tackle
QB – Quarterback
FB – Fullback
RB – Running Back or Tailback
WR – Wide Receiver (2)
SB – Slot Back (2)

12 Defensive Positions

NG - Nose Guard
DE – Defensive End (2)
WL – Weak-side Linebacker (Will)
LM – Left Middle Linebacker
RM – Right Middle Linebacker
SL – Strong-side Linebacker (Sam)
C – Corner (2)
HB – Halfback (2)
FS – Free Safety

Canadian Football 101: Glossary of Terms

(See diagram above for context of some terms.)

A-Gap: The gap between the centre and guard on the LOS (see diagram above)

All-Star: Each year the best players at each position are selected by the media and coaches to form an All-Star team.

Assignments: Whatever a player at any position is coached to do based on the coaches' game plan; players are required to complete their assignments for the success of the team. Dedication, teamwork, and discipline are needed for every player to learn their assignments and execute them in the game.

Backside (BS): Refers to the side of the field away from the offensive play. If the offensive play is attacking to the right side of the field, the backside of the play is to the left.

Backside edge: Refers to the outside area (edge) on the backside of the offensive formation or defensive box.

Backside guard: The offensive guard on the backside of any play.

Blitzing front: Refers to the alignment and posture of the defenders in the box, and how many of them are likely to chase down and tackle the quarterback.

(Your) block: Every offensive player may have an assignment to block a particular defensive player, based on the game plan — coaches will hold you accountable to complete "your block."

Blockers: Any players who are required to block opposition players for the success of a play.

Box: The defensive area along the LOS, between the DEs, and back to behind the linebackers – generally any defender aligned in this area can blitz the QB, so the OL have to account for them in the pass-protection scheme. Anyone in this area prior to the snap is considered "in the box."

Break-out pattern: A receiver's route (pattern), where he runs straight ahead for a specific number of yards (usually 5–10), then suddenly plants his inside foot and breaks "out" toward the sideline on a 90-degree angle. This is a common quick-hitting pass play because the QB knows exactly where his receiver will be when he throws the ball to him.

Bull rush: When a defensive lineman collides straight into his blocker and attempts to drive him straight back to the quarterback.

Cadence: The rhythmic call of the quarterback prior to the snap of the football. It's important that the offence knows the cadence, so they don't jump off-side before the snap.

Chop block: When a defender is engaged with one blocker high and another player hits him low at the same time.

Convert/extra point: After a touchdown (TD) is scored, the scoring team is given the option to kick for one extra point from the 32-yard line (making the TD worth seven points), or attempt an offensive play running or throwing from the 3-yard line for two extra points (making the TD worth eight points).

Cover teams: Special teams that have to cover the field after a kick, and tackle the opposition player who returns the kick towards them. With the kick-returner and the cover team running at full speed towards each other, this results in some of the highest-velocity collisions in the game.

Cross-stunt: Any stunt where two or more defenders cross paths to rush the quarterback.

Cut block: When an offensive lineman blocks a defender below the waist to cut them down to the ground, usually because the play requires the quarterback to make a quick throw and needs the defender's hands down.

Defence: The group or squad of 12 players on a team that is designated as defenders, who will only go on the field when their team does not have possession of the football. The defence must stop their opponent's 12 offensive players from moving the football towards their goal line and scoring points (see diagram above).

Defensive halfback: A defensive back positioned outside his linebacker, and inside the cornerback, usually responsible for covering the offensive slotback (see diagram above).

Defensive line (DL): The group of three or more larger defensive players, lined up closest to the offence. In the Canadian game, DL must line up one yard back from the line of scrimmage (LOS - see diagram above).

Defensive secondary: The group of five smaller, faster defenders, lined up behind the linebackers and forming the third level of defence (see diagram above).

Deliver a punch: Offensive linemen are trained to deliver an open-handed punch to the chest or shoulders of the defender they are blocking to slow their progress up the field when they are rushing the passer. This is one of the most effective techniques used in the trenches to protect the quarterback.

Down lineman: Anyone on the offensive line or defensive line with their hand on the ground, in a three-point stance.

Downs (three-down system): Each attempt by the offence to move the ball forward on the field is called a down. In the Canadian game, the offence is given three downs (attempts) to move the ball 10 yards (a 10-yard measuring chain on the sideline is used to measure the distance). If the offence is successful in moving the ball 10 yards or more, they are rewarded with a "first down," and the 10-yard chain is moved forward to mark the new distance. If the offence is not successful in moving the ball 10 yards, they must punt the football to the other team, and the opposing offence now has three downs to move the football forward 10 yards. This process continues until one of the teams is successful in moving the football across the goal line for a touchdown, or kicking the football through the uprights for a field goal. In the American game, they use a four-down system, which gives the offence four downs to get 10 yards, making it easier to move the football 10 yards.

Field goal (FG): A team can attempt to kick the ball through the goal-post uprights for a field goal from any yard line on the field. If successful, the field goal is worth three points.

Free-release: When no one is blocking a special teams player covering a kick, they have a free release to run to the football and make a tackle.

Frontside (FS): Refers to the side of the field in the direction the play is being executed. If the play is attacking the left side of the field, the frontside is left.

Great feet: Can be used to describe any athlete with good foot speed and coordination, but usually refers to an offensive lineman with those attributes.

Hard-nosed: When a player is considered by coaches and opposition players to be tough and physical to play against.

Hash marks: The short one-yard markers painted along each side of the field surface inside the numbers. The referees place the football on the closest hash marks before each play, unless the previous play ended inside the hash marks (see diagram).

Individual drills (indy period): Every practice each position coach takes their position group or unit to do drills that focus on skills that are specific to their position.

In the numbers: When an offensive lineman blocks his opponent, he is coached to deliver a blow with open hands to the jersey number on his chest — in the numbers on his jersey.

Linebackers: The group of 3 or 4 defenders, lined up in two-point stances, behind the defensive line (see diagram).

Line of scrimmage (LOS): The imaginary line across the field at the point where the ball is being snapped – the LOS moves down the field with the ball's movement. On a televised game, the LOS is shown by a CGI line for the viewers, but at a live game we can't see it. The LOS is very important because that's where the play starts - the referees place the ball on the LOS to begin any play. Also, on the sideline the first flag to mark the 10-yard chain is placed at the LOS.

Nose guard: A defensive lineman in a three-point stance lined up in front of the offensive centre.

Offence: The 12 members of a team who form the offensive group or squad, and go on the field only when their team has possession of the football. The offence must move the football forward, toward their opponent's goal line, to score points (see diagram).

Offensive install period: This is the period during practice designated for the new plays to be installed by the offensive coordinators. New plays are usually introduced during meetings before the players get on the field. It is important to use good teaching skills and processes to ensure everyone knows their assignments before a play is run in a live team situation later in practice.

Offensive line (OL): The group of five large athletes lined up on the offensive side of the LOS, with the primary responsibility to protect their quarterback from any defensive player trying to tackle him (see diagram).

Offensive tackle: Refers to the right or left offensive tackle positions, which are two of the five offensive line positions on the LOS (see diagram).

Off-tackle power: A hard-nosed run play, specifically attacking the C-gap outside the offensive tackle, and inside the fullback's kick-out block on the defensive end.

On the numbers: Describes when a quarterback throws the football and hits his intended receiver on the numbers of his jersey (i.e., in the chest).

One-on-ones: A period in practice where one defensive player is isolated against one offensive player to improve a particular skill set. For example, the defensive line and the offensive line usually work against each other every practice to improve their pass rush and pass protection techniques, respectively.

Passing game: Any play in which the football is thrown by the quarterback is considered part of the passing game.

Pass protection: Any blocking scheme requiring the offensive line and running backs to pass-block for the quarterback, protecting him so he can pass (throw) the football down the field to his receivers.

Pass rush: When a defensive player's responsibility is to put pressure on or tackle the quarterback, this action is called a pass rush. They need to use pass rush moves to beat the blocking of the offensive lineman, who is trying his best to protect his quarterback. This results in the constant hand-to-hand battle that happens in "the trenches" between the OL and DL.

Pull: When any offensive lineman quickly moves back from the LOS, then sprints to the point of attack to block a defender in another area of the field. For example, a pulling guard usually leads the running back around the outside of the defence on a toss or a screen play.

Punt block: Occurs when the punt return team blocks the punter's kick, while he attempts to punt the ball on third down.

Reach block: A blocking technique where an offensive blocker attempts to reach to the play side of a defender in order to cut him off from the point of attack.

Release (cut): When a professional player's contract is terminated by their respective club.

Redshirt player: An American term referring to a player recovering from injury while practicing with a team, and being paid without counting towards the game day roster.

Rip move: A pass rush move where a defensive player drops his inside arm to the near hip of the blocker, attempting to "rip" it through to get past the OL to the quarterback.

Rouge: Any time the football is kicked from the field of play through and beyond the opponent's endzone, it is worth one point (rouge) — even a missed field goal. This is unique to Canadian football, which has its roots in rugby.

Rundown (practice): The day after the game is usually reserved for a rundown practice, where players do some relatively light trainer-designated conditioning and sprint work, to help work the lactic acid out of the muscles. Usually during a rundown practice, there are no contact drills, to rest the body and begin recovery from the previous game. Football is a very physical "collision" sport, so after a game, it takes a well-planned week for a team to successfully recover for the next game.

Run game (also ground game, or rushing game): Any offensive play in which the football is run for a gain by the QB or running back – not thrown by the QB.

Run-pass-option: A play designed to allow the quarterback to read the defensive alignment and either give the ball to the running back or keep the ball and throw it to a receiver.

Rush: This has a double meaning — it refers to a defensive player attempting to get to the quarterback using a pass-rush move to beat his blocker; it also refers to a running back carrying the ball on the ground or rushing game.

Sack: When the quarterback is tackled with the ball behind the LOS.

Screen pass: When a running back or receiver catches the football behind the LOS and the offensive linemen pull and block outside the box to spring the ball carrier for positive yards down the field.

Second and long: If an offence gets less than 4 yards on first down of a series, this means they need seven or more yards on second down to get a first down (10 yards).

Second level (of defence): Most defences use three "levels" or layers of defenders between the LOS and their own goal line to stop the offence: the defensive line (DL) is the first level, at the LOS; while the linebackers constitute the second level, usually about 5 yards behind the DL; and the defensive backs form the third and deepest level of defence.

Slotback: An offensive receiver, positioned back from the LOS and outside his offensive tackle.

Short yardage package: A special group of offensive plays that an offensive coach designs, used if only one or two yards (short yardage) is needed for a first down.

Special teams/specials: The groups of players (squads) making up the kickoff and kickoff return teams, punt and punt return teams, and field goal and field goal return teams. Because they are not offence or defence and they involve kicking the football they are "special." In the Canadian three-down system, special teams have more importance for field position than in the American game, where four downs make it easier to get first downs.

Spread formation: An offensive formation with all the receivers and running backs spread out across the field.

Stand-up defensive player: Any player on defence using a two-point stance, hence standing up.

Stretch drive: The final group of scheduled season games before the playoffs begin, during which playoff positions are often determined.

Strong side: Refers to the wide side of the field. If the football is on the left hash mark, the right sideline is further from the football, so it becomes the strong side (see diagram).

Stunt: A defensive scheme called in the huddle to create pressure on the quarterback or stop the run game by attacking different gaps.

Swim move: A pass-rush move where a defensive lineman swings one arm up high to "swim" by the offensive lineman trying to block him, while swatting the near shoulder with the opposite hand.

Tailback: The running back positioned behind the quarterback, who generally runs with the ball if the QB give it to him.

Team period: Practice usually culminates with the entire offensive unit (team) executing plays against the entire defence (team), so it mimics a game situation.

The huddle: When the offensive or defensive team groups up before the play to communicate what the play call is for the next play. Usually, the captain will call the play in the huddle before each play.

The pocket: An area approximately 5–7 square yards, directly behind the centre and between the tackles, where the quarterback sets up to pass the ball. If the offensive line protects this area consistently, the quarterback will feel comfortable doing his job throwing to his receivers without getting hit.

The snap: When the centre moves the ball between his legs, from the LOS in front of him to the quarterback or the kicker behind him.

The trenches: The area on the LOS between the offensive line and the defensive line, where hand-to-hand combat takes place on every play between the biggest and strongest athletes on the field.

Three-point stance: When an offensive or defensive player places their hand on the ground, usually at the LOS, this is called a three-point stance (both feet and a hand — three points of the body touching the ground).

When a player is standing upright, they are in a two-point stance because only their feet are on the ground; conversely, if a player puts both hands on the ground, it becomes a four-point stance. The latter would be used by linemen in goal line/short-yardage situations.

Tight end: A larger receiver lined up on the LOS beside his OT, usually for the purpose of blocking on a run play.

Toss action: A running play designed so that the quarterback laterals the football (tosses the football underhand to the side, as in rugby) to the running back as he sprints outside the perimeter of the defence, usually with the guards pulling around the edge to block for the ball carrier.

Touchdown (TD): When a player in possession of the football crosses their opponent's goal line, or a player catches the football inside their opponent's end zone, a touchdown is scored. Each touchdown is worth six points.

Training table: All the food and nutrition provided for the team during training camp, usually designed by nutritionists to help offset the loss of calories during hot practices over long days. A copious amount of food is consumed during camp, especially by the linemen.

Turnover: When the defensive team takes the ball away from the offence, through a fumble, interception, or failed third down attempt.

Two-a-days: During training camp, many coaches choose to run two full practices per day, one in the morning and one in the afternoon, to increase the number of drills and reps they can run in a day.

Two-and-out series: If a team does not get a first down with their first two offensive plays, they may choose to punt the football to the other team on third down, instead of risking a loss of possession too close to their own goal line. This means they only ran two offensive plays in the series, losing possession on the punt — "two-and-out."

Video cutup: Video segments from the game film that are cut up by the video coordinator using coaching criteria and placed in digital folders to help coaches save time when watching film in meetings.

Waggle in: The movement or motion of an offensive receiver to reposition himself along the LOS prior to the snap, to help in the blocking scheme.

Waivers: Before a player is released from one team, they need to pass a waiver period of 48 hours, where another team can claim them under the same terms as the existing contract.

Walk-about: Pre-game, getting partially dressed for the game, then walking and chatting with other players around the field, before returning to the dressing room to complete dressing in full equipment.
Want-to-speed: A player may have a slower time on a stopwatch in the 40-yard dash than they will with the added incentive of game situations; for example, a defensive player chasing down a ball carrier with the ball; or the adrenaline added to a running back being chased by a ferocious defence; or a receiver getting to a ball that seems out of reach — this is what coaches call want-to-speed.
Weak side: Refers to the short side of the field. If the ball is on the left hash mark, the left sideline is closer to the football than the right sideline, so the left is the weak side of the field (see diagram).
Yards receiving: The total number of yards gained by a receiver catching the football on a single play, a game, a season, or a career.

APPENDIX B

RELAXATION, MEDITATION AND VISUALIZATION ACTIVITY

Rationale

Many people find it difficult to fully relax themselves because it's not something that is generally taught as an essential skill. However, I have found that using a combination of psychological techniques, which I've learned over the years, has helped me personally with my game preparation when I played and with my mental health now. It was also a useful tool for my students and players.

Additionally, visualization of completing skills successfully, as compared to practicing the skill physically, has been proven to be the next best thing for improving performance.

Coaches, I used this activity with my offensive line, but it can be used for any position group in any sport.

This is a brief outline of the procedure. For a group, it's best to be led by a leader's voice, but individuals can use it on their own after they learn the technique — this can be useful in any situation where you want to relax and reduce your internal tension, or even get to sleep. In fact, using this technique, I have fallen asleep in the dentist's chair, with her instruments in my mouth. She said it was a first.

Preparation

1. A basic understanding of muscle groups in the human body will help you with this activity.
2. Optional — a prayer or spiritual guided meditation script.
3. Play a relaxing soundtrack softly in the background, and turn down the lights.
4. Participants lie down with a pillow (or some form of neck support), or sit comfortably in a position where they will not need to move.

Relaxation

Leader's narration

1. Put your body in a position where you can stay motionless and relax.
2. Close your eyes.
3. Now, focus on your breathing — breathe deeply and slowly.
4. Put everything else out of your mind, except my voice. Focus only on my voice.
5. We're going to take a journey in your mind's eye to completely relax your body from toe to head.
6. In your mind's eye, imagine that you are inside your feet looking out. Now completely relax all the muscles in your toes and your feet, looking outward from here you can see all the tension evaporate from every muscle in your feet. Your feet are completely relaxed.
7. Breathe deeply.
8. Moving up into your ankles and lower legs, relax all the muscles in this area. Use your mind to relax your calf muscles; in your mind's eye, see the tension evaporate into the air.
9. Moving up into your knees and upper legs, use your mind to relax these muscle groups. In your mind's eye, see the tension evaporate from all your quad muscles and your hamstrings. Your legs are completely relaxed and still. They feel great.
10. Moving into your hips and lower back, use your mind to relax all the muscles in this area of your body. Release the tension in these muscles and, in your mind's eye, see the tension evaporate.

Leader continues with this "journey" to every other muscle group in the body: the abdomen, along your spine, chest, shoulder blades, shoulders, upper arms, lower arms and hands, then the neck, all the way up to the head, releasing the tension from the jaw, face, forehead, and scalp.

Finally, "In your mind's eye, take yourself back into the core of your body. You are now inside your chest, looking at your heart. Breathe deeply, and focus on your heart rate — use your mind to slow it down. In your mind's eye, you can see your heart slow down. Use your mind to bring down your heart rate — slow your heart, relax, and breathe. Now your body is completely relaxed and you feel wonderful."

Meditation

Narration continues

"Now your entire body is completely relaxed and you feel fantastic. You are totally motionless because there is no reason to move and your eyes are still closed. Continue to focus only on my voice.

Imagine that you are now on your favourite beach on a warm summer day. You feel the warmth of the sand on your back, and the warmth of the sun on your face. Your entire body is warm, motionless, relaxed. Continue to breathe deeply and slowly.

You are peaceful and happy, your family is peaceful and happy, your city is peaceful and happy, your province is peaceful and happy, your country is peaceful and happy, your world is peaceful and happy, the solar system is peaceful and happy, the universe is peaceful and happy — you feel calm and at one with the universe. You have no worries and no anxiety. You feel wonderful.

Prayer (optional depending on participants)

In this state of relaxation and mindfulness, the group is perfectly primed for a favourite prayer, or a guided spiritual meditation prepared earlier.

Visualization

Coaches, this is where I would lead my offensive line group through a final preparation for our game, either the night before or the morning of the game. With them in this fully relaxed state, review key assignments, lead them through successful run and pass blocking techniques, visualize being successful against the opponent's best players, visualize themselves winning after a hard-fought game, etc.

To conclude the session, end with a positive statement and leave the room to allow them to come back to reality at their own pace, feeling refreshed, invigorated, in a positive state of mind.

Here is an example of concluding remarks at the end of a playoff visualization; each session is written for a specific opponent:

Visualize yourself knowing where your quarterback is on every pass, and playing with urgency and desperation, to launch yourself for that final push every time we pass the ball, giving him the time he needs. We know that if we protect him, he will have success. No one touches our quarterback and we take that personally!

Guards, see yourself tracking your blitzing linebacker, and having your eyes lasered into his chest, until you knock him off his feet.

Tackles, visualize yourself blocking down to the defensive tackle, and chipping up to the middle linebacker on a perfect down-block, then hammering number 51 as he tries to scrape to the ball.

Understand that a football game is a microcosm of life and that some bad things will happen tomorrow, but you have the confidence in yourself, your teammates, and your coaching staff to overcome any amount of adversity.

Visualize yourself winning the one-on-one battles all game long.

Visualize yourself having fun knocking people down.

Visualize yourself winning the game tomorrow!

ACKNOWLEDGEMENTS

Paulette and the kids get the highest praise for their constant love and support — they are the greatest blessings in my life. I would also like to thank my siblings, John, Janice, and Jeff, for their support in this project and the many conversations we had about the memories we shared growing up.

Thank you to all my former teammates and coaches for their commitment to our winning teams and for sharing the stories that make our game so great.

Also, thank you to my friends Jim Cimba, Todd Fryer, Ray Jones, and Mark Moors for being instrumental as sounding boards in developing the book.

Finally, I am saddened to say that the following people, all mentioned in this book because they had an impact on my life, died before publishing: Jack Frimeth (2021), Ray Jones (2021), Angelo Mosca (2021), Chris Schultz (2021), Bob Laycoe (2020), Glenn Timlock (2020), Don Edwards (2018), Bernie Custis (2017), Rick Klassen (2016), Bill Howard (2015), Cal Murphy (2012), Carey Lapa (2011), Harvey (Tyrone) Jones (2008), Ron Lancaster (2008), Fred Scione (2002), Anne Costello (2001), Tony Antunovic (1998), James Zachery (1994), John Mandarich (1993).